The Dark Side of Early Soviet Childhood, 1917–1941

The Dark Side of Early Soviet Childhood, 1917–1941

Children's Tragedy

By Boris B. Gorshkov

BLOOMSBURY ACADEMIC
LONDON • NEW YORK • OXFORD • NEW DELHI • SYDNEY

BLOOMSBURY ACADEMIC
Bloomsbury Publishing Plc
50 Bedford Square, London, WC1B 3DP, UK
1385 Broadway, New York, NY 10018, USA
29 Earlsfort Terrace, Dublin 2, Ireland

BLOOMSBURY, BLOOMSBURY ACADEMIC and the Diana logo
are trademarks of Bloomsbury Publishing Plc

First published in Great Britain 2023
Paperback edition published 2025

Copyright © Boris B. Gorshkov 2023

Boris B. Gorshkov have asserted his right under the Copyright,
Designs and Patents Act, 1988, to be identified as Author of this work.

Cover image: painting by Neil Gorshkov

Bloomsbury Publishing Plc does not have any control over, or responsibility for, any third-party websites referred to or in this book. All internet addresses given in this book were correct at the time of going to press. The author and publisher regret any inconvenience caused if addresses have changed or sites have ceased to exist, but can accept no responsibility for any such changes.

Every effort has been made to trace the copyright holders and obtain permission to reproduce the copyright material. Please do get in touch with any enquiries or any information relating to such material or the rights holder. We would be pleased to rectify any omissions in subsequent editions of this publication should they be drawn to our attention.

A catalogue record for this book is available from the British Library.

A catalog record for this book is available from the Library of Congress.

Library of Congress Cataloging-in-Publication Data

Names: Gorshkov, Boris B., author.
Title: The dark side of early soviet childhood, 1917-1941 : children's tragedy / by Boris B. Gorshkov.
Description: New York : Bloomsbury Academic, 2023. | Includes bibliographical references and index. | Summary: "This book examines the inter-related issues of children's hunger, homelessness and high mortality in the USSR between 1918 and the outbreak of the Second World War"– Provided by publisher.
Identifiers: LCCN 2023019441 (print) | LCCN 2023019442 (ebook) | ISBN 9781350098671 (hardback) | ISBN 9781350098688 (ebook) | ISBN 9781350098695 (epub)
Subjects: LCSH: Homeless children–Russia (Federation)–History–20th century. | Children–Mortality–Russia (Federation)–History–20th century. | Russia (Federation)–Social conditions–20th century.
Classification: LCC HV887.R8 G67 2023 (print) | LCC HV887.R8 (ebook) | DDC 305.23086/9420947–dc23/eng/20230515
LC record available at https://lccn.loc.gov/2023019441
LC ebook record available at https://lccn.loc.gov/2023019442

ISBN: HB: 978-1-3500-9867-1
PB: 978-1-3504-1569-0
ePDF: 978-1-3500-9868-8
eBook: 978-1-3500-9869-5

Typeset by Integra Software Services Pvt. Ltd.

To find out more about our authors and books visit www.bloomsbury.com
and sign up for our newsletters.

Contents

List of Figures	vi
List of Tables	vii
Preface	viii
Introduction: Street Children, Problem, Historiography, Discourses, and Evidence	1
1 Street Children before the Bolshevik Revolution: Prelude to the Crisis	17
2 Soviet Street Children: Definition, Identity, Demography, Geography, and Origins	43
3 A Revolutionary Childhood: Ideals, Declarations, Challenges, and Realities	73
4 New Economic Policy: Cheka Comes to Play	101
5 A "Happy Soviet Childhood": Stalinist Childhood Revisited	133
Epilogue: Vanished Childhood in the Early Soviet Union	163
Appendix One	171
Appendix Two	179
Notes	186
Cited Materials	208
Index	217

Figures

1	Homeless children at Nikolaevsk train station in Moscow	2
2	F. S. Bogorodskii, Besprizornyi. 1925	7
3	Homeless boy with a homeless dog. Samara. 1930	16
4	Shelter at the Church of St. John the Baptist. Pupils of the Shelter 1900, Russia, Yaroslavl Oblast	19
5	Orphanage in Voronezh, founded in 1848	34
6	Moscow's orphanage	57
7	N. K. Krupskaya	79
8	Homeless children play cards on the street	90
9	Escorted street children in Moscow	102
10	At the Makarenko Orphanage	125
11	Thanks to our dear Stalin for a happy childhood. Soviet poster	161

Tables

1 Special settlers in Siberian GULAG in December 1932   146

Preface

This book is about children and childhood in Russia and the early Soviet Union; it focuses on the period from October 1917 to the outbreak of the Second World War. The Revolution of 1917 and the attending Civil War brought about social troubles, but they were not the root cause of children's tragedy. This tragedy was exclusively the result of Bolshevik population and economic policies that left millions of children hungry and homeless for an extended period. During the civil conflict and later, child mortality in some areas of the country reached 95 percent. In addition, severe problems as regards early Soviet children remained ubiquitous throughout the 1920s and 1930s. This study demonstrates, on the basis of primary sources, exactly how policies of the Bolshevik government caused such extended homelessness and starvation of children. It also considers the situation of the children's population, as well as the efforts of the state to solve these problems. Of particular interest in this regard is the role of the secret police—the Cheka and its descendant the NKVD—in working with homeless and starving children.

The book is intended for a wide range of readers, students, and specialists in the history of Russia and the USSR, researchers on the history of childhood, as well as for the general reader. Students of the periods of Revolution and Stalinism should find this study of special interest. This volume should also be of great interest to students of comparative history: it analyzes the imperial period and thereby bridges the gap between the tsarist and Soviet eras. Researchers of Stalinism should also find fruitful data and analysis because this study considers the problem of child homelessness and hunger in a very broad historical context, from the standpoint of the imperial and Soviet periods, drawing parallels and, most importantly, emphasizing differences. Footnotes provide links to historiography and primary sources, as well as basic facts about events, places, or people, to help the general reader make sense of the historical setting. Bibliographic notes will assist the reader with further inquiries and additional historical research on the subject. The appendix introduces the reader to primary archival sources. The author proceeds from the fact that most readers do not read Russian. In most instances, I have therefore used the English equivalents for Russian terms, which follow immediately in parentheses. In most cases, I have used the standard U.S. Library of Congress method for the transliteration of the Russian spellings of Russian given names, patronymics (middle names), and surnames. Customarily, in Russia people have three names: the given (first) name, the middle name (patronymic), and the surname (family name). The Russian middle name (patronymic) is derived from the father's given name. Along with the person's given name, the patronymic is used as a polite or formal form of address. The names of certain historical figures, such as Stalin, are given in an anglicized spelling form. The names of cities, regions, places, and rivers are given in a manner familiar to those who read English. Direct transliteration is used for titles of Russian-language publications in those notes that contain ideas or recommendations for further reading. I assume that further reading recommendations will be used mainly by Russian scholars who are familiar with the Russian language. For those who do not know Russian, I have provided the titles of some relevant English-language studies.

I began my preliminary research on this topic in 1993 as an undergraduate student in history. During summer trips to Moscow, I began to collect data on street children. My interests, however, are broad and include various social issues relating to child labor, labor laws, and the peasantry, on which I have published three books and numerous articles. At the same time as I worked on peasant and child labor issues, I continued to explore children's hunger and homelessness during the Soviet state's first decades. In exploring such topics in the history of the imperial and early Soviet periods, I am trying to reach an understanding of the 1917 Revolution, its expediency, and essence, with special consideration for Bolshevik power. Over the years (1996–2021), I have worked in state and municipal archives and libraries in Russia. This book offers a view of the early Bolshevik state through the lens of the ongoing tragedy of early soviet childhood.

I would like to thank all those who helped me in collecting materials for this book, all the staff of libraries and archives, as well as all my colleagues who provided indispensable intellectual support. I am grateful to the U.S. Department of State's Title VIII Program and University of Illinois at Urbana-Champaign for financial support. I would like to thank Professor Michael Melancon for his constant intellectual encouragement and support, and my son Neil, who gave me his permission to use his painting for this book cover. I dedicate this book to all children who experienced sorrow and hardship during eras of social destruction under totalitarian regimes.

Boris B. Gorshkov
Chattanooga, Tennessee, USA

Introduction: Street Children, Problem, Historiography, Discourses, and Evidence

Children's homelessness has reached an extent, which can threaten public security ...
Official report, April 16, 1923[1]

Recently, the Mikhailovsky district [of Moscow Province] was faced with the increased cases of a large influx of homeless children of pre-school and school ages ... The homeless are detained by the police and temporarily placed in an overloaded local orphanage...
Chairman of RIC Melnikov, June 13, 1933[2]

In connection with food shortages, the homelessness and beggary among children are growing in Voronezh, in the Chelyabinsk region, and in the Mordovian ASSR ...
From a classified report of state security service
lieutenant Golubev, 1938[3]

Perhaps I should start this book with the obvious—the definition of children. The Merriam-Webster Dictionary defines them as young people, especially between infancy and puberty, and persons not yet of the age of majority. The Free Dictionary defines them as people from birth to puberty, persons who have not reached the age of majority or the stage of maturity, unborn babies, fetus, baby, and a child. In the second edition of the Great Soviet Encyclopedia (1952), they were defined as "the young rising generation of people" and as "persons who have not reached the age of majority." By the late imperial period, the age of majority was determined at eighteen years.[4] All of these definitions lack the fact that children, especially young ones, cannot survive alone and cannot be alone without adult supervision—thus, children are a dependent group of people. In other words, children belong to their parents, guardians, or other legal adult overseers. They belong to their families, households, homes, or communities. Obviously, children do not belong to the street, and they cannot be left alone on the street and in public places without adult supervision. Therefore, it is important to remember that the well-being of children is largely dependent on the well-being of their parents or adult guardians, as well as on the well-being of the immediate environment of the children. This book is about what happened to the children of early Soviet Russia, the millions of boys and girls

Figure 1 Homeless children at Nikolaevsk train station in Moscow. 1920. Source: Open public domain.

who belonged to the street. However, this story cannot be revealed without telling what happened to the inner circle, that is, to their homes and families, who lost millions of Soviet street children.

The quoted excerpts from official Soviet sources may shock the reader. The scale of the tragedy of millions of Soviet children was unprecedented, extraordinary, and unceasing. Hunger, neglect, homelessness, and high mortality rates for Soviet children have plagued the country for two or more decades. When millions of hungry and unattended children flooded the streets, the state perceived them as a "threat to public safety," but the question arises: who is to be blamed? According to contemporary estimates, in 1921–2 the number of "starving, dying and homeless" children reached 7.5 million in Russia and up to 2 million homeless in Ukraine.[5] In the 1930s, when the Stalinist regime imposed extreme censorship, secret reports were again received from various regions of the USSR, in which the central state bodies were informed about the large number of starving, begging, and homeless children, and were again called for urgent measures to combat the problems. Children's homelessness was so out of control that the government had to use its armed forces, armed detachments, and punitive intelligence agencies—the Cheka, and then the NKVD—to cope with the problem. The Soviet state ultimately used exclusively punitive institutions to solve the problem of street children, qualifying homelessness as a criminal offense—vagrancy—with all the ensuing consequences. Millions of early Soviet children were exposed to all forms of human pain, suffering, and misfortune. The geography of children's homelessness and hunger affected all regions of the country without exception, with varying degrees of intensity and persisted throughout the entire period from the seizure of power by the Bolsheviks in 1917 to the outbreak of the Second World War.

The book examines the tragedy of Soviet children in the period between the revolutionary 1917 and the beginning of the Great Patriotic War in 1941. As already mentioned, these years witnessed extreme homelessness, hunger, and high mortality among children. The book analyzes the striking persistence of these problems, albeit at different rates, in the context of the domestic politics of the early Soviet state. It also explores the origins, geography, and dynamics of children's homelessness, hunger, and high mortality during this time. Questions about the extraordinary continuity of the problems between 1917 and 1941 and who was responsible for this require serious research: was it a *force majeure* circumstance that did not depend on someone's control, or was it caused by a human factor, and was there any or a significant connection between these problems and the internal policy of the state? What brought hundreds of thousands of children to the streets, train stations, and markets beginning in late 1918, and what led to even more homelessness in 1920–1 that continued throughout the 1920s, followed by further episodes in Western and other parts of Siberia and elsewhere during the 1930s? This study provides answers to these questions. The book presents a revisionist point of view based on many previously unused archival and published sources.

The book's main hypothesis is that misconceived and vicious Soviet domestic policy caused a general humanitarian catastrophe that precipitated the attendant problems: children's starvation, leading to high mortality rates, as well as separation of children from their families or caregivers and homelessness. In a sense, homeless children were society's response to government repressive actions against it. Moreover, the state's measures to cope with children's homelessness and hunger often exacerbated these problems and created new ones. Millions of Soviet children fell victims of Bolsheviks' *realpolitik*.

In this book the term *realpolitik* refers to politics that rely on pragmatism and practical goals rather than on ideology. This term does not imply "real politics." Originated from German political philosophy, the term "real" in German means "things." Literally, *realpolitik* can be translated as a politics of reaction to things as they are regardless of ideology or moral principles. It is necessary to remember that with the rise of Soviet-era absolutism, the ruling Bolshevik Party, to control and mobilize resources, both material and human, introduced policies of extreme force and even terror to bend the population to its will. These policies supplemented and even supplanted Marxist-Leninist ideology, which did not require anything like the degree of force the government employed. For understanding this phenomenon and its societal consequences, I suggest the term *realpolitik*, a term that signifies policies deployed outside the realm of ideology to achieve certain aims. The term implies a degree of immorality, which certainly applies to Soviet policies toward the population between 1918 and 1941.

Regarding the Bolsheviks, when they assumed control over Russia and were in power, they hardly acted as Marxists or Marxist-Leninists. Most scholars of Soviet studies would agree that the Bolshevik government dreamed of creating a state in accordance with their visions and ideals based on Marxist-Leninist ideas, but what is not generally accepted is that when push came to shove, the Bolshevik government followed the *realpolitik* methods.⁶ It turned out that in order to achieve its ideals, the government used coercion, terror, and repression—all possible means of *realpolitik*—the main sources of enormous ongoing social anguish. In fact, the Bolshevik *realpolitik* prevailed over the Marxist-Leninist ideology, which served primarily to hide the real repressive policy. At times, one might get the impression that those in power in early Soviet Russia suffered from severe mental illness that led to anger, aggression, and impulsive decisions.⁷ Nevertheless, the Bolshevik *realpolitik*, as the main tool for implementing policies to achieve goals, became the main cause of the suffering of millions of Soviet families. As a result, a huge mass of children was thrown out into the street, filling stations and cities. Children concentrated in those places where they could find food. In Soviet times and in light of social neglect, children's homelessness turned into a social catastrophe. Street children fought for life through theft, begging, prostitution, and street trading. Homelessness among children became a real scourge of Soviet society after 1917 and created a breeding ground for the growth of child and, in the long term, adult crime.

In 1918, when they came to power, the Bolsheviks destroyed the traditions of charity and caring for the needy.⁸ The new government outlawed all private philanthropy, patronage, and guardianship and took childcare under state control, but were unable to create any viable infrastructure to replace the abolished institutions. When the government closed the existing charitable infrastructure, this was immediately followed by children's starvation and, as a result, homelessness. Hundreds of thousands of starving children took to the streets. In 1919 and in the early 1920s, childhood tragedies (poverty, homelessness, hunger, and high mortality) were the result of food requisitioning and other punitive measures against a large part of the rural population. This policy greatly affected the immediate environment of children—their families and homes. In 1930, children suffered from the consequences of violent Stalinist collectivization of agriculture and ongoing repression against large masses of the population. Government policies put millions of families and their children at risk. Needy and starving children had to take to the streets to beg, find food, and commit illegal activities to survive or simply to protect themselves from the repressive authorities.

It can be assumed that the problem of street children was not uncommon in the history of any period and any nation. Homeless children existed in ancient Greece and Rome, and they roamed the streets of many cities of the Renaissance and Reformation; they posed an acute social problem during the Industrial Revolution. Homeless children existed in Russia before 1917. However, its size did not reach even 100,000.⁹ In early Soviet Russia, children's homelessness and hunger became extreme, ubiquitous, and unrelenting. The scale, urgency, and persistence of these problems, as well as the high degree of notoriety they gained in the early 1920s, made this issue unique. The fact that many street children were separated, often forcibly and violently, from their parents and families made this problem the most striking. The only strict state censorship during the Stalinist era of the late 1920s and 1930s prevented public debate on or even mentioning these lingering issues.

Surprisingly unique was the use of the term *"besprizornost"*—homelessness—in early Soviet Russia was surprising. The word *"besprizornost"* itself can be translated from Russian as negligence on the part of parents or institutions or homelessness. Street children were called "*besprizorniki*," who were homeless, and everything they embodied was called *besprizornost*. It is noteworthy here that the first edition of the Great Soviet Encyclopedia, published in 1926, defined the term "*besprizornost*" exclusively for children, although this phenomenon could hypothetically refer to people of any age or even to animals. It can be assumed that there were many homeless and neglected adult or elderly people, but they completely escaped official or public attention and were not mentioned in any official or public discourse of that period. *Besprizorniki*—starving and unattended children—became an everyday feature of the time. They engaged in all kinds of activities to survive. In this study, I will refer to them as street children or *besprizorniki*.

By 1924, the state distinguished four categories of *besprizorniki*: (1) minors who lived in conditions that could have pernicious effects on their health; (2) minors who lived without supervision and care; (3) minors who committed beggary, vagrancy, and prostitution; and (4) children whose parents led "a vicious life" that might affect the child's life.[10] Thus, the state considered *besprizorniki* as neglected and unattended street children, who had lost their homes or families, were abandoned by their parents or were separated from their families, while not mentioning the fact of their starvation and sufferings. Cases of child abandonment were particularly widespread in 1920-1, as an immediate response to the Bolshevik *realpolitik* (forceful food procurement, "proletarian dictatorship" and war communism), whereas cases of separation of children from their parents took place during the entire period under examination. Separations markedly intensified and became commonplace during Stalin's agricultural collectivization campaign and the forceful replacement and resettlement of peasant families in the 1930s. During the *dekulakization* campaign (repressions against certain groups of peasants), which occurred simultaneously with collectivization and when hundreds of thousands of peasants were repressed and executed, many children lost their parents or were separated from them. Nevertheless, government internal policies affected the well-being of a significant number of families, especially in rural areas, and produced many starving and homeless children.

Regardless of the officially recognized categories, the state approach made no considerations or distinctions regarding the development of these children, because the concerned authorities tended to categorize them collectively as "morally defective," criminal, and socially threatening masses, an embarrassment to the Soviet polity. None of the Soviet government's earliest acts concerning street children differentiated between homeless, orphaned, or other unattended children, and described them collectively as *besprizorniki*. Street children, who became a disturbing attribute of early Soviet Russian society, represented a variable group of all ages, both genders, and had different social backgrounds and circumstances (with or without living parents). However, what most of them shared—as we will see in the following chapters— were their tragedy and miserable conditions. Most street children could share the definitions of all four categories at the same time because they experienced all these conditions together. Nonetheless, the street children were *children* who needed close adult care and supervision. They were at various psychophysiological stages and in the development of the nervous system, and each stage naturally influenced their behavior and perception of social realities. None of these were considered by government agencies. These aspects are also practically absent from current studies of early Soviet childhood.

As mentioned, the phenomenon of street children was hardly new, but its extraordinary level and the public attention it received from the state were outstanding, starting approximately in October 1920. The terms "*besprizornost*" and "*besprizorniki*" received a great occurrence in the official Soviet press in the early 1920s, when the crisis grew, and magnified significant attention from contemporaries and state institutions. Even, as mentioned above, the Great Soviet Encyclopedia of 1926 linked the entire phenomenon of homelessness exclusively with children and did not attribute it to any other age group. Again, it bears repeating, the virtual absence of public debate about homeless and starving children in the 1930s means only the fact of Stalin's censorship, not the absence of questions that remained secluded in confidential and secret government documents. Throughout the 1920s and 1930s, generations of street children lived in Soviet Russia. By the end of 1920, Soviet government officials recognized the presence of street children as an ominous and the most serious social harm. However, government officials also compared this "harm" to counter-revolution and called for immediate emergency measures to end it. From this point of view, the homelessness of children posed a danger not only to the lives of the children themselves, but primarily to public order and the security of the state, taking into account the Bolshevik *realpolitik*. The perception of street children as mentally handicapped criminals—because children often displayed anti-government sentiments—had a major impact on the government's approach. Practically mentioned only in classified documents, street children were still a serious problem for the state in the 1930s. In 1935, the Stalinist government simply by decree announced the end of children's homelessness and imposed severe sanctions on all minors who walked the streets unattended vagrants. New state laws made vagrancy and begging punishable offenses. At the same time, the state lowered the age of death penalty to twelve years, toughened other penalties for minors and reintroduced imprisonments. Street children, or in fact the struggle of the state and successes in solving the problem they presented, caused an extraordinary wave in the stories and publications of newspapers and magazines. Contemporary art, and later Soviet cinema, contained scenes with street children and portrayed these unfortunate victims of a difficult time. Writers have written success stories about government efforts to help and rehabilitate hundreds of thousands of street children.[11]

Another unchanging reality of this period was the extremely high mortality rate among children. In some cases, it reached 95 percent. The life expectancy of an early Soviet street child was indeed noticeably short, and it is likely that most homeless children did not even make it to adolescence. However, the presence of street children had always been striking and constant and took on catastrophic forms throughout the years between the Revolution and the outbreak of the Second World War. The enormous scale of children's tragedy—homelessness, hunger, and mortality—indelibly marks the history of the first decades of Soviet unofficial childhood. The

Figure 2 F. S. Bogorodskii, Besprizornyi. 1925, Moscow, Tretyakov Gallery. Source: Open public domain.

misunderstood official image of a "happy Soviet childhood," as promoted by the state, can be refuted by the stories of millions of Soviet youths who suffered throughout the years covered in this book.

One aspect of the tragedy of early Soviet childhood—children's homelessness—has attracted the attention of scholars and students of Russian history. This topic received much attention in the 1920s–early 1930s, as well as after Gorbachev's perestroika. Apparently, Russian-language scholarship is both dependent upon and can illustrate state censorship of all scholarly and intellectual products. Nonetheless, its dynamics have changed over time. This issue was originally widely discussed in the mid-1920s by authors often associated with the government. Authors of the 1920s focused mainly on government efforts to eradicate children's homelessness. They tended to attribute the origin of the problem of "moral inferiority" of children (as street children were usually perceived) to the First World War and the Civil War. In the late 1920s and the first half of the 1930s, when the state was defining its propaganda priorities, Soviet studies on this issue emphasized the Soviet state's great concern for children and women, the protection of motherhood, and its efforts to prevent children's homelessness. The authors praised the party, Dzerzhinsky, Lenin, Stalin, and other statesmen for their quick reaction to the problem, great love for children, and a successful end to children's homelessness and hunger. Most of these studies were written by government officials who dealt with the issue of childcare.[12] Beginning in 1935, when the Stalinist state officially "put an end" to the problem of children's homelessness and starvation by decree "on the elimination of children's homelessness," the latter disappeared from research, public discourse, and in any mentioning until the era of perestroika. Following the historian Andrei Aleksandrovich Slavko, I suggest that the state was afraid to raise questions about the negative consequences of deprivation of property and special settlements as reasons for children's homelessness and the revealing of the truth.[13]

Russian émigré literature stressed the consequences of the disastrous Bolsheviks' experiment to impose a system that did not correspond to the economic and cultural conditions of Russia. For example, E. D. Kuskova wrote:

> Of course, all sorts of civil and imperialist wars will produce homeless, both adults and children, but even more destructive [was] the policy of the state itself that does not correspond to the normal conditions of the state and its development. Thus, the destruction of the peasantry—its overwhelming burdens—[was] a constant source of separation of homeless children who [could not] afford to feed themselves at the fertile but impoverished peasant household.[14]

Largely ignored by Soviet and Western scholars, émigrés accounts were close to reality. Indeed, what Kuskova observed in 1918–19 and the early 1920s is true and applicable for the following decade, the 1930s and what corresponds with the recent Russian-language studies.

Regarding the recent Russian-language scholarship about homeless children, the issue is currently under debate, especially in the past few decades. Gorbachev's perestroika inspired some interest in the émigré literature—late Soviet publishers reprinted émigré writings from the 1920s and 1930s. Nevertheless, many fundamental questions about the origins of homelessness among children remain unanswered. Most current Russian-language studies seem to reach no consensus about homeless children's origins. Many tend to follow the old path and stress the period's wars and the transition from capitalism to a new socialist system as the key factors that created millions of homeless children during the 1920s.[15] Historian Natal'ia Viktorovna Semina highlighted political, economic, social, and ideological crises as causes of mass homelessness among children.[16] Distinct studies, which stand out of this tendency, is by A. A. Slavko and A. Y. Rozhkov. The authors explore the problem from the Revolution through the period of collectivization and industrialization and suggested that Soviet population policies were the major cause of the social breakdown and the attending issues of children's starvation and homelessness. According to Slavko, "the repressive policy [of the Soviet state] toward its citizens became one of the main factors of the destruction of the family that lead to children's homelessness."[17] Seconding Slavko, a recent case study about children's welfare in late imperial and early soviet Tambov province, by Pavel Petrovich Shcherbinin, suggested that, when the Soviet state took charity in its own hands and prohibited all private and public initiatives, the province was scrubbed out as much as possible, humiliated, and punished by the new government for the "*Antonovshchina*"—a massive peasant anti-Bolshevik uprising. The result was a humanitarian catastrophe, which resulted in hundreds of thousands of homeless and starving children in this province.[18] Challenging the "neo traditionalism" paradigm,[19] the author found a remarkable break between the pre-revolutionary and revolutionary times—the revolutionary Bolshevik government virtually massacred a large bulk of the Tambov province's civil population regardless gender or age diversity. The soviet policies created hundreds of thousands of homeless and starving children and forced many children to special settlements to Siberia along with their parents. To be sure, this book will discuss the matter in the following chapters.

English-language scholarship has produced a book, *And Now My Soul Is Hardened*, by Alan Ball, and several articles (Ball, Margaret Stolee) and one book chapter (Wendy Goldman) about homeless children during the first years of Bolshevik power.[20] They have realistically described the problem as pervasive and critical. These studies have concentrated on government's policies in dealing with homeless children. The authors discussed the issues of homelessness and delinquency in terms of early Soviet government family policy, and within the context of Bolshevik visions of new socialist upbringing and the official publicized discourse. In this version, early Soviet family policy failed because of Russian sociocultural and economic reality. Allegedly, resulting from the First World War, the Revolution and the Civil War, millions of street children were left to survive on their own way. Assembling in groups, they engaged in criminal activities and developed a sense of independence and unity that in turn made it utterly impossible to socialize and regulate them. One may raise a question about what made the children engage in criminal activities: their assembling in groups, the sense of independence they obtained or something else? This question remains unclear.

According to these historians, the early Soviet family policy of socializing street children collapsed due to Russia's "backwardness," impoverishment, and lack of funds, which destroyed the truly Marxist ideals of family and childhood. "Backwardness" and lack of resources for solving the problem of children's homelessness and crime forced the young state to revive traditional methods of childcare.[21] Alan Ball characterized the phenomenon of children's homelessness as a persistent and serious problem and concluded that it is wrong to blame the government for the millions of abandoned children in the early 1920s and to view them as the result of the Revolution and subsequent "communist politics."[22] Of course, given that the new government abolished all forms of pre-revolutionary charity and claimed responsibility for homelessness and starving children, Ball's argument may be problematic. Ball followed the argument presented in an earlier study by Margaret Stolee that the homeless children of the 1920s "were the victims of catastrophes and social disintegration over which the new government had little control."[23] The question may arise here whether the Bolshevik government had any control over the forceful and violent food procurement campaign or the collectivization of agriculture if the campaigns themselves were initiated and carried out by the same government. Children's homelessness was portrayed as a serious social problem that almost unexpectedly hit the young Soviet state, and the government had little to do with its origins.

It is rather unusual that historians of the early Soviet period tend to follow the official Bolshevik scenario for the problem of street children and rely mainly on published secondary sources. At the time of preparation of their studies, all the main Soviet archives were open. For example, Alan Ball relied heavily on published contemporary secondary reports for his discussion of the causes of children's homelessness and rarely cited archival material. Likewise, Wendy Goldman based her findings about the failure of the early Soviet government to implement new socialist ways of raising and socializing children on Soviet official discourse. Following the paradigm proposed by the state, the study highlights the failure of the late imperial regime and the disasters of the revolutionary and Civil War as the cornerstone of children's homelessness.

Consequently, research into homelessness among children lacks a consistent historical basis. Therefore, it is not surprising that existing studies, exhaustive in detail, overshadow another striking problem—children's hunger and high mortality. Childhood hunger, as mentioned earlier, became the main factor that pushed children onto the streets and forced them to seek all means of survival, including committing crimes. Homelessness among early Soviet children can hardly be explained without a proper study of the general policy of the state in the field of population, or without a thorough study of social conditions in general in the context of the concrete actions of the Bolsheviks. Nonetheless, Stolee, Ball, and Goldman should be thanked for introducing new questions about early Soviet era childhood into English-language historiography and for doing their best to present them.

As already mentioned, existing studies completely ignore the vital issue of children's general living conditions and the reality of the Soviet government's policy as regards governance and its implementation, for which I use the general Bolshevik *realpolitik*. Since most homeless and starving children had families and living parents with whom they lived until they became homeless, the problem of childhood disasters should be analyzed within the context of general Bolshevik policy and actions toward the population. Beginning in 1918, the government carried out well-known brutal food requisitions and other punitive measures against a large part of the peasant population, which could lead to no other result but to cause a catastrophic wave of children's hunger, homelessness, and the subsequent increase in mortality.[24] Historians are aware of the requisition of food from grain-producing provinces (surplus appropriation), but, mysteriously, they do not link this phenomenon to famine in the very same provinces, the main source of homeless children in 1919 and the early 1920s.

It is impossible to explain children's homelessness without discussing the living conditions of children and their families in general, without taking into account the policies and measures toward the population chosen by the state—violence and terror. In this respect, it was not imaginary "Russian backwardness," but specifically Bolshevik *realpolitik*, which became the permanent genesis of the population's impoverishment in general and of children's hardship, in particular. All social strata (workers, peasants, bourgeoisie, clergy, old people, adults, etc.) suffered from the new Bolshevik and then Stalinist government, and children, as the most vulnerable social group, suffered the most. Children's homelessness reflected and perpetuated their hunger and behaviors that the government deemed abnormal and criminal. Children did not commit crimes because, to quote official sources, they "gathered in groups and acquired a sense of independence." Children committed crimes because they were hungry.

Indeed, problems of children's homelessness, hunger, and high mortality should also be considered in aggregate and in a broader chronological framework than has been done so far in order to understand and explain the startling continuity of these issues, as well as to clarify some historiographic omissions. For example, contemporary research into the plight of children in the 1930s suggests that the suffering of children during Stalin's collectivization and repression of the kulaks was *sui generis*, with no relation to earlier periods. It is assumed that earlier Soviet children enjoyed happiness, as official Soviet sources usually state. The anthology *Children of the Gulag* edited by Katie Frierson and Semyon Vilensky and the collection of children's testimonies edited by Frierson *Silence Was Salvation: Child Survivors of Stalin's Terror and World War II in the Soviet Union*[25] are an excellent set of sources for Siberian special settlements, where children were resettled with their exiled parents in the 1930s. According to the editors, the children's population of the GULAG was subjected to the oppression of the authorities and lived in terrible conditions. What these historians do not consider in their comments is that the policies that began with War Communism (1918–21) and continued, with variations, until the late 1920s, had already subjected millions of Soviet children to similar horrendous shock and trauma. The actual continuity between early Soviet and Stalinist times inexplicably disappears in modern studies of early Soviet childhood.

The lack of consistent research into early Soviet childhood leads scholars to speculate that there is a sharp gap between pre-war and wartime perceptions of childhood. For example, in her superb study *Sacrificing Childhood*, Julie de Graffenried implies that Stalin's pre-war ideal of "happy childhood" was abruptly cut short with the outbreak of the Second World War and was transformed into a new ideal—"sacrificing childhood."[26] Like everyone else, children had to work, fight, and sacrifice their lives. Even so, careful study of 1920s and 1930s social and political realities would render controversial any idea of a "happy childhood" in the early USSR. In the fourth and fifth chapters of this book, an attempt is made to fill these gaps in the history of early Soviet childhood by establishing continuity in the history of Soviet childhood.

In addition to Julie de Graffenried's book, among the general studies of Russian imperial and Soviet childhood, the works of Catriona Kelly and Elizabeth White occupy a special place. For any historian of childhood, primary sources are the main problem: children simply left no record about their history and left few tangible traces of their experiences, especially in relation to earlier historical periods. In this way, both researchers attempted to structure the lives of Russian and Soviet children and youth by analyzing state and social institutions and records created largely by adults. Both researchers found that the concept of childhood in Russia was not much different from the European one. Both researchers reveal the state and political interest in childhood in both periods of Russian history—imperial and Soviet. For both, the concept of childhood arose long before the October Revolution of 1917. However, understanding the experiences of starving and street children during the Soviet era was not a priority in these general studies.[27]

As already noted, the entire phenomenon of early Soviet children's tragedy requires a broader historical context, an analytical setting (especially regarding the economic and demographic policy of the state in the period from 1917 to the outbreak of the Second World War) and a wider range of primary sources, including available Cheka and NKVD files. The whole question of the involvement of the special services (Cheka and Cheka police) in the problem of children's homelessness must receive a thorough scholarly attention. In 1921, responsibility for homeless children was completely transferred to the Cheka, a punitive institution and one of the key instruments of the Bolsheviks' *realpolitik*. Its head, F. E. Dzerzhinsky, headed the famous *Detkomissia* (Children's Commission), and his colleague in the Cheka, V. S. Kornev, who headed the armed forces of the Cheka (and later became one of the first leaders of the NKVD), became deputy head of the Children's Commission. Commission Secretary V. A. Nazarov was also a high-ranking officer of the Cheka. Even the headquarters of the Children's Commission were in the premises of the Cheka. Not only the Cheka but all state institutions were engaged and authorized to aid street children. From 1920 on, homes for orphans were transformed into labor communes, where children were engaged in productive work only for a meager ration. None of the above are documented in existing studies. Chapter 4 explores these issues.

It is worth noting that the existing literature on homeless children tends to view street children as a static and isolated category, when in fact it was a dynamic category, as children constantly grew and became adolescents and adults: the nine-year-old child of 1918–21 was almost a matured adult by the end of the 1920s. If the children survived and made it to adulthood, they would then go to work, get married, or join the military. Obviously, street children in the late 1920s or mid-1930s were not the same people as they were in 1918 or early 1920s. But most of the homeless did not survive: the main problem was the horrific death rate (from disease, hunger, and repressions) among homeless children, which is recorded in the state's own statistics. Periodicals and documents show that contemporaries and government officials recognized children's homelessness as "a problem that constantly took on catastrophic forms" until the late 1920s. Even throughout the 1930s, when the government imposed heavy censorship, which meant that newspapers and magazines could no longer write about the issue, government "secret" and "top secret" circulars still described children's homelessness and starvation as "serious and disastrous." Although numbers fluctuated between 1918 and the late 1930s, the problem remained endemic and was clearly one of the causes of a severe demographic deficit, as shown by the 1936 census, which shocked the government so much that its results were not made public.

As already mentioned, official contemporaries of the Soviet state viewed the causes of children's suffering as directly reflecting imperialism and war. Government members and prominent Soviet public figures stressed the economic and social catastrophe caused by the wars of that period. In fact, the language used to explain the childhood crisis as due to wars was laid down by the state in the early 1920s. One of the first official documents stated that "children's homelessness arose as a result of imperialist [World War I] and the Civil War, famine, and has recently acquired dimensions that could pose a threat to public safety."[28] A government representative wrote in 1920: "with every year, the war, starvation and epidemics take more and more lives of parents. The numbers of orphans and homeless children are growing with dreadful speed."[29] The Commissariat for Enlightenment official N. K. Ulyanova (Krupskaya) pointed out that the collapse of social infrastructure was caused by the First World War and the Revolution and made millions of children homeless.[30] Later, the mid-1920s, the state officials began to emphasize Russia's pre-revolutionary capitalist and exploitive past. In a letter dated January 1926 to the Soviet of People's Commissars, an official wrote "the roots of current children's homelessness are in the lawlessness, exploitation and impoverishment of people during the tsarist regime."[31] Analogously, legal language may also cause confusion. The wording of most of the period's laws about childcare and children's protection seemed progressive, and this is what can be misleading if these laws are taken for granted without examining the context and concrete policies and actions of the government.

Along with this explanation, not only did the state put forward the First World War, revolutionary and Civil War as the cause of children's disasters, but some of the first Soviet specialists also suggested an idea that the persistence of children's homelessness and the difficulties of the government to cope with it resulted from the moral and behavioral "inferiority" of homeless children. Thus, children's misdeeds resulted from "imperialist" and revolutionary wars, and from the "moral inferiority" of homeless and starving children themselves. Although later some experts criticized the idea of moral inferiority of street children, the Revolutionary War and Civil War remained prominent in explaining the origins of children's homelessness for many decades.

Here the obvious question can be asked: How and why did the First World War, the Revolution, or the Civil War make vast numbers of children starving and homeless throughout the 1920s and 1930s? We are not talking about tens of thousands or even hundreds of thousands of children, but, according to the official estimates, millions of children, who allegedly became homeless in the late 1920s or 1930s. One may also wonder why and how in tsarist era poverty could have left huge numbers of children starving and homeless even in 1926? Obviously, the First World War, the Revolution, and the Civil War could not account for children's starvation and homelessness permanent problems throughout the 1920s and 1930s. Could 7–12-year-old homeless children reported by the government in 1924 be the result of the First World War or the 1917 Revolution? This is hardly the case. As mentioned earlier, English-speaking and most Russian-speaking commentators have tended to adhere to the official Soviet script. Regardless, the Soviet scenario must be considered critically and examined in a broader historical context using yet unused archival and other evidence.

The question of what led to the appearance of hundreds of thousands of children on the streets and train stations in 1918 and what lead to vast homelessness in 1920–1 and even into the late 1920s and 1930s, when official sources still characterized the problem as the acute, requires further study. In 1918, most street children came from cities and urban areas; in 1920 they were from the South-Eastern and Volga agricultural provinces; and in the late 1920s and 1930s, they still originated from agricultural regions of the USSR. For example, a 1932 report from Western Siberia, a major grain producer, defined the problem of homeless children as "particularly acute."[32] Therefore, the problem of time and place of the outbreaks of homelessness needs further exploration. Why in certain years was there an influx of street children from specific areas? What made these children stray and why did this issue persist in Soviet Russia over two decades after the Revolution and Civil War? What caused the issue to become perpetual?

Extensive archival evidence about children's homelessness and starvation reveals a different point of view than that suggested by the official Soviet scenario. The history of children's homelessness is inseparable from children's starvation and high mortality. A broader historical context, based upon more representative primary sources, is obviously required, especially with regard to the economic and demographic policy of the state during period from 1918 to 1941. Commentators have often attributed the beginnings of children's homelessness to the outbreak of the Civil War, whereas early children's homelessness and hunger exactly coincided with the forced grain requisites from the agricultural regions (and not from areas of the Civil War). Wave after wave of homeless children appeared on roads, train stations, and cities. By the early 1920s, this phenomenon had reached such proportions that the Soviet press reported on it daily in terms that left no doubt about its magnitude. Despite this, during the 1920s and 1930s, new outbreaks of homeless and starving children followed one another in Soviet Russia, albeit at different rates. According to secret documents, in Moscow, NKVD officers took children from train stations and sent them to children's colonies. In April 1933, about 900 homeless children were admitted to the Danilov orphanage in Moscow alone. By all official reports, mortality among street children had reached incredible proportions. In early Soviet Russia, these joint phenomena were endemic. The scale, urgency, and persistence of the problem were extraordinary.

To provide the necessary historical background and to create a comparative context, the first chapter of this book will examine the living conditions of children in the period leading up to the October Revolution of 1917 and explore the traditions of helping those in need in imperial Russia. It will explore the development and evolution of the childcare tradition, as well as the efforts of society, church, and government to help children in need during the last czarist decade. The chapter discusses the activities of imperial charities, the church, and local community institutions. With the coming to power of the new government in October 1917, the state abolished the entire private childcare system, assumed responsibility for orphans and all children in need, and therefore became responsible for the living conditions of minors in the country.

The second chapter will look at demography, geography, and the causes of children's starvation and homelessness. The very first street children appeared in urban areas of the former Russian Empire at the end of 1917–18, when children's institutions were closed or destroyed. But massive streams of homeless children came from the village, from the grain-producing regions of the republic in 1920–2. A huge number of children appeared from homelessness, hunger, and imprisonment. This chapter will analyze the Soviet official discourse about children and the social realities of the government's course based on previously unused archival materials, including the files of the Cheka and its successors, the NKVD, and from the archive of the Federal Security Service. Both the Cheka and the NKVD officially dealt with the problems of children's homelessness and aid to the starving. Existing scholarship has not used these sources. The role of coercive institutions, such as the Cheka and the NKVD, deserves more attention and analysis than it has until now received.

The third chapter will discuss the early Soviet government's perceptions of childhood, as well as the socio-economic and political realities it faced. By prohibiting private initiative and charitable foundations, the government placed all children under the patronage of the state. According to my findings, the early Soviet government had no policy regarding homeless and starving children and acted daily, often harshly and coercively. The early government publicly discussed new approaches to socialist parenting, but children's experience was bleak. Hungry children who were looking for food faced government troops and Cheka prisons. The government dealt with homeless and starving children with arms, suppression, arrest, and evacuation. Orphanages quickly developed into full-fledged labor camps.

Chapter 4 analyzes the situation of children during the period of the new economic policy. The early Soviet state continued to face problems of homelessness, hunger, and high children's mortality on a daily basis. Relief measures were always required. In the face of the new market turn, the Communist Soviet state turned its institutions for homeless children into manufacturing enterprises. Under the auspices of the Cheka, the state organized a trade and production enterprise named "*Larek*" (store). The enterprise widely used the labor of street children and children in labor camps. According to a monitoring agency, *Larek*'s profits, ostensibly for children's aid, mysteriously disappeared. This entire phenomenon is completely ignored in existing scholarship.

The fifth chapter examines Stalinist collectivization and its impact on children. Based on archival and published primary material, this chapter will show the remarkable continuity between early Bolshevik and Stalinist decades in public policy toward children; it will also examine the hardship of children throughout much of the Soviet Union. It was during this period that the Soviet government introduced ordinary criminal courts and the death penalty for children from twelve years of age.

Soviet scholars have long argued that Soviet children enjoyed a "happy childhood" under Stalin, a point of view that reflects the state's official point of view, that is, the soviet concept childhood. Numerous published and easily accessible archives, as well as widely known Soviet laws and policies seem to support the official happy childhood. Even so, careful study of early Soviet children living conditions, within the context of

Bolshevik *realpolitik*, cast doubt on the idea of a happy childhood and instead suggests the children's tragedy. During the years discussed in this book, Soviet children faced the harsh realities of the Bolshevik *realpolitik*. They were mistreated, manipulated, placed in concentration camps, and even terrorized by the early Soviet government. The story of early Soviet childhood is filled with tragedy.

Figure 3 Homeless boy with a homeless dog. Samara. 1930. Source: Open public domain.

1

Street Children before the Bolshevik Revolution: Prelude to the Crisis

Children's homelessness resulted from the imperialist and civil war[s], and from starvation, and recently reached an extent that may threaten public security ...
                    Commissariat for the Enlightenment report, April 16, 1924[1]

Children's homelessness is an inheritance from Tsarist autocracy and capitalist exploitation of labor.
                                        Izvestia, March 12, 1926

A history of street children's experiences in the early Soviet Union without retrospective historical context creates misunderstanding. To better assess the state of childcare in the early Soviet period, it is necessary to provide a brief overview of the imperial and earlier periods of Russian history. First, as the above passages illustrate, early Soviet officials identified the tsarist regime and nascent capitalism as the source of all childhood suffering and despair after 1917. The striking fact is that even in 1926, almost ten years after 1917's October Revolution, the Soviet state still blamed the tsarist autocracy and capitalism for the dire living conditions of millions of Soviet children in the mid-1920s. Secondly, almost nothing has been written about children's hunger and homelessness during the imperial era—presumably, these phenomena did not exist. Existing English-language scholarship hardly explored measures the late Russian imperial state deployed to cope with the children's hardship. Likewise, research on imperial Russian philanthropy is practically absent in Soviet scholarship—in the Soviet Union there was a taboo on researching imperial Russian philanthropy.

In recent decades, Russian scholars have begun to pay attention to this long-ignored issue. The 2005 book by Moscow historian Galina Nikolaevna Ulyanova is an inaugural seminal Russian-language work on charity in the Russian Empire in the nineteenth and early twentieth centuries.[2] The thematic analysis of historian Shcherbinin mentioned in the "Introduction" investigated the topic of caring for needy children in the Tambov region before and after the 1917 Revolution and made a great contribution to this little-studied topic.[3] Nevertheless, some recent Russian-language studies still explain the increase in the number of street children "as a direct consequence of the backwardness of Russia, the economic crisis and the underdevelopment of institutions of social protection."[4]

Thus, the history of child protection, as well as the state and society's perception of childcare in the early days of Russia, remains, virtually, a blank page in the Russian- and English-speaking historiography of Russia, whereas the system of charity and care for children in need was well-established and functioned, albeit imperfectly, until the October Revolution of 1917. Moreover, many of the progressive trends in childcare, education, and juvenile justice pursued by the early Soviet regime in fact existed before the Bolshevik Revolution. In a sense, the Bolshevik "innovations" in education and childcare simply imitated and built upon late tsarist counterparts. Late tsarist society in reality paid great attention to the practical issues of upbringing and education of children.

The following pages suggest that the system of imperial charity arose from a long-standing folk tradition of supporting the needy, and later, with the Christianization and rise of the Russian state, it consolidated into a cohesive social organization of charity. According to Adele Lindenmeyr, an eminent historian of imperial Russian society, the tradition of giving to the poor was part of a religious ideology deeply rooted in Russian culture.[5] The roots of this tradition, however, go back to pre-Christian times, to the polytheistic traditions of ancient Rus, in which there were already the simplest forms of voluntary assistance to those in need. After the adaption of Christianity, charity became an ideology: it acquired a more systematic and institutional character as a moral and ethical obligation necessary for spiritual well-being and salvation.

After the emergence of the Russian state and its centralization under the Rurikid rulers, the idea of state aid to the poor was further widely implemented during the reign of the Romanovs, especially Peter I and Catherine II. Charity was carried out by individuals and by church and state, and since the nineteenth century it had been organized in various civil institutions—charitable societies and charitable foundations. The reforms of 1864 transferred state charity in part to local authorities, zemstvos, and dumas. Thus, by the beginning of the twentieth century, Russia had not only a well-developed system of private and church charity, but also a system of state and local government aid to those in need with an extensive network of charitable foundations and institutions. A significant part of the beneficiaries of this network were orphans and other children in need.

In this chapter, we hope to fill the gap in our historical knowledge of philanthropy in the Russian Empire, especially with regard to supporting children in need, by examining the social practices in the tsarist state and the state policy of charity, which the Soviet government tried to destroy and actually succeeded in doing after the Revolution. It assesses the claims of the early Soviet authorities about the origins of early Soviet childhood suffering by providing a broader historical context for the origins of the vast and endless stream of starving and homeless children after the 1917 October Revolution. In addition, the chapter hopes to contribute to the vast literature on philanthropy in antiquity, the Middle Ages, and the beginning of modern times, suggesting that the nascent concept of philanthropy was already known and functioned well in the pre-Christian peasant community and ultimately grew into a state supported system.

Figure 4 Shelter at the Church of St. John the Baptist. Pupils of the Shelter 1900 Russia, Yaroslavl Province, Yaroslavl; Source: NIVA Magazine Volume 35, 1900. Source: Open public domain.

Tradition of Assisting the Needy

The phenomenon of orphaned and needy children existed from time immemorial in the vastness of the territory from which the Russian state was born. Russia's long history has witnessed numerous epidemics, natural disasters, wars and subsequent deaths, poverty, despair, and family breakdowns. They were a common occurrence and the main cause of children's distress and hardship in those days for all lands. The pre-Christian tradition of ancient Russia to bury wives with deceased husbands was another serious factor that led to the emergence of many orphans.[6] But did these phenomena make children homeless or starving? Had the loss of their parents deprived children of home or refuge? Did mass famine and homelessness occur in ancient or modern Russia, and did the problems at some point reach the level of severity and prevalence that almost instantly reached after the 1917 Revolution? Probably not. Of course, these factors left children in great distress and need, but in no way made them homeless or hungry. In all these tragic cases, the extended family and community dutifully took responsibility and care for their minors and other members in need, and children could always count on foster care or communal assistance.

The structure of the extended peasant family and the communal way of life prevented the possibility of homelessness, severe impoverishment, and children's starvation. The peasants lived in closely related communities, which often consisted of representatives of two or three related clans. Over the centuries, peasant communities had developed traditions and lifestyles aimed at minimizing the potential consequences of humanitarian disasters. Peasant communities voluntarily supported their orphans and the poor. The communal way of life in those ancient times, without much effort, allowed orphans or those in need to find refuge with close or distant relatives. According to the observation of nineteenth-century psychologist Moses Rubinstein, a large family served as "a large community whose members were linked to each other by blood ties." He wrote, "In such family societies, children were in fact viewed as a common heritage, and the loss of one or both parents did not make [children] worse off."[7]

The tradition of Russian peasant communities to prevent child neglect impressed the Prussian observer August von Haxthausen (1792–1866), who wrote that "the Russian peasant commune is one of the most remarkable and interesting social institutions in the world. A man can become impoverished—this will not harm his children: they will still own or receive again their [land] allotment, in accordance with customs and traditions, not as heirs of the father, but as members of the family and the commune."[8]

While von Haxthausen's views on the Russian peasant commune may be idealistic, Russian explorers of public philanthropy and anthropologists emphasize the positive role of the communal lifestyle of Russian peasants and polytheistic culture in caring for the needy and the well-being of members of the community. In fact, pagan and communal traditions were intertwined. The pagan tradition perceived a person as part of a single whole, within which the individual was dissolved in nature and space. This belonging to an integral social structure stemmed from the experience of coexistence, ritual, and work activities, which were organically woven into nature, space, and the emotional world of people. For the individual, there was no opposition to these realities: one is a continuation of the other, and therefore the principles of the existence of the individual and the community coexisted. In my recent book on the Russian peasantry, I called it "peasant ecological mindset" that rested upon very specific circumstances of peasant and community interactions.[9]

The communal principles of human life and survival—the practice of humanitarian protection within the framework of the family and community system—were reflected in specific forms of aid and mutual assistance, among which were traditional religious and mythical cults with various sacred features. The practice of helping and supporting those in need was closely related to the mythological world of the ancient Rus' people.[10] In the spirit of this tradition, families and communes supported and fed their children and all others in need.

Pagan "Pomochi" (Helpings)

Russian-speaking anthropologists have found that many types of charity in Imperial Russia originated in pre-Christian Rus' and survived until the nineteenth century. For example, there were folk labor ritual holidays called *pomochi* (helpings), and were originally associated with the pagan god Yarila, personifying fertility, profit, and harvest. *Pomochi* was a complex custom based on community volunteerism by peasants and a moral commitment to help complete any task or help those in need. The products of this day were distributed among the poor members of the community.

Many nineteenth-century observers who traveled to the Russian provinces left indispensable descriptions of this surviving tradition of voluntary philanthropy. "Helping a fire victim is a natural phenomenon. They will not ask for alms, because even the victims of the fire do not go to beg but wait and are sure that everyone will approach them with a hand," wrote an observer from the Novgorod province.[11] According to Professor of Anthropology and History Marina Mikhailovna Gromyko, an authoritative explorer of Russian popular traditions, peasant charity was "a tribute to an ancient tradition that was once pagan in nature. These actions were performed so as not to break with the custom of the ancestors."[12]

Thus, even before the rise of state in Russia, and the introduction of Christianity, the needy or an orphan could always count on aid and support from the clan or community to which they belonged. Assistance and giving to the needy were habitual and voluntary practices. Although orphans and children in need existed, they could always seek help and protection from their extended family and commune.

"Synovstvo" (Adoptions)

There were many customary ways for caring for and protecting orphaned children through adoption or practices of transferring custody. Adoption was known as "synovstvo" (sonship).[13] Peasant local customs provided for various adoption methods that were also supported by a pagan ritual. Some areas practiced adoption through the rite of a fictional birthing: a woman in imaginary labor was placed on an underwear shirt stained with blood in order to become a stepmother. A man could also stage an imitation of the childbirth giving in a ritual that empowered him to become a stepfather.[14]

In some instances, orphaned children, who possessed no inherited property, were sent to foster families of childless elderly people. This was done for the mutual benefit of both, these families, and the children: the elderly received help from their stepchild and the child received custody, to ensure that the family provided for the future of the child. The adopted children were obliged to help their foster parents in maintaining the household, esteem them, and organize their funeral after they died. Foster children received whole possession of their deceased foster parents' property. For pragmatic reasons, usually peasants were willing to foster orphans because they could increase their allotment of the communal land, obtain additional laboring hands in the future, or receive an allowance from the commune. Orphans could also be assigned to communal parents who took them for nurturing. Children, who possessed some property, were not sent to foster families, but the community assisted them with maintaining the household, according to customary law and tradition.[15] Nevertheless, it should be noted that, having grown up, orphans became equal members of the commune. Along with everyone else, they received allotments of communal land and could start their own households.

Thus, the commune's work of charity had a practical function—to prepare children for adulthood responsibilities.[16] The Russian peasant commune had a mechanism that allowed growing children a smooth passage to adulthood and to becoming full commune members. Children participated in almost all rural activities; they were constantly growing up and learning what they would be expected to do as adults. From age 9 to 10, children were taught basic peasant skills. Boys learned to harrow, mow, and ride horses, whereas girls cared for younger children, and learned how to milk cows, rake hay, and tie bundles of rye. After five to six years, as children reached fifteen to seventeen, they became "full workers"; that is, boys performed workloads requiring male strength, whereas girls worked in the household.[17] Judging by numerous testimonies, the commune effectively generated all social types of people it needed for sustaining itself. Well-known scientist and publicist A. N. Engelgardt (1832–93) observed that "peasant boys count better than the lords' children." He wrote that

> ingenuity, memory, the ability to measure by the eye, hearing, and recognition of smells are developed in them immeasurably better than in our [upper strata] children, so seeing our child, especially an urban one, among peasant children, you might think that he has no ears, no eyes, no legs, no hands.[18]

Even taking a critical stance toward Engelgardt's objectivity, one can certainly assume that for their own sustainability and survival, peasant communes tried to provide for the well-being of their children and to prepare them for adulthood responsibilities.

As we have seen, there were numerous forms that prevented children's impoverishment, starvation, and homelessness in the Russian countryside; these practices became customary law. It is possible to conclude that during earlier times, children's homelessness and starvation hardly presented a severe problem in the countryside, where most people lived, because families and village communes supported their orphans and needy persons in numerous ways.

Institutionalization of Charity

With the rise and centralization of the state, and the introduction of Christianity, charitable activities became the government and church spheres of activity and supervision. This period of Russian history is associated with the early Rurikid rulers and the reign of Prince Vladimir and his successors. This period witnessed the emergence of a legal tradition of benevolence and assistance to the needy. In fact, laws of this time created a legal foundation for charitable endeavors and set forth a tradition of state charity. Eventually, from voluntary practice, performed at free will, either out of personal, religious, spiritual, or socio-economic considerations, charity and support for the needy became obligatory acts, required by law, and encouraged by the state fiscal policy. Charity of the Russian Orthodox Church also became institutionalized, regulated, and required by the state.

"Sell Your Possessions to Benefit the Poor"

According to the Primary Chronicle, Prince Vladimir, "taking the faith of the Savior, lit up with this faith in his heart, became a different person."[19] The chronicler narrated that Vladimir

> loved the Holy Scripture so much that he once heard the Gospel: "Blessed are the merciful, for they will have mercy"; and once again: "Sell your possessions to benefit to the poor"; and again: "Do not collect treasures for yourself on the earth, where the moth destroys and the thieves steal, but collect treasures in heaven where neither the moth destroys, nor the thieves steal"; and David's words: "Blessed is the man who has mercy and lends"; he heard the words of Solomon: "He who lends to a beggar gives to God." Having heard all of this, he ordered every beggar and poor to come to the prince's court and take all that they needed: drinks and food, and money from the treasury. He also arranged this: saying that for "the weak and sick that cannot get to my court, I order to equip the carts" and he placed bread, meat, fish, various fruits, and honey in barrels on them, and on others—kvass, to deliver them around the city, enquiring: "Where is the sick, the poor, or who cannot walk?"[20]

Although the chronicler's words may be visionary and exaggerated, it is a fact that after conversion to Christianity in 996, Vladimir issued a church charter which instituted church benevolence. It entrusted the clergy with social welfare activities and charity and ruled out that the tithe (one tenth) of donations in favor of monasteries and churches should be distributed to the poorhouses and for charity. During Vladimir's reign, churches and monasteries received considerable revenues from their landholdings, as well as from individual patrons. These landholdings and donations were exempted from state taxation, as well as all other sources of the church income, but a tenth of its revenue the church was obliged to spend on charity.[21] In addition to mandatory tithing of churches and monasteries, charitable donations came from private individuals. The forms of these donations varied and ranged from monetary contributions to the grants of land, houses, and other property.

Russian late imperial historians described the reign of Prince Vladimir as a blossoming time in the history of Russian philanthropy that laid the foundation for church and state charity and continued to develop further. In this view, Russians acquired some realization of the spiritual importance of charity for proper moral conduct in a Christian society. Nineteenth-century historian V. O. Kliuchevsky wrote:

> Peasant charity was not so much a means of achieving public welfare, it was a means of maintaining personal spiritual safety: it was more necessary to the giver than to the recipient. It is like in a hospital, where the patient is necessary to learn how to cure illnesses, so that in the old Russian society the lonely and poor were necessary to learn to love the person.[22]

According to historian A. M. Kapustina, in the Russian Orthodox Church charity became the manifestation of Christian love—compassion, likeness to God the Benefactor, self-cultivation on the path to salvation.[23]

Yaroslav's Welfare Laws

After Vladimir's death, the tradition of charity continued, deepened, and became further institutionalized and promoted by the state. Vladimir's successor Yaroslav the Wise supported and required public welfare measures. He set up an orphanage, which provided shelter and education for 300 young male orphans. The Rus' earliest code of laws—*Russian Truth (Russkaya Pravda)*—of Yaroslav required orphans' nearest relatives to provide "a loyal care and patronage for the children."[24] Yaroslav's law code had a semblance of a nascent social welfare program: fifteen articles of the code were entirely devoted to children's protection, as regards their possessions, property rights, and custody. This was the first attempt to compile Russian laws and regulations, and eventually it became the basis for Russia's future legislative policies. The subsequent sets of laws were built in the image and likeness of the "Russian Truth," so that the foundations of social welfare policy were firmly established from the very beginning of Russian practice of written law.

One of the code's articles concerned the practice of passing on property and the protection of the youngest male child. Bearing in mind that unlike the older son, the youngest son is not socially protected, the article ruled that "the father's yard always belongs to the youngest son without division." Before the introduction of the "Russian Truth," youngest brothers could resolve the dispute only by force, now the youngest sons were protected by law. In general, the laws of Yaroslav regarding children's protection were humane for the time. For example, laws determined how property was to be divided between siblings of the same father, but different mothers, or addressed issues when negligent mothers wasted property. For the first time laws protected women, as well: "children cannot drive the widowed mother out of the household or take away from her what had been given to her by her husband."[25] To protect children with one living parent, Yaroslav ordered these children to be transferred to the next of their father's kin if the mother married again. Of course, this was not fair to the mother, but, it seems, this was an assurance against possible mistreatment of children by their stepfather. Apparently, all these developments might be critical for urban areas especially, where popular traditions were weaker and numbers of the needy were greater.

Charity Institutionalized

Thus, in this early period of Russian history, a full-fledged legal and social tradition of caring for children in need emerged. After the death of their parents or other adverse circumstances, children could not only count on help and support from their extended families, communities, rulers, and the church, but it also became the legal duty of these institutions to care for orphans and other children in need. This tradition is well reflected in the literature of Ancient Rus. In the Teachings of Vladimir Monomakh (eleventh century), one reads:

> Do not forget the poorest, feed the orphan as much as you can, give the orphan, and justify the widow, as you would yourself, and do not allow the strong to destroy the weak.[26]

However, it can hardly be argued that childhood adversity was entirely absent during this transformative and turbulent period in the development of the Russian state. The living conditions of most of the population were poor and the infant mortality rate was very high. As already mentioned, epidemics, wars, natural disasters, harsh natural conditions, and lack of medical services were the main causes of child deprivation. In addition to natural and climatic disasters, wars, and epidemics, fires were frequent in "wooden" Russia. Chroniclers recorded forty-three outbreaks of severe famine in Russia up to the sixteenth century—an average of eight cases per century. Here is a description written by a chronicler in 1128 about the consequences of the lack of bread in the country: "Fathers and mothers gave their children to foreign merchants." Similar stories came from Novgorod in 1214–15: "Woe to you, brothers! Parents gave their children as a gift." Obviously, no one at that time, especially a child, could be completely insured against the danger of "sinking to the bottom."[27] In order to solve these social problems, the participation of the state in charity and childcare gradually increased and moved to a new level. State control over charity increased.

Not only a shelter, but teaching values: a Russian Renaissance?

During the sixteenth century, charity became more oriented toward socialization and education of children in need, especially orphans. Although this is denied by most scholars, some predisposition to the Renaissance and Enlightenment may have occurred during this period in Russia. It seems that the state recognized orphans as individuals in need of education and learning to behave in a way that would produce a better society. At least certain aspects of what is usually associated with Catherine the Great's Enlightenment had already begun during the reign of Ivan the Terrible (Ivan IV). This clearly requires serious unbiased scholarly attention.

Albeit a controversial ruler, Ivan was a progressive reformer, and his reforms were aimed at improving the central and local governments, laws, education, and charity.[28] His government produced the first "book schools" in urban monasteries that taught a religious and secular curriculum. Ivan helped introduce printing in Russia and organized a commission to draw a new map of his kingdom. Typography became a new craft, headed by Ivan Fedorov. The printing court in Moscow published religious and secular literature and textbooks. The first grammar and arithmetic books were published during this period.[29]

No less progressive were Ivan's political innovations. The tsar implemented judicial reforms, and introduced a representative body, the *Zemsky Sobor*, and a new code of laws, the *Sudebnik* of Ivan IV.[30] This code of law became the first normative legal act in Russia, *proclaimed* as the only source of law—in fact, it became the first constitution, approved by the *Zemsky Sobor*. Compared to laws of his predecessors, Ivan's laws were more lenient and philanthropic in nature. For the first time in Russian history, monetary fines were officially approved and in certain cases used as an alternative to imprisonment.

To a certain extent, the government tried to expand the rights of the peasantry and its participation in local public affairs. Elected representatives of peasant communes were to participate in the legal investigation and proceedings. The authorities, neither in court nor before the trial, could take a peasant into custody without the consent of the communal elective chiefs, elders, or executives. Worthy to note here is that when the Bolsheviks carried out forceful food procurement, or later the collectivization of agriculture, they arrested whole peasant families, including children, and never bothered to ask for consent from peasant communal authorities. How this impacted early Soviet children's well-being will be discussed in the following chapters. Again, this book considers children not only as an age group, but a group that depends on their guardians and immediate environment, whose well-being in turn directly affects the well-being of their underaged or otherwise dependent members.

Ivan's Charity and Educational Laws

As mentioned, the state began to view children in need as individuals and recognized the importance of providing them with education. A series of Ivan's laws aimed at children's schooling and proper upbringing. The tsar appointed the Patriarchal order to oversee these educational and benevolent activities. Ivan's laws required that "the Church of God feed and support the poor and needy," as well as provide them with teaching and instruction. The 1551 *Stoglav Sobor* (the Hundred Chapter Synod or Council of a Hundred Chapters) of the Russian Orthodox Church introduced a requirement for each church to open schools for orphans in order "to teach the children to read and write," and to create church almshouses for "orphans and those with infirmities."[31] The Council required pious and skilled priests, deacons, and clerks to establish schools for literacy, religious reading, and grammar curriculum. The state also obligated monasteries to create schools, and to teach children secular disciplines—such as grammar and arithmetic. Priests and monks became responsible for teaching children.

These educational intentions and reforms were hardly mere declaratory acts. To implement the policies, the state provided monasteries with financial and material support, thus becoming a patron of benevolence and education. Ivan's laws instituted state funding and supported private endowments to provide for charity and schooling. During his reign Ivan continued to set up charitable institutions and almshouses. Ivan indicated that every city should identify children in need of public assistance and supported building special almshouses for the orphan and infirm, where they would be provided with shelter, care, and education.[32]

It is important to note that these humanitarian efforts also resulted from the acute need to smooth the implications of numerous social and economic problems. While the assumption of a Russian Renaissance during this time may seem provocative and exaggerated, and may raise skeptical questions, this unexplored aspect clearly deserves more unbiased scholarly attention than it has received, especially the educational and charitable efforts of the Ivan IV's government. With the death of Ivan the Terrible, his successor, his son Fyodor I (r. 1584–98), who in fact gave the government into the hands of Boris Godunov, the Rurikid dynasty ended, but the tradition of charity, established during the time of its rulers, continued and flourished.

Godunov's Welfare State

After Ivan's and his successors' deaths, the Russian kingdom entered the Time of Troubles. The early seventeenth century was mainly distressful for Russia—famine, epidemics, unemployment in towns, and internal turmoil plagued the reign of Boris Godunov (r. 1598–1605).[33] The state, however, continued its humanitarian policy. Godunov, ascending the throne, promised that there would be no homeless or beggars in the kingdom. Godunov was known for his piety and generosity. The tsar "did not spare any means and daily distributed huge sums of money to the poor in Moscow."[34] He organized almshouses and, after the outbreak of famine in 1601, set up the distribution of free bread in Moscow, Smolensk, Novgorod, and Pskov, and introduced government regulation of bread prices. Free bread distribution to the needy became a tradition in Russia. To relieve the unemployed and support the poor, perhaps for the first time in Russian history Godunov introduced public works—construction of stone buildings in Moscow and other cities.[35] Obviously, this community service was important because it provided thousands of people with jobs and the means to support their families.

Private-State-Church Benevolence: the Romanovs

It seems that during the reign of early Romanov's rulers, private, church, and state charitable activities coalesced. As the Russian state continued to expand and centralize—developments that implied warfare, civil disturbances, social dislocations, and disintegration of families—the number of orphans and needy children increased. In response, the state, the church, and private individuals cooperated in charity efforts. The state encouraged this cooperation.

The first Romanov ruler, Mikhail Fyodorovich (r. 1613–45), required the patriarchal order to open more homes for orphans, whose numbers grew steadily. His successors, his son and grandson, Alexei Mikhailovich (r. 1645–76) and Fyodor Alekseevich—Fyodor III—(1676–82), respectively, organized special agencies that dealt with charity and opened houses for street children, where they were taught literacy, trades, and science.

Alexei began a tradition that he, his court, as well as the clergy and noble citizens, visited prisons and almshouses, and distributed alms on Christmas and Easter eves, the days of commemoration of military victories, or the birth of heirs. Alexei attempted to combine private, church, and state charity, while the state also remained a patron and overseer of charity. In 1670, the tsar formed an "Order" for the construction of almshouses and assigned all almshouses to the department of the patriarchal house. The state provided funds for and supervision of monasteries' charity and educational programs for orphaned children, in addition to private donations and the tithe that monasteries received. His successor, tsar Fyodor Alekseevich, in 1682, created an organization of state funding for church-state charitable institutions for the chronically ill, beggars, and orphans.[36]

Thus, supported by the government, monasteries became shelters for many orphans and abandoned children. The cases of child abandonment were frequent. Unable to save their children from starvation, some parents left them by monasteries gates. Monasteries set up schools where these children learned reading and writing, as well as arithmetic and geometry. The monks took the foundlings and sheltered them in special huts, where the children received a bed, food, clothing, and necessary care. In church and monastery orphanages, in addition to foundlings, orphaned children of monastic peasants and others found refuge as well. Besides schooling, children learned trades and performed work they could do according to their strength and abilities: cultivated the land, grazed the monastic cattle, helped in the haymaking, etc. The number of orphans kept in monasteries varied. According to historian I. N. Shamina, in 1632, in the patrimony of the Nikolo-Ozersky monastery in the Vologda region, orphans occupied seven buildings; in the Arsenyevo-Komelsky monastery, in 1677, they all lived in one building.[37] A special children's shelter for orphans also functioned in the Pavlovo-Obnorsky monastery of the Vologda diocese. The monastery sheltered up to ninety orphaned peasant children where they received an education and helped with the maintenance of the monastery.[38] According to surviving documents, the Novgorod monastic community had several monasteries that hosted beggars in special rooms for needy adults and children. The Virgin Monastery, for example, sheltered 600–700 needy people, including children, pilgrims, and patients.

By the end of the seventeenth century, Russian churches housed about 60,000 shelters for the poor and orphans, where they received boarding and education.[39] As mentioned, this was especially vital for the urban areas, where traditional forms of assistance were inadequate or absent. Thus, although orphans and the children in need existed and were perhaps numerous, the state used various means and initiatives to support, educate, and socialize them. Starving and homeless children hardly created a problem that would be identified as a threat to national security, as in fact happened during the post 1917 Revolution decades and as the Soviet state itself defined it.

Benevolence among Old Believers

In the Old Believer version of Orthodoxy, in addition to the above-mentioned features of church benevolence, it was important to teach about the four gifts, which is instructed in the Old Believer verse about John the Baptist, given by the Old Believer merchant V. P. Ryabushinsky in his Moscow Merchants:

The Lord has sent four gifts. Already as the first gift—the cross and prayer. The second gift is love and charity. The third gift is prayer at night. The fourth gift is a reading of the Book.⁴⁰

The building of churches served the cross and prayer. Love and charity stood for almshouses, hospitals, free canteens. Night prayer were icons, the collection of which had become widespread among the Old Believers. Reading the Book explains the book culture of Old Believers and their efforts to preserve old books. The Old Believers assumed that they were the ones chosen by the Lord for eternal life; therefore, they must preserve their peace, their community at any cost, and for this they all had to help each other.⁴¹ One can hardly imagine a needy orphan or a hungry child in an Old Believer's community.

Petrine Benevolence' Pragmatism

The era of Peter I (commonly known as Peter the Great, r. 1682–1725), witnessed profound militarization, state-promoted industrialization, and intensive and constant warfare, which produced many orphans, as well as wounded and needy persons.⁴² At the same time, as a result of prolonged wars and military campaigns, there was a significant population decline during his reign. It is impossible to provide any statistics on homeless and needy children during this time; let us assume that they did exist in significant numbers. Apparently, the state approach to child support became more pragmatic and orderly than it had been before. To deal with the new issues, the state needed stable revenue, systematic tax collection, and an efficient use of human resources. Government control over philanthropy increased, and philanthropy became more regulated and more closely monitored, and it became more compulsory than voluntary. Laws of Peter prohibited beggars and vagabonds from streets and either sent the ill and children to almshouses and orphanages or employed these capable of doing work to industries or military. According to sources, Peter became concerned about growing numbers of professional vagabonds who wanted to take advantage of the charity system.

According to a series of decrees of the Senate, churches and monasteries were required to organize and maintain hospitals and childcare institutions. In order to improve hospitals' finances and means of church charity, the state required monasteries to submit accounting books for reviews on a regular basis.⁴³ Under Peter the Great, the organization and maintenance of almshouses and hospitals became the responsibility of state departments: first—the Patriarchal department, then, from 1701, the Monastic; from 1721 all charity came under control of the newly formed Holy Synod and thereafter, from 1724, under the finance department (*kamer-kontora*).⁴⁴

In order to deal with the population decline, Peter encouraged the opening of shelters where illegitimate children were admitted with anonymity as regards their origins—perhaps an opportunity for serf children to escape servitude. With this measure, Peter I in fact institutionalized an earlier monasterial practice. Peter's reforms introduced legal norm to support illegitimate children and unwanted babies, who were often victims of infanticide. For fear of being publicly shamed, mothers often killed their illegitimate newborn babies. Under the new decrees, the reception of unwanted children was confidential and arranged in a way that no one could see the person who left the child. The state created and funded a network of shelters and foundling homes for abandoned babies. These establishments were entirely funded by the state. When infants matured, they were placed in almshouses or foster families.[45] The same law required financial compensation for nursing women.[46]

In June 1718, Peter issued a decree which sent orphaned and impoverished street children to the cloth court (i.e., cloth manufacturers) and to other manufactories to learn trades. Children over twelve-year-old were turned over to sailors to learn naval arts and navigation skills (and other pertinent practices).[47] In addition, since most almshouses and hospitals were overcrowded, the state tried to place orphans into families for upbringing and education. Peter I identified new sources of funding for "state hospitals" and children's homes by increasing the collection of money from those entering into marriage, establishing a deduction from the salary of any ranks and other fees. Funds were allocated from the treasury for the maintenance of pupils and the payment of service personnel.

During 1721-4, the state took over the administration of the church with a series of decrees and by the introduction of "Holy Governing Synod" or the "Spiritual Collegium," as the head of the Russian Orthodox Church. Under the conditions of state-bureaucratic administration of the church, many long-standing charitable traditions became regulated, and voluntary, merciful deeds turned into a duty. In particular, on July 29, 1723, the Synod, by its official order, introduced financial support of poor parishioners as a duty of church parishes. Church elders were instructed to collect charitable donations from believers, sell wax candles, and use these funds for charity for the poor members of the parish, including orphans and single widowed mothers and widows.[48]

Catherine's Enlightened Approach

Under the Empress Catherine II (r. 1762-96), the system of charity witnessed an Enlightenment turn and further institutionalization.[49] Like her predecessors, she supported charitable schools and shelters, but her approach emphasized virtue and the cultivation of good morals in children. Educational houses provided "good upbringing," and their main task was not only giving children a shelter but also transferring them to "good" families and homes, where they could have proper upbringing. The purpose of the empress was to create a stratum of educated and industrious people, who would serve the homeland and master various crafts. She stimulated development of a "middle class"—a group of educated professionals and conscious citizens. The children's homes obtained workshops and trained children to become doctors, village teachers, midwives, nannies, and personnel for the merchant fleet. Catherine followed a principle that all children who have been deprived of a parental care should have the right to guardianship from the state; care for these children should be no less dutiful than the care of parents they gave to their own children.

In the early 1770s, the Senate established foundling homes for illegitimate children in Moscow, St. Petersburg, and other cities across the empire. After being wet nursed, many children were transferred to the countryside to foster families, where they remained until the age of 21. Wet nurses received some monetary compensation from the state. This laid a foundation for the charity of illegitimate children through the empire. It is important to note here that foundling homes received children from all social estates and children were treated equally and all became free persons.[50] The idea of creating such houses belonged to the well-known philanthropist and teacher Lieutenant-General Ivan Ivanovich Betskoy (1704–95). Betskoy believed that through the upbringing of orphans and illegitimate babies it would be possible to raise a new "breed" of people—knowledgeable and well-educated. His opinion was also shared by well-known Russian teachers of that time—the chairman of the Commission on the establishment of public schools P. V. Zavadovsky and the former director of schools in the Temeshvar district of the Austrian Empire, F. I. Jankovic-de-Mirievo, invited in the 1780s to work in Russia.[51]

Orphanages were government institutions and included a complex of separate buildings. Each building housed a specific group of children, according to their age and gender. The babies were sent to the nurses in the village; children from two to seven years old, sent to foster families to the countryside, were under the supervision of a district doctor and a curator; children aged 7–11 remained in orphanages, where they received education and training. Upbringing and education included the foundations of faith; the classes were equipped for the study of literacy, arithmetic, geography, and there were also various workshops for learning crafts. Upon reaching the age of 18 to 20, the pupils, receiving a free passport and one ruble, were released from the orphanage. Both graduates and their children remained free persons forever and could not be serfs afterwards. They had the right to buy houses, shops, join the merchant class, manage their property, or engage in trade. Young men received a land allotment a serious privilege in the conditions of serfdom.[52]

The empress's reforms tried to change the socio-economic structure of Russia, which in turn affected charity. In 1775, Catherine created a two-tier system of public charity management: regional public charity management bodies and local government bodies based on estates and an orphan's court, in charge of guardianship and orphan affairs. The governing bodies included the noble guardianship and the city orphan's court and worked on the principle of self-financing.[53] Catherine's legislation created a network of charitable institutions in forty provinces of the empire. The regional bodies oversaw supervision, organization, and funding public schools and orphanages. Rural and urban communities and parishes under the control of local authorities were required to feed the poor, not allowing them to become impoverished in the future. All social estates had a responsibility of helping disabled members of society. In 1785, Catherine's government created trusteeships to manage charitable institutions. From the second half of the eighteenth century, according to some scholars, there was an emerging interest in the child as a person and attempts to provide children with legal protection.[54] But as discussed earlier, these tendencies had already emerged during the reign of Ivan IV.

Some local case studies illustrate the activities of regional charitable bodies established by Catherine's government.[55] These provincial charitable bodies, established during 1777–9, had the goal of coordinating and funding all provincial institutions of charity. The imperial government donated 15,000 rubles (worth about 317,000 dollars today) to each provincial body and thereafter this amount was to be funded annually by local provincial governments. Over a period, these local bodies received numerous private donations. For example, in 1781 they received charitable donations from the district nobility.

However, the attempt to create a nationwide network of childcare facilities for orphans was hampered by several serious problems. State-controlled orphanages turned out to be ineffective: due to the high density of inmates, they often turned out to be hotbeds of infections, which led to mortality and morbidity among inmates in these homes. For example, over the four years of its existence, more than 82 percent of the 3,147 infants of the Moscow Orphanage perished. Thereafter, the government used foster families and paid these families 2 rubles per month.[56] The Moscow Orphanage, consisting of 4,300 villages in the Moscow, Tula, Vladimir, Tver, and Ryazan provinces, maintained 30,000 wet nurses and foster families raising up to 40,000 children. Some 2,000 villages of the St. Petersburg, Pskov, and Novgorod provinces were assigned to the St. Petersburg House, in which 18,000 wet nurses and foster parents nursed and housed 25,000 children. Nursing mothers received an allowance for children until they attained the age of 15, after which the children remained in families until the age of 21.[57]

The issue of high infant and toddler mortality was persistent throughout both the imperial and soviet periods with some important differences that will be considered later. Therefore, the policy of needy children's welfare relied on a combination of foster care and non-state orphanages handled by individual philanthropists and the Russian Orthodox Church. Nevertheless, Catherine established state system of public and private charity which flourished until the 1917 October Revolution. Her successor Paul I appointed Empress Maria Feodorovna as the head of all social institutions in Russia; these later became known as the "Institutions of the Empress Maria." Over the thirty years of her activity, many charitable hospitals, orphanages, experimental orphanages for deaf and blind children, almshouses, etc. began to function. After the death of Maria Feodorovna in 1828, institutions named after her continued to develop and grow. In 1854, they were transformed into the Department of Institutions of the Empress Maria.

Nineteenth-Century Philanthropy

During the nineteenth century, Russia went through a remarkable economic and institutional transformation with attending new social realities and challenges. The rapidly growing capitalist economy and the growth of cities eroded the old social and family ties that in turn undermined traditional practices of caring for the needy.

These developments forced various social segments to seek ways to adjust themselves to new challenges, a process that was uneven and turbulent. At the same time, the changes in the economy created new social needs and precipitated the rise of civil society, which, by definition, became actively involved in politics and social issues. The century started with the Napoleonic wars and the Russian 1812 campaign with its grim consequences. All of these led to widespread homelessness, both in cities and the countryside, and an increase of children's hooliganism and delinquency. The state relied on tradition and pragmatism in dealing with these new challenges. As before, the government relied on the placement of orphaned and homeless children in various children's institutions and foster families.

As mentioned earlier, placing children in childcare institutions had severe shortcomings. Orphanages and other children's homes became overcrowded and standards in these homes seriously deteriorated, as the numbers of the needy children increased. Children's homes lacked adequate provisions, medical services, and necessary personnel, which lead to extremely high infant mortality rates. The mortality rates among infants and toddlers in these homes reached 75 percent—even so, this was lower than in early Soviet childcare institutions. It was against this circumstance that the imperial government prohibited the organization of new children's homes in 1828 and discouraged sending foundlings to childcare institutions.

Some attempts were undertaken to find ways to help mothers in need so that they could receive government subsidies and raise their toddlers themselves. The government paid the needy mother a certain cash amount to raise her infants at home until they reach the age of 7. The number of mothers who wished to receive this subsidy became so high that the government had to cut the amount of assistance and Empress Maria Feodorovna Charity System subjected the process of approving subsidy applications to greater scrutiny. In 1837, a government decree introduced a requirement that all babies brought to orphanages, without exception, be sent to foster care families for adoption and prohibited their return.[58] The government held that these actions could reduce child mortality rates.

From the mid-1860s state support for children in need was carried out in two directions. The first was the Department of Institutions of the Empress Maria Feodorovna, which included charitable foundations and institutions for children; the second was local zemstvo institutions established for the care of orphan and other children in need. In 1869, general supervision of orphanages was transferred to the chief manager of the IV department of His Imperial Majesty's Own Chancellery. The Russian Orthodox Church also continued to host and create additional shelters for children in need. As mentioned, the Russian church took upon itself the fulfillment of the most important childcare functions: upbringing, education, treatment, and charity. By the nineteenth century almost all the major monasteries provided homeless shelters and kept orphanages. Consequently, by the time of the October 1917 Revolution, virtually all monasteries and churches maintained orphanages and schools for children from all social strata. In addition, the church made significant financial contributions to charitable foundations and individual childcare institutions.

Middle-Class Philanthropy

In addition to state, public, and church charity, many private individuals became actively involved in benevolence, especially toward the end of the nineteenth century. Many entrepreneurial families engaged in charity work: these included the Abrikosovs, Alekseevs, Baevs, Karzinkins, Lepeshkins, Morozovs, Tretyakovs, Bakhrushins, and numerous others. Orphanages founded by merchants received full state support, in addition to their personal funds. Additional funds came from the church as well. A couple of examples will illustrate the activities of these private individuals. In 1849, merchant and honorary citizen Mark Pimenovich Pimenov organized the Nikolaev orphanage in Petrozavodsk, which became the first private charitable institution for children in Olonets province and one of the oldest in Russia. Pimenov donated a wooden house and initial funding for the maintenance of this orphanage which operated for almost seventy years mainly on public funds. At least one-fifth of the annual subsidy came from the local representative body, the zemstvo. Other sources of support of this orphanage came from the interest on the institution's capital, contributions from the trustees and elders of the orphanage, donations, income from workshops, and rentals.[59] This institution survived until 1918 when the new Bolshevik government closed it down.

In 1913, the endowment of all charitable institutions of St. Petersburg amounted to about 8 million rubles. In March 1910, the All-Russian Congress of Philanthropists stated that 75 percent of the funds for St. Petersburg were formed

Figure 5 Orphanage in Voronezh, founded in 1848. Source: Open public domain.

based on private voluntary donations and only 25 percent came from the state. According to rough estimates, at least 27 million rubles were distributed in Russia annually in the form of alms.

Bakhrushin's Charity

The most remarkable example of Russia's middle-class benevolence comes from the Moscow Bakhrushin family, responsible for creating orphanages, shelters, schools, and theaters; the Bakhrushins also sponsored arts. In 1895 the brothers Bakhrushin donated 600,000 silver rubles to Moscow to create an orphanage for children of the Orthodox faith, mainly among Moscow residents. In addition, the merchants gave the city land in the present-day park area of Sokolnikov—now close to downtown Moscow.[60] By 1905, the shelter contained 150 scholarship holders. The orphanage had a home theater, fruit orchards laid out in front of each house with the help of the hosted children, several chicken coops, pigeons, and open-air cages for geese; there were also an infirmary, a laundry room, and a bathhouse. Thus was the first family-type orphanage in Russia. On holidays, buildings were decorated with electric garlands, and in the evenings, readings were held with a magic lantern. The female members of the Bakhrushin family taught at the shelter's school. In addition, the brothers also built stone houses and organized shelters and homes for single mothers. In total, the Bakhrushins created about a dozen professional schools, laid the foundations of three museums (including the famous Bakhrushin Theater Museum), and helped create four theaters. The brothers built ten temples and systematically subsidized seventeen temples, and three monasteries. For philanthropy, including donations to the Church, this family spent more than 6 million during the late nineteenth and early twentieth centuries.

The Bakhrushin orphanage and school's main task was to prepare children for independent life, for which they were not only taught to read and write, but were also given a profession, depending on their inclinations. Many chose at that time the newest and most promising—electrical engineering—as the main craft. The shelter also taught carpentry and maintained a locksmith workshops with a forge. Already during their studies, adolescents professionally carried out third-party orders and earned some money. The Bakhrushins continued to participate in the life of scholarship holders even after they left the shelter at the age of 18.

By the beginning of the twentieth century, charity for children in Russia was at its peak. There were six charitable institutions for every 100,000 inhabitants of the European part of Russia. According to data for 1900, 82 percent of charitable institutions had been created by and operated under the patronage of private individuals, followed by estates (8 percent), urban entities (7 percent), and zemstvos (2 percent). By 1902, a total of 11,400 charitable institutions and 19,108 parish boards of trustees were registered in the Russian Empire.[61] This broad network supported the creation of educational institutions, the maintenance of houses for poor children night shelters for vagrants, canteens, outpatient clinics, and hospitals. During this period, charity took on a secular character. Personal participation in charitable endeavors was perceived by society as a moral act. Charity was associated with the nobility of the soul and was considered an inalienable affair of everyone.[62]

Late Imperial Reforms and Challenges

The late nineteenth century witnessed important institutional shifts regarding children and childhood. New laws regulated childhood, childcare, education, and child labor in industries which increased heavily toward the end of the century. Rapidly waxing civil society in Russia addressed numerous social issues, including those related to children. During the second half of the century significant changes took place in the development of education, especially in pedagogy. Russian late imperial pedagogues searched for humanistic, spiritual, and moral approaches to child development. Russian pedagogical society was concerned about self-improvement of the individual child, free education for children, and reform of education. Russian educators, physicians, and lawyers actively discussed such issues as child abuse and children's industrial employment and its implications for children and for society, as well as its regulation.[63]

With the purpose of protecting children from abuse, the Society for the Care of Poor and Sick Children (Blue Cross) was created in St. Petersburg in 1882. In 1892, this society established a special department for the protection of children from cruel treatment, harmful exploitation, and potentially corrupting and generally harmful influence on them from the persons on whom they depended. The department acted through district trustees, who had been empowered to access places where the interests of minors were violated; the trustees collected information about all cases of child abuse, tried to prevent abuse, in extreme cases brought them to the attention of the police and the prosecutor, and tried to get the children out of disastrous situations. In 1893, the department opened a shelter for children taken away from their parents. Founded in Moscow in 1883, the Society for the Care of Poor Children in 1887 expanded its activities by organizing a special department for the protection of children, after which it was renamed the Society for the Care of the Poor and Children in Need of Protection. The society committee informed the authorities about crimes against children, took the victims into the custody, and located attorneys to protect the interests of the victims in court.[64]

To deal with the increasing urbanization and the weakening of the institution of the family, the late imperial state regulated the status of so-called "illegitimate children." Earlier, they were eligible for adoption. The law of June 3, 1902, "On Approval of Rules for Improving the Situation of Illegitimate Children" established the recognition of children born in invalid marriages (recognized as such on the grounds of violation of the conditions of marriage or the presence of obstacles to its conclusion) as legitimate and abolished the restriction on the legalization of children born as a result of adultery if the child's parents married. The law gave parents freedom of choice for determining which of them would have custody of the child born in an invalid marriage. The state's protective function manifested itself in the decision of this issue by the board of trustees if the parents did not reach an agreement.[65]

Correction through Education vs. Coercion

Earlier, during the era of the Great Reforms in Russia, significant changes took place in the development of education, which emphasized humanistic, spiritual, and moral directions in pedagogy. The pedagogical community dealt with issues of personal self-improvement, free upbringing, and educational reform. The main aim of the state and society was to prevent juvenile delinquency. The state focused its efforts mainly on the development of a legal base of preventive policy, whereas imperial civil society took practical steps to prevent delinquency in the first place. Methods of preventing juvenile delinquency arose solely by public initiative. As described below, the Russian public began to deal with the issues of appropriate legislation, as well as raising and training and children.

Public activities aimed at solving issues related to the protection of children from the corrupting influence of prisons, the organization of education and upbringing, the creation of special institutions for juvenile convicts, and the organization of their post-penitentiary education. At that time, children were usually kept in prisons together with adult criminals. This raised the issue of the influence of the criminal environment on children. Therefore, the task was to bring the children out of prisons. For this purpose, special correctional institutions were established, which included child offenders and children of prisoners serving sentences in prisons, as well as homeless, poor, and/or abandoned children. Congresses of these correctional institutions for juvenile offenders took place and became active in the development of preventive measures and in the search for more perfect forms of operation. The congresses helped in the development of juvenile justice laws and in the creation of juvenile courts.[66]

In 1870, A. N. Strekalova, a public activist, founded the first correctional orphanage in Moscow. The orphanage, which later became known as the Rukavishnikovsky Orphanage, hosted children aged 10 to 15 who were under investigation or who had been convicted of various offenses. The orphanage used a re-education system that excluded the corporal punishment traditionally used in institutions of this kind, and instead relied on clear rules, expectations for behavior, well-organized supervision, and systematic work. The orphanage provided elementary education within the scope of the curriculum of public schools and a thorough knowledge of a craft necessary for later life.

Correctional institutions for juveniles worked closely with the courts, and only court decisions could place juveniles in these institutions. Juveniles who had served their sentences often choose to stay there: they lived and worked, sometimes for several years, in these shelters. In Russia at that time there were several types of correctional institutions for minors: shelters, labor colonies, etc. In total, there were about a hundred correctional institutions in pre-revolutionary Russia. According to the law "On educational and correctional institutions for minors," dated April 19, 1909, such institutions were of an educational and preventive nature and should be called educational and correctional institutions. In these institutions, where the internal routine of life was similar to that of correctional institutions, children had to undergo preparation for life as adults—in other words—socialization as adults, a very important social service for any state. Minors received general, vocational, and physical education.

Earlier, the Criminal Code of 1903 limited the use of the death penalty to men between the age of 21 and 70 for serious crimes (murder, etc.) and women of the same age for attacks on or threats against the emperor, his family, or his power. The law also eliminated prison sentences for all crimes committed by minors. The 1903 law stated that

> a criminal offense committed by minors between the age of 10 and 17 who could not understand the value and meaning of what they did, or could not control their actions, is not imputed. These minors should be under the responsible supervision of a parent or guardian.[67]

No punishment was applied for a criminal offense for a child under 10 years of age.[68] Compared to other countries and the USSR, juvenile and criminal justice of the late imperial period in Russia was more highly developed and more humane.[69]

Child Labor and Education

For our future story about childhood experiences in early Soviet Russia and to provide a historical background, it should be noted that in the late tsarist state, child factory labor was strictly regulated, and the institution of factory inspectors was introduced. (As we will see below, dramatic economic, social, and cultural changes attracted many Russian children to social and political events in the Russian Empire in the last decades of the empire.) Many adolescent children worked in manufacturing, services, or street vendors. In those days of early industrialization, child labor was a common and grim reality in every industrialized country. Russian late imperial laws regulated the employment of children in industry and ordered children to attend school. A law of 1882 prohibited the employment of children under the age of 12 and limited the working day for children between the ages of 12 and 15 to eight hours. A law of 1884 introduced compulsory schooling for children aged 12–15 and obliged these children to attend school.[70] The government made many efforts to place children of factory workers in schools and childcare establishments. A series of laws prohibited the employment of children who reached 12 but had not completed at least two years of school.[71] On the whole, the tsarist Russian authorities, teachers, and educated people did not consider the factory workshop as a place of learning. As the following chapters will illustrate, the Soviet government, on the contrary, viewed child productive labor as a measure for upbringing and education.

Children's Socialization and Involvement in Political Activities

One of the most interesting phenomena of the last decades of the empire was the above-noted participation of children in the empire's social and political events. Most of these children were employed in production. In addition to providing new educational opportunities for working children, factory labor also facilitated their rapid involvement in public and political life. Factory children worked side by side with adult workers and often lived in the same crowded areas with outsiders. These children, of course, were not homeless or starving, but represented the growing generation of politically motivated and involved citizens of Russia. Numerous primary sources on the workers' movement shed light on children's participation in demonstrations and strikes and, even more surprising, on some occasions in initiating and leading role. The record of the workers' movement during the late imperial period contains a significant number of strikes started by working children. Child and juvenile workers were quick to question the existing social and political order. State officials reported that young workers rejected family and religious values, ignored existing social values and norms, and were disobliging and disrespectful of authority.[72] Some contemporaries noted growing generational conflict in the last decades of the empire. This conflict epitomizes the development of a new culture among younger generations. This culture emphasized protest and resistance to official morality and rules exemplified by the state, church, and parents, as well as social freedoms and equality. Thus, in the last imperial decades, children were actively involved in the sphere of adult activity, including criminal activity. How did this affect children's homelessness and hunger under the first Bolsheviks? Most of these late-imperial teenagers became adults by 1918 and had little or no impact on child homelessness in the 1920s. However, the tradition of protesting official morality and rules among the younger generations had not faded away. The Bolsheviks willingly took advantage of youth protest culture, but for their own purposes, which will be discussed later in the book.

First World War and Its Impacts on Childcare

As mentioned, at the beginning of the twentieth century, according to the All-Russian Congress of Philanthropists, 75 percent of charity funds came from private voluntary donations and only 25 percent came from the state. In 1902, there were over 30,000 charity endowments in Russia, which funded children's homes, shelters for homeless children, free dining rooms, hospitals, and clinics. Charity had become more secular and personal participation in charity was considered an act of good morals and virtue.[73] As noted, in 1913 private donations to all charitable institutions of St. Petersburg alone amounted to about 8 million rubles ($4,112,000 for 1913 and $114,882,218 today). According to rough estimates, at least 27 million rubles ($13,878,000 for 1913 and $387,727,489.09 today) were distributed in the country annually in the form of alms. Although the growth in the number of orphans continued, the extent of children's homelessness never presented a serious socio-political issue.

In 1915, the late imperial government introduced a new public charity law, which laid care for orphans upon local rural communities and governments (zemstvos). Resulting from wartime, this measure would later come under criticism from contemporaries, who indicated that neither local communities nor local governments paid due attention to orphans. When orphans inherited property left by their deceased parents, the communes appointed a guardian (usually a relative or a villager) to take care of the orphan and his or her property. Local communes also appointed foster parents. In some cases, orphaned children would pass from one foster family to another until they grew up and could live on their own. However, the economic conditions of most families worsened during the war. Villagers often could not support orphaned children properly. In addition, foster parents occasionally exploited orphans' property and labor and provided them with inadequate support.[74] The state and the public were aware of these issues and, in addition to the local communes, organized private and public empowerments to support rural and urban orphans. For example, the Alekseev and Romanov Committee made significant donations to support orphans. The local trustee committees of the Empress Maria Charity Fund also founded children's homes for rural orphans. During the war, however, this fund directed its major efforts to the support of soldiers.[75]

Regardless, the number of institutions providing care for children was hardly adequate to the growing children's population. In 1911, there were 14,439 children of preschool and early school age in 438 shelters in Russia. By 1917, there were 538 children's shelters in Russia with 29,650 children. A significant proportion of shelters belonged to private charitable institutions. Some shelters belonged to church and military departments or to the Ministry of Internal Affairs. Shelters that housed juvenile offenders were strictly regulated. Many of these shelters were self-supporting and self-sufficient because of the involvement of children in productive activities.

Regardless of earlier measures, the First World War had an appalling impact on the welfare of the empire's children. By January 1914, there were 862 orphanages providing shelter and care for 31,651 children. These orphanages were financed by private endowments, 73.8 percent; local zemstvos, 15.1 percent; city governments, 7.8 percent; and state budget, 3.3 percent.[76] The war created millions of orphans, caused deprivation among millions of families, drove masses of refugees with young children from their places of permanent residence and curtailed education of children in schools. One can also not discount the unhealthy influence on the still fragile psyche of children of rampant militarism. A contemporary wrote:

> By the end of 1916, large cities were already overflowing with masses of street children, the number of child delinquency in large cities more than doubled, and juvenile delinquency itself became more dangerous and aggressive.[77]

In March 1916, the All-Russian Conference on Wartime Childcare gathered in Petrograd to discuss orphan's relief. The conference outlined a set of measures to combat the growing children's homelessness. These measures were only partly fulfilled due to government's lack of effort and funding. Only city trusteeships for the poor in some urban areas could arrange modest assistance to families and take some measures to protect refugee children, for instance by setting up playgrounds that distracted street children from the city streets.

Some tsarist government officials and educators saw the solution to the growing problem of rural orphans in creating a network of agricultural shelters in rural areas where children could receive care and education while learning agricultural methods.

As we shall see, the new Soviet government also tried to employ this tsarist government approach. To implement the idea, the tsarist government began to set up agricultural shelters but apparently their number grew slowly owing to wartime economic hardship. According to a 1915 report, there were about seventy orphanages in the countryside that could hardly accommodate the existing number of orphans. By one estimate, in 1916 the number of children under twelve, that is, not eligible for employment, who lost one or both parents reached as many as 5.5 million.[78]

It goes without saying, the revolutionary ferment that swept through the year 1917 further worsened children's plight. School life came to a standstill, food supplies deteriorated, public attention was diverted toward politics, and the few measures taken by the Provisional Government for child protection were paper projects rather than real relief measures. Children's vagrancy worsened and then reached enormous proportions during the Civil War and the famine that followed. Many children's institutions were forced to close, and inmates who had been sheltered and educated at state and public expense ended up on the streets. By 1917, there were 538 shelters for children in the Russian Empire and the number of children they sheltered reached 30,000.[79]

According to estimates, before the October 1917 Revolution, the number of needy children roaming streets, markets, and railroads, most orphaned during the First World War, was slightly under 100,000.[80] The number of orphans was particularly high in the countryside, the main area of military recruitment. Although insufficient, the ideas of the tsarist and later the Provisional Government about how to deal with these children were at least practical and appropriate for the predominantly rural problem it was. What is important to note is that these children's misfortunes directly arose from the First World War.

Even so, until late 1917 there was a tradition of caring for children established by the state and common law and rooted in folk customs and religious traditions. Before the Revolution, most orphans were neither starving nor homeless. The situation changed dramatically after the 1917 Revolution, when private and public charity was banned and when the countryside became the main source of homeless and starving children. Toward the end of 1920, what had been a wartime problem became a vast crisis of homeless children. The real question is what had happened to these millions of children—many of whom had had living parents in 1917—but who by 1920 would be characterized as "starved, abandoned and unattended street children"?

Conclusions

The skeptical reader may have some reservations about my very positive story about children before the Revolution. Of course, the late imperial landscape varied greatly depending on the region, ethnic composition, and royal legislation, and consequently, children's experiences were very diverse. As I discussed earlier in this chapter, adversity in childhood was not uncommon. Even so the imperial Russian society used various ways to save needy children, and the government did not destroy all existing traditions and institutions for caring for children, as did the Bolshevik government did immediately after 1917.

As noted earlier, historians and Soviet government officials generally emphasize war, famine, and epidemics, factors supposedly beyond the control of the young socialist government, as the main reason for the escalation of child homelessness in the 1920s. In this view, the war and the ensuing epidemic and famine created to thousands of orphans whose parents either died or were separated and lost. Obviously, the Revolution paralyzed the entire economic and social infrastructure: important aspects of the economy stopped functioning, social institutions experienced widespread collapse, and the entire childcare system deteriorated, although, as yet, neither children's starvation nor homelessness was as serious as they would become in 1919–20. What can explain the sheer scale of the phenomenon after the October 1917 Revolution, not to mention its continuity, and what caused these factors in the first place? Answering these two key questions involves comprehending what happened to the thousands of institutions that had provided socialization, support, and shelter for orphaned or needy children before the Revolution. Furthermore, why did children's starvation and homelessness become persistent problems throughout the 1920s and the 1930s? In the existing historiography, these questions remain unanswered and, mostly, not even addressed. The following chapters offer detailed research and analysis that go far beyond the claims of contemporary Soviet government officials, not to mention Russian and non-Russian historical analysis.

2

Soviet Street Children: Definition, Identity, Demography, Geography, and Origins

People busily sauntered around; the rings and whistles of steam locomotives blended with street merchants' calls; and in the middle of this lively scene, at the entrance to a public restroom, lay a barely moving small grayish heap. Suddenly, one of passengers stumbled over it and stopped ... Peering at it, the passenger asked in perplexity: "Hey, little boy, why are you lying here, what for?" "I lay down here," the boy said, losing consciousness ... His small skinny body twitched and trembled, whether in a terrible fever or a death agony, it was hard to say. Improbably tattered hemp sacks barely covered his exhausted body. Parasites teemed all over him and his shivering arms made unconscious scratching gestures. "Little boy, where are you from? Who are you? What are you doing here? Where is your mother?" the gathering crowd asked. The boy was silent, probably not understanding or even hearing the questions. Only at the word "mother" did his bleary eyes open and he tried to rise. "I have no mother ... she is lost" he said and again lowered himself to the ground.
                                               "Deti," *Pravda* (March 10, 1921)

... the revolution that we have experienced is one of the reasons for [children's] homelessness. What is a revolution? Revolution is the destruction of the old, outdated, obsolete order, old ties, old family relationships, and old social relationships. A revolution means the elimination of all this and the establishment of new ties, new relationships, a new social organization.
                    N. K. Krupskaya, ("O detskoi besprizornosti," 1924)
                             in *Pedagogicheskie sochinenia*, vol 2, 169

The reasons for children's homelessness are exclusively social: it is created by the capitalist exploitation of the masses.
                                      Great Soviet Encyclopedia (1927), 783

With these mournful words, quoted at the beginning, in 1921 the leading Bolshevik party newspaper *Pravda* described the situation in Soviet Russia, where the Bolsheviks had come to power in October 1917. These words and this situation marked the unofficial story of early Soviet childhood—a story that millions of urban and especially rural children experienced every day during the first decades of the Bolshevik regime.

It is almost impossible to find any such description of the living conditions of children in the country from earlier times, and I doubt that it ever existed. In 1921-2, the number of starving and homeless children in need was unprecedented, extraordinary, and shocking—over 7 million. Even more shocking was the 95 percent infant mortality rate, especially in childcare institutions.

The massive flood of suppressed children in the streets, markets, and railways was one of the many startling and disturbing facts of this troublesome time. These children depressed the feelings of many adult observers who themselves had gone through too much turmoil, suffering, and despair. Hungry street children survived through begging, theft, picking pockets, peddling, prostitution, and other survival strategies that the state considered criminal, antisocial, deviant, and even counter-revolutionary. Perhaps not a single contemporary traveler who found himself in cities, on railways, or in markets could avoid encountering *besprizorniki*, as street children were usually called in official and public discourses. Many street children became targets of abuse, crime, violence, human trafficking, and exploitation by adults and criminals.

Although the Great Soviet Encyclopedia comments cited above emphasized the cruel nature of "capitalist exploitation of the masses," Soviet street children fell victim to abuse by the newly formed state regime and its *realpolitik* policies. But for the regime itself, this was justified. As Krupskaya cynically put it, the Revolution consisted in the destruction of everything old, even if the new revolutionary regime was unable to create a new infrastructure for children in need, except for numerous abstract concepts and ideas that were never implemented. Moreover, the state did not hesitate to use *realpolitik* (excessive coercion and violence) to implement these abstract concepts and ideas. This chapter explores the definitions, demographics, geography, and origins of child homelessness and hunger between 1914 and 1941, in conjunction with the Bolshevik *realpolitik* policies.

Definition and Identity

In the Introduction, we defined the category "children." Now let us define homeless children as the state identified them. Paradoxically, the Soviet state categorized and defined identity by decrees. By a decree of June 11, 1921, the government singled out four categories of homeless- *besprizorniki*—classifying them exclusively as children, as indicated in the Introduction: (1) minors living in conditions that could adversely affect their health (without food, clothing, and shelter); (2) minors living without supervision and guardianship; (3) minors who have committed begging, vagrancy, and prostitution; and (4) children whose parents lead a unprincipled life that affects the child's life.[1] Thus, according to this decree, the definition of *besprizorniki* applied to underage teenagers and children whose parents were serving sentences in prisons, as well as minor beggars, homeless children, children-speculators, and juvenile criminals and prostitutes. In September 1921, the government adopted a resolution "On the legal protection of minors." Minors who were not under proper parental or guardian supervision or home were classified as street children living in conditions that could adversely affect their morals and health. The state also considered as homeless or abandoned these children whose parents and guardians "abused their power, forcing or persuading their children to criminal activities, such as begging, debauchery or connivance, or who were placed at the disposal of beggars, criminals, vagabonds, and the like."[2]

In a more concise form, this definition was included in the Soviet by-laws of departmental acts. The regulations on the protection of children developed by the People's Commissariat of Education of the RSFSR contain a list of categories of street children. In particular, underage children and adolescents under the age of 18 were considered homeless if they were "abandoned by their parents or persons replacing them, without any supervision and care." In addition, children of the same age group who were subjected to violence by adults were classified as street children. Among these categories of street children, there were those who were not provided with the necessary "minimum of upbringing and education stipulated by the current legal provisions." Minors were also considered homeless in the event of "the corrupting influence of the home environment; the minors themselves lead a vicious way of life, as well as begging or vagrancy; or doing any kind of trade."

The first edition (1926) of the Great Soviet Encyclopedia identified the homeless or unattended (*besprizorniki*) as "a child completely separated from his family, associated with the loss of a permanent place of residence and work ... as the most acute form of being neglected" associated with lack of care for minors by parents or guardians. The phenomenon of homeless children was associated with "minors [who were] deprived of educational supervision and care and [who] lived in conditions harmful to their social condition and health." It can be assumed that there were other age groups of homeless or unattended people—which in fact were numerous at the time—or, for that matter, stray animals, but only children became the subject of special attention in official and public discourses in the early 1920s. In addition, the coercive and punitive institutions of the state became especially interested in the problem of children's homelessness. Obviously, the government worried about street children more than any other age group of homeless people.

In general, the encyclopedia's definition was valid and applied to children who had been in parental or institutional custody and became homeless and constituted a disturbing feature of life in early Soviet Russia. The question of whether the children were orphans or had one or both parents, or living guardians from whom they were separated, or whether they had been in the custody of a state childcare institution from which they had run away remains unclear. The encyclopedia's definition clarified that

> homelessness should not only apply to children who have lost their parents (or guardians) and homes. If parents (or guardians) deprive children of food, treat them roughly, seduce them into crimes, have a destructive influence by their own example, then the children of such parents are also considered "*besprizorniki*."[3]

The second edition of the Great Soviet Encyclopedia (approved for publishing during Stalin's reign, in 1952) contained no entry for "besprizorniki," while mentioning them under "deti" (children). As mentioned in the Introduction, after 1935 this subject, which shed a very bad light on the Soviet government, was written out of all discourses or even mention for several decades. Or perhaps they were "defective" in the Soviet government's eyes and deserved no place in Soviet "scriptures." Some contemporaries identified street children with deviance and considered them as morally "defective" and inclined to asocial behavior and crime. The nickname "defektivnyi" (the defective one) was in frequent utilization in popular parlance during these times, although in the mid-1920s some educators and officials of the Commissariat for Enlightenment urged against labeling street children as defective. Officials often referred to homeless children as a "mass," or "threatening mass."

The vast majority of street children were eight to fourteen years old but outwardly never looked their age. Street children lagged behind their peers in physical development, because they constantly smoked, sniffed cocaine, and drank moonshine. The homeless child was distinguished by a strong self-preservation instinct, increased excitability, and, as noted, a habit of using artificial stimulants: drugs, alcohol, etc. Many of them began sexual activity early. They were infected with one or another disease, including typhoid, scurvy, intestinal infections, and dystrophy which all resulted from their lifestyle and miserable living conditions. Sexually transmitted diseases, including syphilis, were commonplace among them. Without exception, street children, hungry, and dressed in rags, with exhausted faces and hoarse voices, became a typical phenomenon of cities and industrial centers: an experienced eye would catch them in the market crowd, among the trading stalls, by the carts of visiting peasants. The noisy market, where they sell, buy, steal, beat—this is their sea, in which they catch their profit, their kingdom, their school, their place of "work." Their house? A house is a luxury, they don't have a house. They are the "slums."[4]

The outward appearance of homeless children was far from childish: "They amaze with their thinness, exhaustion, pallor, sallow color, and some kind of senile expression on their faces; some no longer have teeth, some black roots stick out, their eyes have sunk in, with huge bruises … They themselves say about themselves: 'That's how I am because I sniff cocaine.'" In appearance, a 15–16-year-old teenager would seem to be no more than 10–11 years. Homeless children lived anywhere: in pits, ruins, dungeons, old wagons. "I remember well these absolutely unthinkable ragamuffins," notes A. Obrosov, "all covered in mud and lice, roaming near asphalt boilers, warming themselves by fires … inhabiting attics and basements …"[5]

Demographics

As mentioned, the extent of homelessness and starvation among children was extraordinary and unparalleled, especially during 1920 through 1922, when the number of homeless and starving children reached 7.5 million. Was the figure of 7.5 million accurate? All official statistics on homeless and starving children are either fragmentary or nonexistent. The available figures on homeless children are random and controversial. It seems that the state had no precise knowledge about the number of homeless children at any given time and much less is known about the numbers of starving children. For example, there are virtually no official statistics on homeless children for 1917 and 1918. Some sources, however, suggest that by the end of 1918, there were already 3.5 million homeless children in Russia.[6]

Regardless, historians and contemporaries' accounts usually indicate that the years 1921–3 marked the peak of children's homelessness. According to some official sources and studies, the numbers of homeless children reached from 4 to 9 million in 1920–3 and never got below 2 million during the 1920s. According to officials of the Commissariat of Enlightenment and Soviet historians, by the end of 1920 the number of street children ranged from 5 to 7.5 million.[7] A. V. Lunacharsky, the Commissar for Enlightenment, believed that the number of homeless children in 1922 was 9 million.[8] According to stateswoman and education commissariat official N. K. Krupskaya, there were over 2 million homeless children by the 1930s. A 1927 figure from a government agency reported 6 million starving children and 700,000 homeless in 1921; in 1923— 1.4 million starving and 400,000 homeless children, respectively. The same source suggested a decline of starving and homeless children during the following years: in 1926 and 1927 there were 125,000 and 80,000 reported starving and homeless children respectively.[9] The first edition of the Great Soviet Encyclopedia suggested the figures of 7 million homeless children by 1922 and 334,500 by 1926.[10] The second edition (1952) of the encyclopedia, which excludes the word "homeless" and only briefly mentioned the phenomenon, provided no statistics on street children, but praised Joseph Dzhugashvili (Stalin) and the party for solving this problem and making Soviet children happy.

The available statistics on homeless children in fact are hard to comprehend and their numbers—hard to count. Obviously, no one gathered data on homeless and starving children systematically and no one could possibly count them. It was virtually impossible to count all children even in children's homes because of the high fluctuation and changeable turnout. Therefore, the data on homeless children is very contradictory and fragmentary, a factor that clearly suggests that the issue had spun out of control. Even some contemporary observers recognized that suggesting any reasonable accurate number of homeless and starving children was impossible because Soviet institutions gave different numbers on these children and there were no centralized statistics, and the information from localities was varied and incomplete.[11]

Recent Russian-language studies tend to accept the number of 7 million. Historians A. B. Rozhkov and Slavko suggest the figure of 7 million homeless children in 1921–2 as realistic.[12] Slavko as well as some contemporary observers pointed to the inadequate registration of street children during the 1920s. In 1924, for example, forty-three provinces of the Russian republic reported to the central state authorities the existence of only about 235,000 homeless children. Furthermore, according to Slavko, the reporting local institutions likely purposely lowered the numbers of homeless children they reported.[13] According to historian T. M. Smirnova, by 1921, in Soviet Russia, not only was the number of street children and children in need of placement in children's institutions unknown, but also the number of orphanages, schools, and other children's institutions, as well as the number of their inmates.[14] Therefore, the reader may never know the exact numbers of street children regardless of any effort applied. I merely suggest that the number was high enough to make the Bolshevik government talk about the problem itself, often with alarm.

Nevertheless, the decline of the number of street children reported in the late 1920s likely resulted from the simple fact that these children were growing up and becoming adults. Another crucial factor in the decline was the unprecedentedly high child mortality rate, especially among street children. In the famine-stricken regions of Russia, mortality among children approached 80–95 percent. In October 1921, the Bolshevik party newspaper *Pravda* reported 95 percent of mortality among children in the Volga and other southeastern regions of Russia.[15] The child mortality rate was particularly high among toddlers under the age of 3.[16] Even in some childcare institutions, the mortality rate was registered at 95 percent. Children simply died of starvation.[17] The newspaper *Krasnaya Zvezda* of the Petrograd Military District on March 29, 1922, reported that "by the beginning of 1922, more than 11.2 million children died of starvation."[18]

Paradoxically, even with this extraordinary mortality rate, *besprizornost'* remained a continuing and disturbing problem throughout the years of the 1920s and 1930s,[19] as was acknowledged by state agencies. Obviously, the direct source of children's starvation and homelessness that so stubbornly persisted throughout decades was Bolshevik policy. It is worth mentioning that, perhaps unsurprisingly, all statistics and information on children's homelessness and starvation during the 1930s, when Stalin was at the helm, became closed from public circulation.

One may wonder about the proportion of this sizable figure to the general population of the early USSR. Although it is practically impossible to suggest any accurate proportion of homeless and starving children to the population of Russia or the USSR, nevertheless, it would be worthwhile to attempt an informed guess. At the beginning of the twentieth century, the Russian Empire was a country with a very high birth rate, especially in the countryside. During the First World War and the Civil War, the birth rate, for obvious reasons, declined, but by the mid-1920s, during the New Economic Policy, stabilized and returned to the pre-war level. According to the available data for 1914, the population of European Russia, excluding Crimea, reached 72,037,615 inhabitants with the overall imperial population of 178,378,800. The Russian empire lost about 8–10 million lives in the First World War. The 1917 Revolution, the Civil War, and the period of the Bolshevik *realpolitik* also claimed lives of over 20 million people in Russia, according to some estimates. The available data for 1920 reveals that among the Russian Republic's population of 66,485,972 inhabitants, over 37 percent (24.6 million) were individuals under 14, and 9 percent (5.9 million) were adolescents between ages 14 and 18.[20] Thus, one may assume that almost one-quarter (about 23 percent) of children under 18 were homeless in 1920–1. This figure, however, might be higher, particularly in the localities primarily impacted by children's homelessness and starvation. According to Slavko, if in 1917, 1 percent of children were homeless in Moscow, by the mid-1920s the figure reached 50 percent. Other sources suggest 1–2 percent of all Moscow children were homeless in 1917 and 25–40 percent by the mid-1920s. These estimates seem accurate.

Almost four-fifths of the Soviet population lived in European Russia. A considerable number of people lived in Central Russia—about 38 million, including the Central Chernozem region (17 million), Central Industrial (11 million), and the Middle and Lower Volga regions (10 million)—the latter of which was the place of origins of most homeless and starving children in the early 1920s. Moscow and St. Petersburg provinces were the most densely populated, with 2.4 and 2.1 million people, respectively. More than 2 million people inhabited the cities of Viatka, Samara, Saratov, Ufa, and Kazan of the Volga region, as well as Voronezh, Orel, Tambov, and other cities of central Russia. These areas also were seriously afflicted with children's starvation and homelessness during the 1920s. It is to highlight the fact that during this time although life expectancy was lower there, the rural population predominated. Consequently, the majority of children lived in the countryside.[21] Hence local percentages of homeless and starving children to the overall local populations might be greater than 23 and even surpass the 40–50 percent figures cited above.

Information on the mortality rates in rural areas during the war years is also fragmentary, whereas data for large cities is somewhat fuller. For example, in Moscow in 1917 the mortality rate was 212 persons per 10,000; in 1918, this figure reached the slightly higher figure of 218. With the onset of food problems in the first half of 1919, the mortality rate soared to 504 persons per 10,000; in the second half it fell to 390; in 1920 it rose again to 462 people. Things developed similarly in Petrograd, where the death rate in 1920 reached 506 people per 10,000 (in 1914 it was at the level of 215 people).[22] How many victims of food shortages died from starvation, and how many from diseases that they could have survived with a normal diet and level of immunity cannot be estimated. As mentioned, children's mortality, especially among infants and toddlers, in some areas reached 95 percent. Children's population numbers remained high because fertility rates remained high—their level depended on regional specifics—especially in rural areas. So, for example, in 1910, on average, in fifty provinces of the European part of Russia, there were 5.3 births per each marriage.[23] (Perhaps as a family survival mode, parents chose to have more than normal numbers of children.) Considering the high child mortality rate and the consistently high numbers of homeless children at any given time, one may suggest that the overall numbers and proportions of homeless and starving children were enormous.

The post-war demographic stability did not last long: by the end of the 1920s, there was a strong population decline that accelerated after Stalin's 1929 collectivization. Even so, as noted, statistics on homeless and starving children became classified. During this period and forward, even through the years of Gorbachev's perestroika, the Soviet state imposed strict censorship, closed controversial document collections, and prohibited inquiries and data collecting on issue that could compromise the government. Thus, no one could collect systematic data on homeless and starving children during Stalin's collectivization. Even today only some fragmentary figures are available. Despite the officially announced "liquidation of homelessness" in 1935—by a decree, which pronounced homelessness among children to be a resolved problem,—the numbers of homeless and starving children remained high in certain localities, as reflected in numerous confidential and top secret reports of the local NKVD during the late 1930s. Thus, it is impossible to estimate the number of homeless children or their percentage to the population during the 1930s. Even so, the systematic classification of documents that identified the presence of homeless and starving children as an alarming and serious issue indelibly signifies the magnitude of the problem.

Children, by definition, live with their parents or guardians and in families or childcare institutions. The most common type of urban family was the nuclear family, consisting of a married couple and children. Large extended families also remained in Russian cities but prevailed in the countryside. The economic basis of all types of families was either ownership of the means of production or, alternatively, employment. Financial leverage was in hands of the head of the extended family, usually the grandfather of the married sons.[24] Although extended families were typical in the countryside, small nucleus families (parents and children) were widespread in urban areas, especially during the period of this study. Therefore, childcare institutions were crucial in cities and in other urban and industrial areas where employed parents did not have other members of family to fend for their children. The issue of how the Bolshevik seizure of power transformed childcare institutions and how these developments affected children's homelessness and starvation will be explored further in this and subsequent chapters.

The social background of besprizorniki depended on their geography, timeframe, and origins. Earlier, in 1918 homeless children had quite diverse social and ethnic backgrounds but were mostly urban orphans. During the 1920s and 1930s, homeless children were of rural origin and of diverse social, ethnic, and religious backgrounds. In 1918–19, most street children were urban orphans from closed childcare institutions; in the 1920s and 1930s, they usually had living parents. Virtually all religions and denominations in imperial Russia exercised some social control over their younger members and also had long-standing traditions of charity and support for their members and families, as explored in the first chapter. After the Revolution, child-raising traditions and childcare institutions were largely destroyed. The social, religious, and ethnic diversity of the children who become the subject of this book reflected the geographic diversity of their origins.

Geography

The geography of children's starvation and homelessness varied: it depended on time and origins. The geography of children's homelessness and starvation coincided with the regions affected by the famine and was very wide—from the south of modern Ukraine, the Volga region (from the Caspian Sea to Udmurtia) to the South Urals, and parts of Kazakhstan. Famine resulted not only because of unfortunate weather conditions and the poor 1921 harvest, but primarily from geographical policies of the Bolshevik government, as will be explored later.

The earliest homeless and starving children were urban orphans from childcare institutions that the new Soviet government began to shut down in late 1917. The first waves of starving children from the industrial centers flooded streets, markets, and railroad stations, and many tried to move to Petrograd and Moscow, where they believed they could survive. But Moscow and Petrograd already had their own street children. Thus, Petrograd and Moscow railroad stations and marketplaces became the earliest areas where large-scale children's starvation, homelessness, and delinquency emerged in 1918. Many street children then tried to move south, where they thought they could better survive. Pushed by need, children sought refuge in any convenient place in a given city. In warm Krasnodar, for example, they huddled near the Alexander Nevsky and Catherine's Cathedrals, merging with a colony of adult homeless people. "They behave too freely," complained the clergy, "sleep, eat, undress and look for parasites, gamble and shower passers-by with abuse."[25] Nevertheless, at this point the state hardly noticed them: there is no *official* data on homeless children for 1918. The central and regional newspapers remained silent about homeless children, as well. Thus, the question is what happened to the childcare institutions that provided care for children in late 1917 and 1918 in urban Russia? According to the citation from N. K. Krupskaya, the Revolution destroyed them, because of the very nature of a Revolution. This matter will be explored in this and the following chapters.

Children's homelessness accelerated sharply in 1919 and toward late 1920 became an alarming problem involving millions of kids. During these years, the geography of children's misery shifted to the countryside, where most children lived. Alongside earlier orphans, now there were millions of starving and homeless children in the countryside. Children's starvation reached enormous proportions in Orel, Voronezh, and Tambov—and especially the Povolzh'e (Volga) provinces, including Samara, Saratov, Tsaritsyn, and Orenburg provinces.[26] While most street children were rural and had Russian orthodox background, many of those who came from the Volga regions in 1920 had diverse ethnic and religious origins. Children, most of whom had one or both parents alive, fled these devastated areas and moving to the southern regions of the Caucasus and Crimea, or to big cities such as Moscow and Petrograd, in hopes of finding occasional earnings and other means to survive.

The numbers of unattended children moving throughout the country grew relentlessly. Homeless and starving children clustered in cities around large train stations, piers, or marketplaces throughout the 1920s.[27] This movement of children continued throughout the 1920s and the early 1930s. Hungry street children from all over the countryside, dressed in rags, with shrunken faces and hoarse voices, became a typical phenomenon of many provincial centers. "Homeless children overwhelmed markets, train stations, streets, huddled in ruined buildings, wandered on communication routes, etc. It can be said that during this period a wave of children's homelessness began to overwhelm the entire childcare system," wrote a contemporary commentator.[28] Another commentator wrote in Pravda in December 1920:

> The large influx of street children from the north and west does not allow the departments of public education to expand their work on a large scale, but even to organize it at all. Children in huge numbers, sometimes 100–150, flood all the large junction railway stations.[29]

In January 1921, the Kharkov leadership informed the central authorities about the arrival of homeless children from the Great Russian provinces, especially from Oryol and Kursk.[30] The Bolshevik party newspaper *Pravda* wrote in September 1921:

> Facing the absence of food, parents bring their children from villages to the nearby city and leave them at the markets and on streets. On market days, the admission of homeless children to institutions increases by a factor of two to three times. There is also an increase in the placement of children in institutions for the protection of infancy.[31]

Stalin's collectivization and dekulakization campaigns further exacerbated the tragedy of Soviet children during the 1930s. Now, the geography of children's homelessness and starvation coincided with the collectivization campaign—it encompassed the entire countryside and Siberia. Although the geography of collectivization was state-wide, the areas that endured the direst weight of the policy were the black-earth regions of the south, the Volga region, Ukraine, and Western Siberia, that is, the major grain-producing areas. The most active period of collectivization occurred between January and March 1930. In January 1930, the Central Executive Committee of the Soviets and the Central Committee of the Bolshevik Party made a decision about accelerated total collectivization, which, according to the new plan, should be accomplished in one to two years. This decision established several special regions where the reform should proceed to completion as soon as possible and created a special commission to develop a collectivization schedule. The regions of North Caucasus and the Volga were scheduled to complete collectivization in one year, by the spring of 1931. Other grain-producing regions were to complete collectivization by the spring of 1932.[32] Alongside collectivization, the government decided to liquidate the kulaks—officially identified rich peasants, especially those who used hired labor.

As a result, a new wave of homeless children emerged to an alarming extent in Western and Eastern Siberia, where collectivization victims—the kulaks—were usually sent to with their families. In 1932, classified letters and telegrams from Siberia informed the central state authorities that homelessness and beggary among the region's children had taken on a mass character, particularly in Omsk, Novosibirsk, and Tomsk, and widely spread across Siberia. Classified telegrams from local authorities urged the central government to deal with the growing problem. Children's homeless grew alarmingly in other areas heavily affected by collectivization as well.[33]

Origins

Thus, the question here is what happened to the over 7 million children who became homeless in 1921? And what happened to the numerous children who became starving and homeless during the late 1920s and the 1930s? In the Introduction, we defined as children not only persons of a certain age but as a dependent group of underaged individuals. Therefore, to assess the origins of children's starvation and homelessness, one must examine this group, always keeping in mind their adult guardians and their immediate environment. To answer what happened to these underaged individuals, therefore, one must explore what happened to their parents, guardians, or institutions that cared for these children.

War Communism, Children, and Bolshevik's *Realpolitik*: The Era of Requisitions

In addition to consolidation of power and creating a legal basis for an ideal socialist society and day-to-day solutions to the problems of the old regime, the early years 1918–21 experienced widespread state requisitioning of children's institutions. Between 1918 and 1921, the Bolshevik government conducted War Communism policies, which involved mobilization of the population, compulsory labor, forced nationalization of resources, various revolutionary taxes, requisitioning of buildings for state and party needs, forced requisitions of foodstuffs from peasants, and terror in the areas controlled by the new Soviet state. Private industry disappeared almost entirely; the transportation system collapsed; private trade was gradually suppressed to be replaced by rationing and by government distribution of food and other necessities of life. These state policies acutely deepened social breakdown, caused outright famine, and brought about unprecedented children's homelessness.

The effects of "War Communism" came immediately: food and fuel supplies collapsed and after mid-1918, people in the cities began dying of hunger and cold. Cities were sites of devastation. Many people moved from the cities to the countryside, a process rendered easier by the fact that many urban residents were newly arrived from the villages who had kept strong ties with their extended families in the village. This was an important factor because after the Revolution, many families with continuing ties to the village returned to the countryside. As a result, during 1918–19 the numbers of rural children significantly increased. An eyewitness wrote in Izvestia: "Our cities are literally dying out. Between May and October 1918, Moscow has lost 1,200,000 people. The condition of the children remaining in the cities is critical."[34] According to some studies, by the end of 1918, there were already 3.5 million homeless children in Russia.[35] Homeless rural children no one bothered to count.

The thousands of homeless children who roamed urban streets in 1918 reflected in great part state policies toward charity. The first massive influx of street children occurred in industrial cities because of the closing of private, public, and church childcare institutions and schools, and measures government took to eradicate private and church charity and benevolent endowments. Having prohibited private and public charity and taken responsibility for the needy children upon itself, the state thus became the sole patron of support for all children of the republic. In stark contradiction to official declarations about state child support, the best premises of closed children's homes were given to newly established party and government institutions, as was attested to by numerous letters from teachers and pedagogues. Public, church, and state institutions that had provided care for hundreds of thousands of orphans and needy children were closed or destroyed, forcing most of their inmates to rely on themselves to survive. Many starving children became homeless because they roamed in one direction or another looking for food—"bread please, bread" were street children's habitual words: the state failed to fulfill its commitments to needy children. It is perhaps worth repeat that no official data about homeless children exists for 1918 and official data for early 1919 dealt with orphans in remaining childcare institutions only. Certainly, the state did not trouble itself with the problem of homeless children at the time.

Paradoxically, requisitioning food and premises from children, the actual Bolshevik policy has attracted no attention from those who have studied early Soviet childhood. Regardless, the question of what factors prompted the Bolsheviks to pursue a policy that seriously undermined the already deteriorating living conditions of most children and their families exists and demands attention. Of course, state policies hardly favored children. To some degree, one can understand and accept official statements—the government needed food to feed starving cities and the Red Army. Even so, massive grain requisitioning caused rural starvation and forced innumerable children to the cities, where they also starved. Furthermore, the seizure of buildings for alleged state needs from schools and other childcare facilities or the removal of all food from the countryside, a policy that endangered innumerable peasant families, should not be taken lightly. Once again: as noted above, most Soviet children lived in the countryside and peasant families usually had many children. Any policy that stripped food from the countryside would automatically cause mass starvation, including of children. Obviously, Bolshevik *realpolitik* prevailed and overshadowed all other motives. The paranoia of the leaders of the Revolution and the early Bolshevik government will be discussed later in this book. Here, I will quote Lenin's instructions in his telegram on how to deal with insurgent peasants dissatisfied with the Soviet government's food policies, as of August 5, 1918:

1. Hang (hang them so that the people can see) at least 100 notorious kulaks, rich men, bloodsuckers.
2. Publish their names.
3. Take all grain from them.
4. Take hostages. Make sure that people can see and tremble for hundreds of miles around.[36]

Already in 1918, a series of decrees instituted "forceful requisitions" of buildings for government, army, Cheka, and party needs.[37] This policy had very serious consequences for orphanages and their inmates. In many instances, the new government seized the best mansions and buildings that had housed tsarist childcare institutions, including orphanages and shelters, and passed them on to the newly created state, party, or military agencies, usually without offering any suitable alternative.[38] With the agreement of local Soviets, the property of children's institutions (whether orphanages or schools) was taken and turned over to other organizations, a measure that forced children and staff out. This was done by the authorities in 1918, 1919, and following years, precisely when the numbers of orphans, homeless, and starving children rose precipitously because of the state's food policies: an already existing crisis found itself turned into a catastrophe.

In December 1918, Commissar for Enlightenment Lunacharsky complained to government head, V. I. Lenin that "the power given to the Army to unconditionally take over educational institutions' buildings leads to hundreds of children being turned out into streets and to the termination of education." He asked for an urgent response.[39] This complaint and others, however, were ignored: the party, Soviets, the army, or any other state agency continued to seize buildings of childcare institutions. Officials of the Commissariat of Enlightenment endlessly reported that various government, party, and military institutions were taking premises (buildings and land) from already equipped and functioning orphanages and schools.[40] Official highly publicized statistics create the impression that the early Soviet government created thousands of new orphanages and children's homes during these years, but the reality was quite the opposite. Newly created children's homes were mostly located in highly inappropriate areas and buildings, such as industrial plant premises or urban slums.

According to primary sources, the practice of appropriating buildings from children's institutions continued during the early 1920s, presumably until the last good buildings were taken from school and turned over to one or another party or state organization. In early January 1921, a non-party conference in Nizhnii Novgorod Province issued a resolution that pointed to the

> weak work of the Department of Public Education; all the teaching staff is starving, and, consequently, cannot devote themselves to the cause of Public Education, and the best school premises are occupied by administrative state institutions, and schools have been transferred to less appropriate premises.[41]

In early March 1921—the peak of children's homelessness—an official of the Moscow department of the Commissariat of Enlightenment complained that,

> all the best school buildings are occupied with one or another [soviet or party] institution and other school buildings, if they exist, are ruins without window glasses, doors, with floors and roofs destroyed.[42]

On March 9, 1921, the party newspaper published a teacher's letter with grave concerns that children may have the impression that "the tsarist regime sheltered them, gave them a chance to grow up into good persons, and take a good path in life, whereas Soviet power takes all that away from them."[43] In fact, this concern reflected the reality—indeed, it was the late tsarist government and the entire childcare system that provided orphanages, education, and care for children. Tsarist-era orphanages and children's institutions usually occupied excellent buildings built by the prominent architects of the time. As suggested in Chapter 1, late Imperial benefactors spared no expense for noble causes and charity. Ironically, not to mention tragically, it was the Bolshevik state, which proclaimed childcare the sole responsibility of the state, that confiscated the best premises from needy children.

The letters and concerns expressed in them in the context of the scale of child homelessness and hunger, as well as the actions of the government, give the impression that the government was in fact indifferent to the child population in 1918–19 and, as already mentioned, barely even noticed children's homelessness and starvation. As early as December 1921, the chairman of the Council of People's Commissars, Lenin, insisted that buildings could be confiscated by the state from children's institutions only in "extraordinary circumstances." Even so, the condition of "extraordinary circumstances" also extended to compaction—i.e., "increase in population density"—of the premises of children's institutions.[44] The "extraordinary circumstances" gave the authorities the opportunity to take advantage of this and interpret it in a way that suited their needs, but not the needs of children. Here, readers should acquaint themselves with another phenomenon of the early Bolshevik government—compaction (*uplotnenie*)—an increase in population density in residential apartments and buildings of institutions. Because of high general population mortality and resulting children's homelessness, orphanages quickly became overcrowded, despite these institutions' high mortality rate due to the rapid spread of infectious diseases. Most street children who entered the overcrowded orphanages had already been exposed to syphilis, gonorrhea, and scabies: the new Soviet state's response was to declare the institution overcrowded, expel the children back into the streets, and employ the structure (hopefully disinfected) for state or party purposes. The new government's policy toward orphanages also paid no attention to norms of fire protection.

Individual stories of Russian orphanages are remarkable. For example, the Imperial Moscow Orphanage, which maintained a hospital for needy parents, was established by the government on September 1, 1763. Its history after the bolsheviks came to power constitutes a micro-history of orphanages after the October Revolution, which in turn provides an illustrative snapshot of the new Soviet state's childhood policies. This institution belonged to the state and was under the patronage of the Empress Maria Charity System. On the coat of arms of the house, a pelican was depicted, which, according to a legend, fed its chicks with its own meat. The inscription on the coat of arms read: "He does not spare himself, feeds the chicks." The orphanage received tax and financial benefits. It was run by trustees and guardians. The orphanage had a vocational school with a six-year period of study and taught algebra, trigonometry, practical mechanics, physics, chemistry, and drawing. After training, there were three years of practice upon completion of which students received a master's degree. In 1868, the school received the status of a higher educational institution and subsequently became the basis for Russia's famous Bauman University. After the October Revolution, the orphanage was liquidated, and its buildings were occupied by a Soviet institution, the House of Labor. From 1922 to 1962, it housed the Research Institute of Pediatrics, after which the entire territory was transferred to the Academy of Strategic Missile Forces, a designation that ended in 2016. Regardless, during the entire soviet era, no orphans were housed or received training there.

Regardless, the most violent requisitioning campaign carried out by the government pertained not to housing but to the unprecedented and brutal food procurement; this campaign affected most children in Russia, as most lived in rural areas. As we have seen, in 1920, the geography of children's homelessness shifted to the countryside. During 1918–21, the government carried out unrelenting food requisitioning from peasants to supply starving cities and the Red Army, as well as, claimed the government, landless people.[45]

Figure 6 Moscow's orphanage. Source: Open public domain.

Prodrazverstka (i.e., food requisitioning), in fact, had first been introduced in 1916 to feed the Russian Army, as well as urban areas; this program applied only to grain. The tsarist food supply ministry's program, as well as the Provisional government ministry of food's similar program, failed in their attempts to provide the army and urban areas with supplemental grain (the issue at this point was not starvation but feared shortages). Both programs attempted to combine moderate grain requisitioning with state grain market regulation models. These policies, never fully implemented, had not threatened peasant families with starvation. Although cities experienced bread shortages throughout 1916–17, there was no mass famine in cities and urban centers, much less in the village.[46] Nor were there recorded massive outbreaks of homelessness among children. Available data indicate only that by 1917 there were 538 orphanages on the territory of Russia with 29,650 children.[47] As mentioned, no statistics on homeless children for 1918 exist. Under the new Bolshevik government, beginning during fall 1918 and continuing throughout 1919–20, all food supplies in the countryside became objects of procurement, a policy vigorously executed. This quickly placed rural families under grave threat.

In early 1918, the head of the government V. I. Ulyanov (Lenin), in a letter to the Commissar for Provisions, wrote that "in light of the critical situation with food we must not spread our forces too thin, but concentrate them on the central provinces where it is possible to take large amounts of grain."[48] Orel, Penza, Samara, Saratov, Kazan, and Tambov provinces were defined by the government as possible areas for procurements. The grain cereal levy defined by the government was often twice as high as some areas had ever provided. For example, the grain levy for Saratov Province was 31,100,000 *puds*[49] (1 *pud* equals 16 kg), whereas the estimated cereal surplus for the 1918 harvest was 22,143,000 *puds*. The cereal levy for Tambov Province was 36,000,000 *puds*, while the estimated cereal surplus was 16,157,000 *puds*.[50] When the first grain requisition decrees were discussed in local Soviets during the summer of 1918, the government authorities always demanded that they be fulfilled; in the words of one local official, "requisitions must be carried out at any cost."[51] One must wonder: at whose cost?

In January 1919, the People's Commissariat for Food Supplies issued an urgent order on accelerating food requisitions at an amount that was far beyond the country's agricultural production capacity. The cost turned out to be high indeed—it claimed lives and made homeless millions of adults and children. More than 20 million people were placed on the verge of extinction, and by the spring of 1922 the number of deaths from starvation exceeded 1 million people. Infant mortality was as high as 95 percent.[52] Thus, the question arises: Was the new regime concerned about children and their education and well-being? The answer is no. The state's food demands from the rural population reflected not only indifference to rural children, but also cruelty to both children and adults—millions of rural families. The campaign seriously worsened the economic situation of most people, provoked violence in the countryside, and caused unrest and mass famine.

In addition to food procurement, the government introduced the One Time Emergency 10 billion Revolutionary Tax (also known as the "emergency tax") on all but the very poorest citizens of the republic with the supposed goal of redistributing finances in order to benefit the poor. The Emergency Tax impoverished most rural families because most were unable to pay it.[53] Ostensibly aimed at the rich, the tax in fact affected the majority of the population in cities and in the countryside. This tax and the food requisitions placed peasant families on the edge of starvation. When the peasants failed to fulfill the required levy, in February 1919 government authorities responded with the threaten that the state "will permit no resistance."[54] The reader must be reminded that "the peasantry," often portrayed in histories as an ignorant mass, consisted, after all, of living men and women—adults, children, and elderly people. Thus, the weight of forced food requisitioning, plus confiscatory taxation, fell not on a "conceptual peasantry," but on concrete men, women, adults, and children. The policies of Prodrazverstka shattered the well-being of most families. Children and the elderly, the most vulnerable groups, suffered the most. The reader must also be reminded that most children lived in the countryside.

Analyzing this period of early Soviet history, all Soviet and some English-language histories exaggerated the impact of the Civil War and the drought and presented them as the only cause of early 1920s mass famine, whereas the predatory nature of the prodrazverstka campaign and the revolutionary tax was completely hidden. For example, according to historian G. D. Fadeeva, "the problem of child homelessness became especially acute in 1921, when a catastrophic drought broke out in Russia. The harvest was gone, grain reserves were depleted, there was no hope for a harvest. The situation in the country became disastrous. An unprecedented famine hit 37 provinces with a population of over 40 million."[55] However, archival records indicate that the famine began earlier. According to a report, by January 1920 the first cases of famine were reported in Vyatka and Nizhny Novgorod:

> The situation is becoming disastrous. Children are losing their parents en masse and are dying of hunger themselves. Hundreds of hungry children roam the roads, occupy the rooftops of southern trains, storm markets and food docks.[56]

The politics of food procurement led to chaos and huge popular protests in the countryside. The Soviet government deployed certain social and generational groups against one another or against other groups and incited social hatred. The state used the Cheka, police, and armed food detachments to secure food orders. These detachments hardly differed from the bandit groups. For example, a discouraged local policeman reported from the Ushimsk district, Tobolsk (Tyumen) province (Western Siberia) to the central office at the end of December 1920:

> [I am asking] once again, Comrade Chief, to pay attention, because here in the localities the work has infinitely fallen, and in particular the organization of our Communist Party. The localities have completely become a dead end, all local organizations have lost spirit. Even our party comrades, echo that are we are lost, we are on the verge of death, etc.
>
> Dear comrade, is it pleasant to see what our Party members are doing? Is it pleasant to hear the words of that a citizen who, two weeks ago, was devoted to the Soviet regime in body and soul, who was on the eve of joining our comrade ranks? Now, these comrades [peasants] tell us: comrade communist, what are you doing to us, taking the last shirt from the peasant, etc.?
>
> And in fact, take a closer look at what is happening: in winter, sheep are sheared, [the detachments take away wool] the last boots, mittens, [wool] from fur coats are cut, the peasant's cattle are confiscated, schoolchildren who go towards enlightenment are taken off their shoes. Is it really necessary? If so, then why did we, Communists, say that we are the defenders of the working people? Why did we say that we do not have violence, etc.? How pleasant it was to listen when we told the peasant: give, comrade, your surplus. And what? Two weeks later, the wagon trains were pulled, and during this time all the barns are filled.
>
> See what's being done. Now the poor and middle peasants are looking at us through their fingers, the wives of the Red Army are crying from the unbearable allocation, the children have nothing to go to school: their clothes have been given to the allocation. Let's see or listen to what our dear comrades have to say about this.[57]

A document dated January 2, 1921, states: "Upon the arrival of food detachments, instead of [grain] appropriations, geese were confiscated, clothes were taken from people, including children."[58]

Requisitions were done so harshly and mercilessly that in 1919–21 peasants often simply refused to produce agricultural commodities. Enormous areas, previously abundant in agricultural products, were empty and devastated.[59] At this point, personal recollections are worth mentioning. A relative of my stepfather, Natalia Filippovna Boltovskaya, recalled her childhood experience in Saratov province. As a teen during the revolutionary years, armed government officials raided her village, forcefully confiscated all grain and all foodstuffs, and answered objections with the cynical remark "you will die like dogs here." In reality, she lost her both parents, after which she fled to Moscow with her older sister.[60] Boltovskaia's recollections are well supported by numerous primary sources. Requisitions of children's institutions' premises in cities and foodstuffs in the countryside severely affected most children and revealed serious problems with early Bolshevik governance.

Numerous published and available primary sources reveal that the revolutionary tax and the food procurement severely affected most of rural dwellers. One resolution of a local peasant meetings, which could stand in for countless others declared that

> on January 4, 1919, we, the undersigned citizens of Simbirsk province, Buinsky district, Tarkhanov county, the village of Shaimurzino, 207 householders, … passed a resolution on the emergency tax—we cannot pay the tax due to the lack of capital.[61]

A report of the management department of the NKVD's provincial executive committee on the situation in a Volga province communicated that

> according to available information from private sources, the emergency tax is partly levied through repressive measures and in an amount exceeding the originally levied amount … The peasants congregate in meetings, which are held in a heightened, even excited mood. Most peasants do not want to pay the tax, but when the soldiers arrive, the noise immediately dies down. … The defaulters are summoned one at a time and asked: why did you not pay 200 rubles?—I have no money.—If you don't have 200 rubles, then bring in 400 right now.[62]

A document from Saratov provincial archive provides how the Atkarsky county

> food conference [of local government officials], convened on January 17, 1919, decided that all surplus grain, as well as the number of livestock due, must be handed over no later than February 15. Persons who have not fulfilled this will be declared opponents of Soviet power, and all grain, fodder and livestock will be confiscated from them.[63]

Here I must remind the reader that the grain levy for Saratov Province was over 31 million *pud*, while the estimated cereal surplus of the 1918 harvest was 22 million. During this arch-revolutionary time, anyone, including a child, declared "an opponent of Soviet power," in other words, an enemy of the Revolution, ultimately became subject to a revolutionary tribunal with severe consequences.[64]

Almost all food supplies that remained in peasants' possession, even for the next sowing season, were seized during the first year of food procurement, in 1919-20. Peasants were left with virtually nothing. The revolutionary tax and procurement affected mostly average peasant households—most rural families. "Kulaks"—who habitually had large families with many children—were struck especially hard by the procurements and were taxed at unjustifiably high rates. Fearing the prospect of forced sale or confiscation of food supplies, peasant families began to take preventive "measures." All surplus and stocks of bread were to be "utilized"—they ate it, mixed it into animal feed, sold it to speculators, simply hid or brewed moonshine. Initially, the "surplus grain appropriation" was extended to bread and grain fodder and later to potatoes and meats. That year many peasant families survived on what they had kept for the future seeding.

A peasant from a Viatka province wrote to the government chair, Lenin, in early 1920 that the food requisition authorities

> do not take into account any norms, and also do not take into account sowing seed—they take everything. In Vazovsky county, I observed many cases where oats were raked out before grain. What can we expect in the future from present village conditions? Here's the thing: the food authorities obviously had nothing to do, first they took away, tortured the peasant, brought [the grain] to the bulk point, then it was blown on a simple winnower, and they say that they sorted it out. They took it from a man for 41 rubles, and they will give it for 100 rubles, get it—it smells a little musty. No Comrade Lenin, this is not politics! It is necessary to pay the most serious attention to labor productivity in the countryside, and to give the peasant human living conditions! They took everything from the village, and what did they give back to the village—nothing! Two yards of lousy calico … but the peasant does not need your rags! Give him a plow, a sickle, a scythe, give him an iron, anything helpful for agriculture.[65]

The catastrophic conditions in the countryside caused by the emergency tax and procurement campaign were further aggravated by the unprecedented spring 1921 drought that undermined the harvest that year. Only 20 million puds of grain were harvested in the Volga region, while in 1913 yields had reached 146.4 million puds. In Samara province, for example, winter grain fields perished already in May, and spring grain fields began to dry up as well. The absence of rains and the appearance of the "filly" locust, which ate the remains of the surviving harvest, caused the death of almost 100 percent of the crops by the beginning of July. As a result, more than 85 percent of the population of the Samara province was starving.

Much the same can be said about other provinces. In a telegram, the Deputy Head of the Politburo of the Ishim District of Tyumen Province (Western Siberia region), I. V. Nedorezov, informed the provincial Cheka that:

> The mood of citizens is terrible because of hunger; today [in] Abatsk, citizens gather in crowds: children, old people, mothers. They ask for bread. We have no way out. The citizens definitely declared: if you don't give us bread, then we will go

to the collection point ourselves and take the quota for a month. I ask you to take action, otherwise I will relinquish responsibility for what will happen not today—tomorrow, Apr 15 [1921].[66]

Despite the massive famine, the Bolshevik state continued to forcibly confiscate food and used the army to force peasants to surrender so-called "surplus" food, which was never surplus. For example, in a telegram to the Tyumen Provincial authorities, commander of Soviet troops of Tyumen province, G. A. Burichenko stated:

> By virtue of the categorical order received from Comrade Lenin about the immediate removal of grain from the Ishim and Yalutorovsk districts to the railway for dispatch to the center, I issued a combat food order for my group, which broke grain regions into combat areas, appointed commanders and commissars of the sectors, assigned to each sector military commander, and began to transport bread to the railway ... The attempt of our military detachments to take [bread] by force led nowhere, since open demonstrative shooting at the crowds that surrounded the grain bins and tried to plunder them did not take any action, and the peasants, on the contrary, took their wives and children, together with whom they again surrounded the grain stations, insistently demanding to shoot them all together with their children and wives and then only take out bread from them.[67]

Regardless, food requisitions in various forms continued to place rural families at a great risk of starvation and death throughout the Civil War period. Most people had nowhere to get foodstuffs other than from their own reserves, which had been confiscated by the government. The Bolshevik policy of food procurement had no historical equivalent but the British East India Company's land confiscations that led to mass starvation in India. Famine in early soviet Russia became real and spread to many regions. According to Russian historian A. M. Kristalin, the food procurement campaign was a major cause of famine in the Volga Basin and other regions during 1921–22.[68] It must be added that this campaign was also the major cause of homelessness and mortality among children in 1920–2, as numerous primary sources confirm. For example, a September 1921 report stated that

> Samara [city] and Samara province are currently undergoing an ordeal. Hunger strangles both adults and children with its bony hand. It is estimated that this winter there will be at least 300,000 hungry children and 3,500,000 adults. Various surrogates have been eaten in villages and towns for a long time; acorns and quinoa are considered the best of them. Very often they grind tree bark, watermelon rind, roots of various herbs; in the worst cases they just eat greens, meadow, and marsh grass. It is clear that because of this, epidemic diseases are developing among the population and mortality has reached appalling proportions, especially among children. The most amazing pictures can be seen where they eat grass: swollen stomachs, face and legs with huge swelling, dim eyes, terribly sluggish movements—these are the results of consuming this type of food.[69]

According to a January 1922 article in the central party newspaper *Pravda*,

> in the rich steppe districts of Samara province, which abounded in bread and meat, nightmares are happening, an unprecedented phenomenon of rampant cannibalism is observed. Driven by hunger to despair and madness, having eaten everything that is accessible to the eye and the tooth, people decide to eat a human corpse and secretly devour their own dead children. In the village of Lyubimovka, one of citizens dug a 14-year-old girl's body from the grave, cut the corpse into several pieces, folded the body parts into cast iron skillet [for cooking] … When this "crime" was discovered, it turned out that the girl's head was "cut in two and scorched." The cannibal obviously failed in cooking the corpse.[70]

The surplus appropriation aggravated the epidemiological and health situation in the countryside as well. For example, in the Volga region, in 1921, mortality from acute infectious diseases was over 469,000, in 1922—over 515,000; simultaneously, the flow of refugees—adults and children—increased as well.[71] The region's starving population, initially estimated at 25 million people, was subsequently estimated at over 30 million.[72] A grim description of the sufferings of the starving population comes from the speech of the Chairman of the Samara Provincial Executive Committee V. A. Antonov-Ovseenko:

> Millions of people are starving, and this is not just a simple word about malnutrition, it means that people have nothing to chew, that they are gnawing on the frozen ground, that they are going crazy with the misery that has befallen them.[73]

There were also many recorded cases of infanticide and cannibalism involving orphans.[74] Antonov-Ovseenko spoke with tremendous force in 1921 at the IX Congress of Soviets about the suffering of the starving population of Samara province: "We have information about how children are taken deep into the steppe and left there to die, how distraught mothers slaughter their children so that they do not just die before their eyes."[75] On February 20, 1922, the head of the Spasskaya canton Soviet militia reported an incident in the village of Apakov in the Yukhmachinsky volost:

> Citizen, Royava Lukerya and her tenant, Tyshktnaya Varvara, with two girls, on February 17, 1922, strangled an orphan boy Philip Sorokin who had stayed overnight, chopped him into small pieces, and ate him. The investigation carried out by the chairman of the council of the Apakovsky society found cooked human meat in the amount of about 2 1/2 pounds.[76]

A 1922 brochure from Samara province described the following horror:

> In terrible despair, people go mad. Children gnaw their little hands. Mothers kill children so as not to see them starve to death. In Romashkovskaya, Andronovskaya, and Usmanskaya counties cases have been officially established when people, distraught and wild from hunger, eat the dead.[77]

A telegram of February 27, 1922, described a scene from the village of Burmeteva: The Serazedinov family

> boiled their dead 5-year-old daughter Polmarui in a cauldron for food. During the search, it turned out that some parts had been eaten together by the family, including the surviving 12-year-old Kadychai girl because of hunger. The offender [mother] has been arrested.[78]

Children's misery during the early and mid-1920s became endemic and must be linked primarily to the procurement campaign, during which uncounted numbers of street children fled starving areas. As living conditions of millions of Soviet families deteriorated, the number of starving children and homeless exploded. The child mortality rate in the food procurement regions approached 80–95 percent. According to one official, mortality among these children reached a "catastrophic level."[79] "The condition of the starving Povolzhie" (the Volga Basin Region), wrote A. Serafimovich, "is terrible; the condition of the region's children is impossible. They die by the thousands; the survivors are incredibly thin and pale. Skin and bones—that is a Povolzh'e child."[80] According to an estimate, of 1,304,425 children in the Tartar republic, 326,106 have disappeared within three months of 1921. Many died and many others became homeless.[81] The Commissar for Enlightenment Lunacharsky in an August 1921 article loudly entitled "We Shall Not Forget Children," wrote:

> In Saratov, on the Volga bank, ... there is a new constantly growing population: thousands of utterly neglected homeless children. Nobody cares for them, nobody feeds them. They live on begging, prostitution, and robbery. They have nowhere to go! In general, we are facing a crisis; orphanages have not been repaired for a long time. What are we going to do? The number of such premises, for example, in Saratov, is drastically reduced, and the children arrive, endlessly, endlessly.[82]

The children, except for a few high-level articles, were in fact forgotten by the new Soviet regime.

The massive influx of homeless children into large cities during 1919–20 from the food procurement districts was one of the costs of this ruthless policy. Children who had previously been evacuated from starving cities hoping to find food in the countryside now left these rural areas *en masse* because there was nothing to eat there: peasants refused to provide shelter for these children because they and their families were also starving. In many cases, peasants took the initiative by bringing their children to the offices of the People's Commissariat of Education. A spokesman for the local enlightenment commissariat said that about fifty children are abandoned in Samara every day.[83] These children were abandoned either by their own parents or by foster families where they had been sheltered. Another government official cited incidents of deliberate poisoning of foster children by "desperate peasants."[84] Parents abandoned their own biological children as well; according to one report, "as a result of the onset of hunger, mothers bring their children to the [Soviet] executive committee and leave them."[85] Giving up children was perhaps the best thing starving peasants could do to save their children: parents had no other option.

By the end of 1920, the scale of the peasant anti-Bolshevik movement increased and continued over the following years. In addition to Ukraine and Siberia, it broke out in the southwest, in the Tambov region, in the Volga basin, Tyumen, and other regions. Children also took part in peasant protest. In its proclamation to all workers, peasants, and Red Army men of the Tyumen province, dated June 21, the 3rd Tyumen Provincial Congress of Soviets stated:

> We know that many have a wound in their souls, many have lost their close relatives, fathers and mothers, brothers and sisters, even children; many have been stripped of property, bread, seeds; many were not even allowed to sow the fields, but still we need to suppress in ourselves these understandable feelings, and reestablish relations with the returning rebels so that they are not afraid to return to their farms.[86]

In reality, in response to peasant resistance to surplus appropriation, the local Cheka and food supply authorities habitually arrested entire families of rebellious peasants, including children and the elderly, and put them all together in prisons. A message from one government official stated that children brought with their parents from the Tambov region are being held in Moscow "concentration camps."[87] How can the Bolshevik laws prohibiting the imprisonment of children be assessed if government security forces arrested children and sent them to concentration camps with their parents? An even more obnoxious alternative would have been to transform these children into the homeless category. The best policy would have been to adjust to peasant demands, which were more likely to have been reasonable than those of the Communist state.

Hence, one cannot discount the likelihood that the very policies of the early Soviet government caused the perpetuation of children's problems during 1918–22 and beyond. Prodrazverstka and the population policy of the early Soviet government became an impetus of continuous children's homelessness and starvation during the 1920s. The state's measures to cope with homeless children also contributed to this never-ending tragedy. During the 1920s, homeless children often originated from mismanaged children's orphanages, which in fact turned into labor colonies for children. The inmates of these colonies used any possible means to escape. Children's homelessness of the 1920s was the direct consequence of the new government's internal policies. Despite all that had been done, at least on paper, in December 1922 there were official reports that "conditions of republic's children's population were terrible, and children's homelessness was growing catastrophically."[88] Similar reports came in the following years throughout the 1920s.

Stalinist *Realpolitik*: Children's Homelessness Perpetuated

The source of children's homelessness and starvation in Soviet Russia seems to have an ongoing nature—namely, state population policies based on *realpolitik* perpetuated the issues. Stalinist collectivization of agriculture well exemplifies this. Collectivization further compromised the conditions of peasant families already under extreme stress, sparked once again actual starvation, and further aggravated children's already harsh lives during the 1930s. Some historical context here is necessary.[89] Historians usually describe collectivization in the Soviet Union as a transformation from "traditional" and "backward" agriculture to a new socialist and communist model, albeit with attending repression of a certain specified social strata—the kulaks. Nevertheless, one should remember that collectivization (setting up both kolkhozes and sovkhozes) involved the entire countryside—millions of peasant families—adults and children. Collectivization and the repressions carried out against certain social groups produced social chaos and created the potential for social and inter-generational conflicts. It sharply reduced material standards and expectations for most of the population. Even so, the reader should be reminded that most children lived in the countryside, as a result of which we must explore the effect of collectivization on children's starvation and homelessness' origins during the 1930s.

Following *realpolitik* principles and methods, the Bolsheviks and their new leader, increasingly dictatorial Joseph Dzhugashvilli (Stalin), ruthlessly executed the collectivization project. Peasant families were forced to join collective farms under threat of harsh sanctions, arrest, and imprisonment. The *realpolitik* of forced collectivization involved all possible measures to expedite the process, from brigades of the Communist Youth Union who agitated among peasants, to police who arrested recalcitrant peasants. Simultaneously, the government, facing food shortages in urban centers, once again imposed food procurement on peasants. During 1928–9, the state used various repressive and sometimes violent policies in order to obtain grain. This further aggravated already deteriorating conditions in the countryside. The government compensated peasants for grain but at a rate hardly adequate for purchases of very high-priced manufactured goods; only a few peasants could pay these prices. Peasants from the Penza province village Lomovka, S. N. Petelma and F. I. Murazanov, wrote to the central authorities on January 26, 1929, that:

> we have many poor peasants in our village who do not have enough of their own bread to feed their families until the next harvest. And they are not able to buy any, because bread is very expensive on the market—4 rubles per pud [16 kg] of rye. All this hit the poor strata of the village very hard.[90]

This clearly resulted from the state's population and economic policies. In villages, continued forced grain procurements, accompanied by mass arrests and devastation of farms, led directly to mass starvation and mortality. "Due to significant mortality cases, the population threw corpses into the cemetery, courtyards, sheds, etc.," according to one of numerous "highly classified" reports. "Up to 100 human corpses have accumulated in the cemetery [of a certain village], lying on the surface of the earth … Most are children and men."[91]

Nevertheless, in 1930, the party decided to speed up collectivization with the goal of completing it in one to two years. According to the decision, all peasants' land plots, including the land of earlier cooperatives, were to be established as publicly owned and transformed, on the given concern, into a single land area. Also, all working animals, livestock, seed, feed stocks, and tool outbuildings were to be socialized. Household facilities, dairy cattle, small agricultural tools, etc. could be retained for peasants' personal utilization. General community meetings were to approve membership in the kolkhoz. Kulaks and persons deprived of their voting rights because of various violations were not accepted. By late February 1930, 50 percent of agriculture was in collective farms throughout the Soviet Union, which doubled the official five-year plan for collectivization. Thus, the stage had been set for the future immiseration of millions of Soviet children.

The collectivization of agriculture led to the reality that affluent and middle peasants, now labeled as kulaks, virtually disappeared from the village. Those peasants who had been forced onto collectives naturally displayed little concern for the outcome of their labor. Additionally, the state essentially confiscated a large part of what was produced. Peasants realized that regardless of how much they increased productivity— exclusively at the cost of their heightened labor efforts—the state would take away almost everything. In kolkhozes, farmers received no cash payment for their work except for the low amount prescribed by the so-called workdays (*trudoden'*). Thus, families of collective farms got little money or produce to sell for extra sorely needed income. During later years, after terrible hunger broke out in many food-producing areas, they were allowed to retain enough to barely sustain their families.

During the first five years of the kolkhoz experiment, the volume of agricultural production decreased by 14 percent, compared to the pre-war years. There was a decline in grain production by 10 percent, a decline in the number of cattle by one-third, and the number of sheep decreased even more. Similar declines were observed in all areas of agriculture. In the future, this negative trend was to some degree gradually overcome but during collectivization's initial stages, the effect was overwhelming. At the same time, state food procurements doubled, some of which was exported, obviously one of the principal causes of hunger during 1932–3 in many agricultural regions of the Soviet Union (the Caucasus, the Volga region, the Ukraine, and Kazakhstan in particular). Authorities registered cases of cannibalism in many starving areas. According to various sources,[92] the famine claimed the lives of between 3 and 5 million people—adults and children. These developments were the direct results of the Bolshevik government's policies (*realpolitik*). Despite the weak harvest in 1931–2, the government sold abroad almost the entire stock of grain, leaving almost nothing for the domestic market. This homicidal sale was done for the sake of industrialization. Industrialization intensified at the price of millions of peasant lives.

Having reached the maximum depth of decline in 1934 after terrible famine, in 1935–7 the birth rate in Russia increased slightly, but never returned to the level that had existed before 1933. In 1935, when Stalin uttered his famous words that "life has become merrier," and "the birth rate is higher, and the net increase is incomparably greater," the total fertility rate in Russia was almost 40 percent lower than in 1927. As for the natural increase, it was almost twice as low as in 1927 (11 vs. 21 percent).

Already in the early 1930s, the classification of demographic information was in full swing, gradually turning into outright falsification. In particular, the 1937 census was declared "sabotage," and a new census was carried out in 1939, the results of which were more acceptable to the country's leadership. Both demographic institutes were liquidated—the one in Leningrad in 1934, the other in Kiev in 1939. Demographic publications almost disappeared. Violent repression fell upon the demographers themselves. The concealment of information about demographic processes in the USSR had reached an inconceivable limit. Even the total population of the country was not known. Only in 1959—six years after Stalin's death and twenty years after the census—of the 1939 population—was a new census carried out, thanks to which statisticians felt something like stable ground under their feet and were able to calculate necessary demographic indicators. The result of the 1959 census and its comparison with the 1926 census made it possible to judge the demographic results of Stalin's rule. What are these results?

Collectivization immediately spurred sharp peasant resistance.[93] All kinds of violent acts took place, from the burning of crops as a means of slowing the process to the hanging of local authorities in their areas. Some villages even compared the administration that was in place to the antichrist and suggested that they were entering the end times. There were also many peasants who looked at the restrictions that were placed on them as a second installment of serfdom. These factors clearly suggest how much the peasants hated the very idea of collectivization. Although Stalin saw his methods as a success for the Soviet Union as a nation, peasants disagreed. Peasants did everything they could to try to end the transformation taking place. In the early 1930s, many peasants tried to peacefully protest collectivization, both through writing letters to the government and by speaking out at local meetings. However, when these attempts were not taken seriously, the peasants turned toward violent acts. According to various statistics, there were 346 insurgencies in January 1930, which were joined by roughly 125,000 people. Already in February 1930, the number of protest actions grew to 736 with 220,000 people. During the first two weeks of March 1930, 595 riots took place joined by 230,000 peasants. In March of 1930, the authorities reported 1,642 insurgencies in Belarus, the Central Black Earth region, the Lower and Middle Volga regions, the North Caucasus, in Siberia, in the Urals, Leningrad, Moscow, West, Ivanovo-Voznesensk, Crimea, and Central Asia. The insurgencies involved about 750,000–800,000 people. There were over a thousand insurgent villages in the Ukraine in March 1930 alone.

By March 1930, the disastrous results of the early stages of forced expedited collectivization (*realpolitik*) finally alarmed Stalin. In a famous (or better infamous) article titled "Dizzy with Success," published in the party newspaper *Pravda*, Stalin blamed the local authorities for the extremes of collectivization.[94] Stalin accused local leaders of imposing the unreasonable pace of collectivization with the goal of impressing the government with high numbers and their willingness to use of force. He also now urged careful consideration of the diversity of geographical conditions of the vast USSR when determining the pace and methods of collective-farm development, a first belated nod toward ecological circumstances.

This "dizzy success" had been achieved with the use of violence and by total neglect of the ecology of local conditions. For example, 70 percent of the Tyumen region of Western Siberia had been collectivized by March 1930. This region, with its arctic and subarctic climate, was not agricultural; its peasants engaged in some subsistence agriculture, fishing, and deer herding. Nonetheless, completely inappropriate collectivization was ruthlessly pursued by the OGPU (secret police) and prosecutorial power, plus that of specially assigned plenipotentiaries to identify the "criminal activity" of kulaks and all prosperous elements. Peasants everywhere sent thousands of letters of complaint, stating that they were all the same and all hungry.

Despite mass terror, this forcefully created collective farm system began to disintegrate already by the spring of 1930; by May 1930, only 20 percent of farms remained as kolkhozes. But this in fact only represented a government breathing space, spurred by Stalin's "Dizzy with Success" commentary. The party reaction followed immediately. On March 14, 1930, the Central Committee of the Communist Party (Bolsheviks) issued a resolution "On the Fight against Misrepresentation of the Party Line in the Collective-Farm Movement." After this criticism, many artificially created collective farms began to collapse. The process of collectivization slowed down but did not end. For example, severe repression quickly resumed in the Tyumen region and elsewhere, where the original collectivization campaign had not yet occurred. According to a decision of the local Tyumen Bolshevik party committee, 3,200 households were to be deported to GULAG (prison camp) settlements in February 1930 and 750 households in March. In June the local party committee demanded the arrest of 290 households deemed in violation of collectivization norms; deportees were to be sent to construction sites and peat works. The key issue seems to have been whether an area had experienced the first stage of collectivization; if it had not, the campaign could proceed, even during the party's "retreat" in other areas.

The first victims of the collectivization campaign were kulak families. The reader should be informed that kulaks were not so identified as individuals, but as entire families with habitually large numbers of children, a fact ignored by the party and its leader. Earlier, in February 1928, the newspaper *Pravda* published an article "Exposing the Kulaks." The author attacked kulaks and reported that rich peasants dominated rural areas, exploited the labor of their hired workers, and had entered local party organizations (cells) and even led some of these cells. Soviet party-controlled media started publishing reports about kulaks' malicious activities. Thus, stigmatization and exposure of "enemies" had begun. The Soviet authorities advocated and promoted forceful expropriation of grain stocks, at first as a "temporary" emergency measure. These forcible seizures of grain discouraged farmers from expanding production and, as a result, it hurt poor peasants, who lost work opportunities (hiring their labor to other better-off peasants). The temporary emergency measure soon turned into the dynamic ruthless policy of "eliminating the kulaks as a class." The original concept of a kulak, the wealthy peasant, was soon expanded to mean any peasant plus family who opposed collectivization. From a social category it underwent a transformation into a political one (*realpolitik*). Children of kulak families were treated accordingly, that is, as offspring of enemies of the state.

Stalin personally formulated the policy of eliminating the kulaks as a class. He assumed that kulaks should be destroyed in open battle and deprived of their livelihood, including the use of land, tools, and the right to lease land and machinery and to employ laborers. Thus, the elimination of kulaks, or *dekulakization*, had started and intensified during 1928–32 with the suppression of anti-kolkhoz peasants and kulaks. In January 1930 the party issued a resolution "On Measures of Liquidation of Kulak Farms in the Areas of Complete Collectivization." The government divided kulaks into three categories, which included counter-revolutionary peasants and organizers of terrorist attacks and uprisings, the richest kulaks, and a third quite sinister category, "the rest of the kulaks." These categories were obviously and deliberately vague: any peasant risked being deemed a kulak. The heads of families of so-called counter-revolutionary and terrorist kulaks were arrested and their cases were transferred to the so-called *troika* (a Russian term signifying a group of three), a special tribunal of three members, representing the police, regional party committees, and the prosecutor's office. The alleged kulak's family members, including children and infants, as well as the kulaks themselves, were subject to eviction to remote areas of the USSR, mostly to western Siberia. Infants were allowed to stay with their mothers in prisons until they attain two years of age and were then transferred to children's colonies. Members of the third ambiguous category, "the rest of kulaks," were settled within their province on a specially allocated area, outside the kolkhoz lands, where they operated, under mysterious circumstances and unknown fate, as *edinolichniki* (individual farmers), portrayed in 1930s films.

The resolution demanded that the first category of kulaks, counter-revolutionaries, and organizers of terrorist attacks should be liquidated by immediate imprisonment in concentration camps. At this point some parallels with the Nazi Germany may be valid. As a repressive measure, the OGPU (political police) proposed to send to concentration camps 60,000 kulaks of that category and to evict 150,000 kulaks and family members of the second category. The deported peasants (kulaks of the other categories) were placed in specially created settlements in uninhabited or sparsely populated areas. The concentration camps and special settlements operated under the authority of GULAG, one of the instruments of Bolshevik *realpolitik*, founded in April 1930 (the new Soviet state, opened its first concentration camps as part of the Red Terror during the fall of 1918, after an assassination attempt on Lenin). The state confiscated all property of the deported peasants, giving each a one-time payment of 500 rubles.

The government categorized people and punishment clearly, at least in the statutes, but how to identify a counter-revolutionary or how to differentiate a rich peasant from a peasant farmer with an average income was not spelled out. There was absolutely no criterion for determining a "kulak." Consequently, most peasants who merely objected to collectivization were designated kulaks or even counter-revolutionaries. There were instances in which even local poor villages were dispossessed. Most peasants who suffered from collectivization and the related repression were hardly suspect of anything. They merely fell victims to Bolshevik *realpolitik*, in this case anti-peasant policies.

Collectivization had a devastating impact on the lives of millions of Soviet children; their families were deprived of their means of existence—land and property; and many families perished in labor camps or in wilderness areas of the far north where people were brought and left without any means of survival. This campaign proved to be the worst nightmare for numerous peasant families and their members, adults, and children. Perhaps no country imposed an agrarian policy that resulted in such disastrous consequences (dispossession, mass resistance, forced relocation, famine, devastating mortality, and homelessness among children) as the Soviet Union's collectivization and nationalization of agriculture.

As mentioned, Bolshevik policies caused mass homelessness among children in food-producing areas of the countryside during the Civil War food procurement campaign (1918–21). Now, anew, a wave of homeless children emerged to an alarming extent in Western and Eastern Siberia, where collectivization victims were often sent. During 1932 classified letters and telegrams from Siberia informed the central state authorities that homelessness and beggary among the region's children had taken on a mass character, particularly in Omsk, Novosibirsk, and Tomsk, widely spread areas of Siberia. Classified telegrams from local authorities importuned the central government to deal urgently with the growing problem. Children's homelessness grew alarmingly in other areas heavily affected by collectivization as well.[95]

Conclusions

According to official statistics and documents about street children, as well as official state periodicals, the central government hardly noticed their presence in 1918–19 and therefore was not concerned about them. Even so, the tragedy of early Soviet childhood hardly resulted from abstract circumstances, supposedly reflecting wartime and Revolution, as the official language claimed in 1921 and on. It reflected very concrete factors. The First World War created economic hardship and political chaos, but policies of the government that took over in October 1917 further aggravated and sharply deepened the crisis. Official Bolshevik policies resulted in mass children's starvation and homelessness that lasted for decades. As the geography of children's starvation and homelessness suggests, the problems coincided with the Soviet state's population policies beginning in 1918–19 and continuing throughout the 1920s and 1930s.

Thus, children's starvation and homelessness became widespread and protracted, reaching the level of millions of children. The total number of children who were homeless and starving in the 1920s and 1930s can only be estimated. The answer to the question of what happened to these millions of starving and street children in the 1920s and 1930s lies in the realm of Bolshevik politics. As Amartya Sen observed, famine is rarely the result of drought or spoiled crops, and it rarely happens due to a country's absolute food shortages.[96] Excuses such as drought, rain, or crop failure cannot justify government policies that lead to hunger. In the following chapters, the problems of children's starvation and homelessness will be examined in the context of Bolshevik and Stalinist *realpolitik*.

3

A Revolutionary Childhood: Ideals, Declarations, Challenges, and Realities

The environment has a huge impact on person's upbringing.
    N. K. Krupskaya, September 20, 1918[1]

In a bourgeois state, whether it be a monarchy or a republic, it makes no difference— the school is an instrument for the spiritual enslavement of the broad masses of people.
    N. K. Krupskaya, 1918[2]

If a fighter, a personality is not raised from a child, then this will prevent us from creating a lot, will prevent us from creating a harmonious society.
    A. V. Lunacharsky, 1924[3]

The state should be the ultimate guardian of the child. This formula contains the main requirement for the state. As the supreme guardian, the state considers parental authority only as a form of childcare subject to state supervision.
    P. I. Lyublinsky, 1924[4]

Paradoxically, during the revolutionary years homeless children were of little priority to the newly formed government, which directed its attention and energy to the fulfillment of its main task—the liquidation of tsarist and bourgeois institutions and the creation of new ones—according to the vision of its theorists. Although the state and party media, as well as some official documents, mentioned children's starvation, this issue did not overly bother the government: during 1918–19 it was not discussed as an important issue in the mainstream media and did not receive widespread publicity. During that period, the government made several mostly declarative decisions and adopted laws that addressed children in general, as an age group. It seems inexplicable that during 1918 street children, who already roamed the streets of Moscow and Petrograd en masse, did not concern the government until mid-1920 to early 1921. In 1919–20, crowds of hungry children left the starving regions of the Volga provinces and Ukraine and moved to Moscow and other urban centers or to the south (the Crimean Peninsula mostly), overwhelming trains, stations, and markets. By mid-1920, their number had swelled into millions, to the point where the government viewed them as a threat to public order and safety: homeless children engaged in "counter-revolutionary" and criminal activities, often just to get food for survival. It was true—children's crime had skyrocketed over the years during the food appropriation campaign, and it is also true that, at this point, for the first time, the government turned its attention to street children. However, the state viewed street children not as a social and pedagogical problem, but as a political one. Some Bolshevik officials viewed street children, especially adolescents, as a potential obstacle to the creation of a real socialist society, as a threat to public security, and as a source of counter-revolution. The government acknowledged that such children were deprived of food and moved from starving rural areas to places where they believed they could find a means of survival. The government had created several agencies for child relief associated with the enlightenment and state charity commissariats and had also identified several preventive measures to restrict the movement of children on the railways, detain them, and return them home or to childcare facilities. The government issued a series of decrees that required priority attention to children in the supply and distribution of food, issues that will be discussed later in this chapter.

During 1920, the state finally became seriously concerned about the problem of street children. From this moment (two years after the actual beginning of mass homelessness), the issue began to receive unprecedented official publicity. Leading party and state newspapers *Pravda* and *Izvestia* launched a prominent publication campaign with articles about street children and their conditions with calls for urgent assistance. Authors wrote in *Narodnoye Prosveshchenie* (People's Education), *Na Putiakh k novoi shkole* (On the Way to a New School), *Narodny Uchitel'* (People's teacher), *Vestnik prosveshcheniia* (Bulletin of Education), *Krasnaia Nov'* (Red new), *Detskii dom* (Orphanage), and other Soviet pertinent periodicals about the theory and practice of combating homelessness. The media launched discussions on the acute problems of homeless childhood.[5] The Bolshevik government turned to the public for help. In November 1920, government agencies organized the Children's Week campaign and charity trains initially aimed at gathering some foodstuffs in exchange for manufactured goods in the countryside to help the starving children of Moscow and Petrograd.[6] It was only then that the government paid attention to mass starvation and homelessness among children nationwide, especially in the starving regions of Volga and other provinces. This chapter will explore the proposed and widely publicized ideals versus hidden realities of early Soviet childhood, focusing on early Bolshevik policies regarding childhood in general, the conditions of starving street children, in particular, and immediate government action to help street children. This chapter also attempts to assess the related policies and day-to-day practices of the early Soviet government.

Revolutionary Ideals, Declarations, and Challenges

It is generally accepted that Soviet children had enjoyed a happy childhood. This may be true for later periods of Soviet history but is certainly not the case for the first decades of Soviet power. Early Soviet childhood was full of tragedy and suffering for most children. During these decades, children were not the government's top priority; rather, the government prioritized propaganda and discussions about children's upbringing and education in such a way as to cultivate the loyalty of the new generation and its adherence to Bolshevik ideals. Likewise, early on Bolsheviks lacked a clear understanding of childhood. The latter would be formulated later, with Stalin's assumption of power and the development of official state agitprop.

Revolutionary Childhood: Propaganda First

The Bolshevik government quickly created tools for public mobilization and propaganda, which later became a powerful resource for the Soviet state in formulating new concepts of Soviet childhood, womanhood, and family, and helped to steer the building of a new society on what was viewed as a true socialist track. It seems that throughout 1918–19, propaganda and social mobilization were among the government's most important concerns, along with its relentless attempts to consolidate the power of the Bolshevik Party. In May 1918, Lenin expressed grave concerns to Enlightenment Commissar Lunacharsky about his inactivity in preparing good quotes and inscriptions on public buildings in St. Petersburg and Moscow and gave him an order to paint some public buildings with propaganda slogans. Lenin noted that "we need revolutionary and socialist inscriptions on public buildings." "It is necessary to select a commission and immediately draw up a list, a draft of inscriptions, sayings and quotations." As a result, the Soviets' newspaper *Izvestia VTSIK* announced an appeal by Lunacharsky to hold a monumental agitation competition for the best inscriptions and sayings. The announcement impelled everyone to "work out and send in short, bright, telling words that would make passers-by think and, perhaps, spark a bright idea or a sharp revolutionary feeling in their souls."[7] And again, on September 18, Lenin sent a telegram to Lunacharsky expressing indignation that nothing has been done in the field of monumental agitation, and what was done was bad. On September 19, when Lunacharsky sent Lenin materials on the draft coat of arms and press of the Council of People's Commissars, he assured Lenin: "Every effort is being made to implement the plans of monumental propaganda as soon as possible."[8]

The early Bolshevik state spent huge amounts of money on propaganda and agitation, at the expense of funding for social and humanitarian needs. The state created an extensive, highly bureaucratic propaganda network. In December 1918, when the new government's popularity plummeted and the need for propaganda became acute, the government created the Department of Soviet Propaganda. In 1919, the state introduced the Women's Department under central and local Bolshevik party committees to promote political activity, propaganda, and the mobilization of women. This department was responsible for promoting Soviet policy toward women, children, and families in the years to come. In November 1920, a new Main Political and Educational Committee of the Russian Republic (*Glavpolitprosvet*) emerged from the Information Department of the People's Commissariat of Enlightenment to become a separate state agency. Nadezhda Konstantinovna Ulyanova (Krupskaya) became the chairwoman of this committee and was tasked with formulating a political and educational agenda, as well as conducting agitation and propaganda activities in the spirit of the ideals and aspirations of the Bolshevik Party. This institution oversaw reading rooms, clubs, libraries, schools for adults, Soviet party schools, communist universities, etc. Krupskaya was considered the greatest authority in the field of education and became a chief Bolshevik advocate for school, educational, and childcare reforms. In the annals of Soviet pedagogy, she was reputed to be the main theoretician of the Soviet education system.[9]

The activities of the newly created bureaucratic offices, however, did not find large popular support. Moreover, certain policies of the department provoked strong resistance and hostility from many women, who feared that these policies would destroy their families and provoke separation of parents and children due to increasing government interference in family life, as well as in the issues of childcare and education.[10] However, as we will discuss later, many of the USSR's early actions and policies regarding children served primarily propaganda purposes.

"Home Environment Is Inappropriate for Proper Soviet Upbringing": Constructing the Ideal Soviet Childhood

Regarding childhood, it can be assumed that some pre-revolutionary tendencies in understanding the importance of children and their upbringing continued after the Revolution. In the last decades of the empire, among teachers, local zemstvo reformers, and representatives of the professional intelligentsia, there were lively discussions about the upbringing and education of children, as discussed in Chapter 1. They stressed the applied disciplines and practical knowledge that would prepare children for adult life, as well as cultivate good morals.[11] Early discussions of Bolshevik theorists about children also centered around the upbringing and education of children along practical lines. But the Bolsheviks also seemed to understand the political value of children and wanted to instill in them a sense of political purpose and achievement that were far less pronounced before 1917. The Bolsheviks hoped to raise a generation ready to sacrifice their lives for the Revolution and the ideals of communism. Here, the argument of historian of Soviet childhood Julia deGraffenried about the Soviet concept of "sacrificing childhood" during the Great Patriotic War (as the Second World War was called in the Soviet Union)[12] is quite applicable to the earlier years and, perhaps, can be dated to the Bolsheviks' coming to power in October 1917.

Bolsheviks envisioned the ideal person for the new society—the new Soviet person, whom some thinkers would later sarcastically call "*Homo Sovieticus*"[13]—and wanted to imbue Soviet children with ideas about communism, class struggle, the meaning of Revolution, and the roles of the people in this new socialist community. The interests and priorities of the state were placed above the interests of people who had to sacrifice themselves every moment in the name of the ideals of the new people's state. The logic was obvious: if the proclaimed state is a people's state, then there can be no exploitation of the people a priori and people are obliged to sacrifice and create in the name of their state.

The Bolsheviks tried to formulate new concepts and approaches to raising and educating children in this imaginary socialist community. These approaches were clearly articulated and revolutionary. As Krupskaya, who never had children of her own, pointed out in 1918, Soviet children should be taken away from the corrupting influence of the old capitalist regime—in some cases even from their families,—because "the home environment of the majority of the population cannot be conducive to child development."[14] Krupskaya believed that children should be placed in an environment of a new kind, in a school of a new socialist type, capable of creating a new socialist personality. She wrote in 1924:

> If the peasant is thoroughly imbued with an individualistic mindset, then this can be said even more about the married peasant woman, all whose interests are enclosed within the narrow sphere of her own household. Married peasant women are a particularly dark element, especially alien to the public realm. There are, of course, exceptions, but this is the general rule.[15]

Such a contemptuous characterization by Krupskaya and other Bolshevik officials of most of the population—millions of peasant families—should not be taken lightly. Obviously, Krupskaya and other Bolshevik theorists, including most of the Women's Department of the Bolshevik Party, used rhetoric to justify the Revolution, their rise to power, and their policies, as well as to emphasize their political significance to society. However, this rhetoric reflected their views on society, which, in turn, influenced their policies and decisions. According to Russian researchers of Krupskaya's heritage, Krupskaya did not visualize or believe in the role of mother and family in child-raising. Krupskaya viewed women primarily as representatives of their class, and not as mothers and members of their families and had inherent disrespect for the family, which, supposedly, played a destructive role in Soviet reality.[16] In this understanding, children were alienated from their parents and existed outside of their families. Thus, the early Soviet state tended to view children as an extra-family social category.

It is most likely impossible to understand the motivation of childless leaders, like Krupskaya. They seemed to want to "improve the well-being" of children, but the question arises: whose? Perhaps the following explains many of the strange actions of such politicians: neither they nor their descendants would have to live with the catastrophic consequences of their decisions and policies.

Paradoxically, it seems that Bolshevik theorists were more interested in their own ideals than in the lives of those who directly affected by the policies born of these ideals. Apparently, Bolshevik theorists viewed children as convenient plastic material to be shaped into any desired form, unlike older generations, who fixed their thinking back to tsarist times. It should also be noted that during the late 1920s, 1930s, and later, Soviet cultural production, especially films, tended to portray older generations in a derogatory light. The state expected advancement through its own participation in and control over the lives of children through education that reflected the ideal of the state in its exclusive role in caring for and raising children. This approach, in turn, also faced contempt from the population, as mentioned earlier. A contemptuous attitude toward most of the population could hardly bring about any other response.

These new perspectives on the role of the state in the lives of children were reflected in Soviet legislative initiatives and activities that led to the introduction of new laws, which, as a rule, assumed more active state intervention in matters of childhood, education, and childcare. From a legal point of view, the state took control of the education and training of children, taking legal responsibility for the well-being of the young republic's minor dependents. Moreover, it should be understood that the state also assumed control and responsibility for the rationing, distribution, and consumption of food and goods for the entire population, thereby transferring the welfare of Soviet families into its own hands.

Ideal Soviet Education: Is Child Labor Ever Possible?

The answer to this question was negative for opponents of child labor in imperial Russia, as illustrated in my book on child labor.[17] Imperial Russian laws gradually prohibited the work of children under 12 and required education for employment of children over 12 years of age. Certain types of work and work at night were completely prohibited. Late imperial educators allowed child labor only as part of apprenticeship and training. For the early Bolshevik government, employment of children was not only possible, but became compulsory as part of Soviet "socialist education." Thus, for Bolshevik educational theorists like Krupskaya, the answer was yes.

Even so, Krupskaya was a Bolshevik politician and propagandist and always used rhetoric for political and propaganda purposes. Addressing population that did not read theoretical works on pedagogy, her statements sometimes seem contradictory. For example, in her 1917 article, "The Urgent Task of Workers Is Labor Protection of Children and Adolescents," she demanded a prohibition of hired productive labor of children and adolescents under 16 years of age.[18] Here, I must note that child labor had taken a turn during the wartime era. Obviously, children under 16 would be better off studying than earning money for living. But, justifying the need for compulsory universal education, Krupskaya insisted on the required combination of education and productive labor, and emphasized that the work of children ages from 12 to 16 should be compulsory because there was an economic necessity for the country.[19] In her view, labor was a great educational force: "only labor educates citizens."[20] In other words, for Krupskaya, state economic needs justified the compulsory labor of children. Thus, on the one hand Krupskaya seemed to be protecting children when she spoke about prohibition of child labor, whereas on the other, she justified compulsory labor of children for state and educational needs. After a careful reading of Krupskaya's works, it can be assumed that she borrowed many ideas about education and upbringing from the late tsarist times, but added several of her own radical revisions, perverting, in fact, the meaning and idea of school education. According to the 1916 Ignatiev school reform that stressed practical and lab training, labor courses had been included in the curricula of higher primary schools and seventy-two academic hours were allocated annually (288 hours in total) to these courses. However, these practical lessons were optional, and were used at the discretion of the school and the teacher.[21] To the contrary, Krupskaya insisted on the obligatory involvement of schoolchildren in labor activity.

Figure 7 N. K. Krupskaya. Source: Open public domain.

One may ask an obvious question: What distinguishes a working child hired by a capitalist manufacturer from a child working for the state virtually without pay allegedly because of the "economic needs" of the state? Perhaps the difference may lie in the fact that under capitalism, child labor was not compulsory, depended on circumstances, and by no means was universal, whereas for the Bolsheviks, child labor became an obligation supposedly required for the education of all children except those from elite families. The idea that "only labor teaches" would soon be implemented in schools, children's homes, and correctional institutions of the Soviet Union. Government officials advocated the concept that a true workers' government would never abuse or exploit child or adult laborers; in reality, children and many adult workers either received no wages or were paid at the lowest rate. The supposedly "workers" state became a cruel and oppressive exploiter of working children and adults. From the first days of the Bolshevik government, Soviet schoolchildren were obliged to work. Was a 10–14-year-old Soviet pupil happy to wake up at 6 in the morning and work on a state or collective farm field every day during the harvesting season? I leave this rhetorical question for the reader to answer.

Childcare Ideals, Declarations, and Challenges

In 1923, on behalf of the Children's Commission of the All-Russian Central Executive Committee, E. Khazanova wrote:

> After the October Revolution, the state took under its patronage all the children of the republic, becoming, as it were, their supreme guardian, Soviet power. From the very beginning, the Revolution established very broad care for children, trying to give the rising generation the best conditions and, by all means and forces, to promote their normal healthy development, both physically and spiritually.[22]

Following the official Bolshevik scenario, scholars of Soviet childhood usually note that "the Soviet government from the very first days of its existence began to take care of children."[23] In reality, these promises remained largely on paper as unfulfilled laws and declarations.

Acting in accordance with their ideas about childhood and the role of the state in education and upbringing, the government adopted many laws that both implicitly and explicitly influenced the lives of millions of Soviet children and their immediate environment. Regardless, the policy and tradition of caring for needy children preexisted earlier the USSR (see Chapter 1). At certain points, some early Soviet laws deepened and widened policies already began during the late imperial decades.[24] Regardless, many relevant early Soviet decrees had great social and political potential for children and women and were truly progressive for that period. For example, one of the government's first decrees, the act on civil marriage, issued on December 18, 1917, equated "illegitimate children" to children born in legal marriages regarding the rights and obligations of parents to their children and children to their parents. If the father of the child of an unmarried woman refused to recognize his paternity, then the mother of the child had "the right to prove his paternity in court."[25] This law, in fact, was an abbreviated version of the imperial law of June 1903 on "Improving of the situation of illegitimate children" (see discussion in Chapter 1). In December 1917 the government introduced a significantly simplified the divorce process. During the process, divorcing parties could choose surnames for both themselves and their children. Previously, according to the tsarist legislation, children of divorcees were given paternal surnames. The new laws also allowed parents to determine the place of residence for their minor children. Divorced parents had the right to determine the child support amount or, if they were unable to do so, this could be set in the local general procedure court.[26]

In 1918, the government introduced the first family law code with many revolutionary provisions. The code reinstated and reinforced the earlier decrees of December 1917 and proclaimed equality between men and women in civil marriages. In general, the family code was aimed at protecting children and women, as well as fathers. Innovative provisions introduced paid maternity leave benefits for women during pregnancy and afterwards—eight weeks before and eight weeks after childbirth—without loss of jobs and salaries, and seven months benefit for breastfeeding mothers when her paid maternity benefits had ended.[27] The code also prohibited adoption (a provision soon rescinded) and declared that all needy children were considered to be under state guardianship; these provisions and commitments established state policies toward children for the following years.

Certainly, these new laws manifested the state's great commitment to new concepts of the socialist family and parenthood, as well as the government's desire to create ideal laws for a socialist society; in the global context, they were the most advanced. However, the worth of this and other laws must be assessed within the context of Bolshevik *realpolitik*, namely the revolutionary extortion tax and surplus goods appropriation from which most Soviet women (and children), in the countryside and cities, suffered. Thus, the provisions on maternity leave in the much-publicized new family code hardly had any beneficial effect on most young Soviet women; all too often, the government's de facto policy toward women and their young children raises questions about the government's intentions.

Among many other decrees the new government introduced, several would directly affect the lives of children and their immediate environment. Earlier, in December 1917, the newly established Commissariat for State Charity terminated all imperial children's shelters and institutions that had been under the patronage of the Empress Maria Charity System, which in February 1917 came under the guidance of the newly established social welfare department of the Provisional Government. As mentioned in Chapter 1, by 1917 this system funded thousands of shelters and educational establishments for children. The system provided socialization, support, and education for over 70,000 children and adolescents under 18. This system no longer fit the new regime's ideals and its vision of socialist childcare. All former Imperial private and public establishments for children, including shelters, orphanages, and schools were transferred to the new Commissariat for State Charity for the purpose of financing, management, and maintenance.[28] In 1918, the Council of People's Commissars transformed charters and foundling homes into children's homes, which were subsequently transferred to the jurisdiction of specially created commissions under the Commissariat of Enlightenment without creating alternative funding for these childcare institutions. Furthermore, funding for the Commissariat for State Charity, which took charge of childcare, was hardly a major government priority at that time because of the sharp economic crisis. As a result, most childcare institutions were either closed or functioned only nominally.[29] Later, as the next chapter will illustrate, during the New Economic Policy, most old and newly created children's homes were transformed into labor communes where children were required to engage in productive labor to support themselves and their labor communes. As described above, the Bolsheviks justified child labor as a means of proper socialist education. The material conditions in these communes were poor and the treatment harsh, with the result that children often ran away and tried to survive in the streets, all too often by committing crimes.

Even so, the early Bolshevik government didn't see street children as a serious problem. Paradoxically, despite the growing number of street children and orphans, and the unsatisfactory situation with in childcare institutions, the state eliminated all public initiatives and foundations, prohibited adoptions and foster care, and established state custody over all needy children, so that the latter fully came under state guardianship.[30] The state took over the issues of childcare and education, thus attempting to take control of the minds of younger generations, an approach fully consistent with Bolshevik ideals. Acting in accordance with its ideological views, the government broke the pre-revolutionary social and religious traditions of charity, education, and caring for children in need, taking matters into the hands of the state.

Facing Street Children

In 1918, the government could not help but pay attention to street children but did not seem to view them as a serious problem. The early ordinances, laws, and activities were extended to all urban children. On September 23, 1918, the Council of People's Commissars introduced a resolution on the creation of a fund for "baby food." The decree stated:

> All local Soviets have "to organize a "Fund for baby food" by levying a tax on the population. The size, form and procedure of taxation are determined by the Council depending on local conditions.[31]

The tax percentage ranged from 10 to 50 percent of income. In Moscow, by a resolution of the Moscow City Soviet, all enterprises and institutions were required to pay 10 percent of their income amount of the Fund. All private traders were charged 50 percent. All food items issued by local food authorities to children inclusively henceforth were to be provided free of charge at the expense of the state. The regulation also applied to food items given to children by food authorities on ration cards both from food shops and from public diners. The decree was extended to the largest factory centers (cities, large settlements, etc.) of the following provinces: Arkhangelsk, Vladimir, Vologda, Ivanovo-Voznesensk, Kostroma, Kaluga, Moscow, Nizhny Novgorod, Novgorod, Cherepovets, Olonets, Petrograd, Pskov, Tver, Severnaia Dvina, and Yaroslavl. The People's Commissariat of Food could extend this provision to individual cities and factory centers in other provinces.[32] Thus, the state proclaimed the feeding of urban children, including the homeless, as a state matter and responsibility, which left behind most Soviet children who lived in the countryside. The introduction of this and other policies resulted from some state officials' increasing anxiety about street children in cities and reflected a realization that there were unattended and homeless children who needed help and protection because of their high vulnerability to being abused by adult criminals or, in some cases, certain state agencies; likewise, criminality among children had increased precipitously.

Despite the sharp increase of juvenile crimes, the Bolsheviks wanted to implement an ideal juvenile justice system in a socialist state with an emphasis on education and rehabilitation. In January 1918, the state abolished criminal courts and imprisonment for minors under 17; the Government's head, Lenin, and People's Commissar of Justice Isaak Sternberg (a Left Socialist Revolutionary) signed a decree "On Commissions for Minors" under the "exclusive auspices of the Commissariat of State Charity." These commissions were to consist of at least three people and included representatives from the departments of state charity, public education, and justice, one of whom was a doctor. After considering the case of minors, according to the decision, the commission either released the defendants or sent them to one of the shelters of the Commissariat of State Charity. Children in need of correction were not to be sent to prison, but to a special institution run by the Commissariat of Education, Health, or Social Welfare. The People's Commissariat of State Charity also developed instructions for commissions and shelters.[33] The decree extended to hundreds of thousands of starving and homeless children, as most of them had committed crimes to survive. Potentially, these children could take advantage of this law and escape being sent to prison. However, according to primary sources, the juvenile commissions "did not justify their mission" and acted instead as criminal courts.[34] At this point, let us remind the reader that, as discussed in Chapter 1, criminal courts and juvenile imprisonment were already suspended in the late imperial period, and therefore, in this regard, the Bolsheviks cannot be credited with novelty. Despite the efforts of the Soviet government, the number of crimes committed by minors, mostly street children, grew as the causes of child delinquency increased.

The financial difficulties of the Commissariat of State Charity limited its ability to create an adequate number of commissions for juvenile affairs, as well as a nationwide network of special children's institutions. Thus, the commissions had no place to send errant children. Also, the commissions had a management problem. Initially under the authority of the Commissariat of State Charity, the commissions were transferred to commissariats of Education, Justice, and Health: in reality they were instructed and managed by none of them.[35] To solve this problem, on January 14, 1919, the government transferred the commissions to the authority of the Commissariat of Education, which also had neither resources, nor the necessary authority.[36]

Like most early decrees and efforts of the Bolshevik government, the abolition of imprisonments for children was declarative and propagandistic for the most part and the reality was usually the opposite, a matter that will be explored further in this chapter. The adoption policy of the family code also was challenged when the government realized existing harsh realities and retreated from that part of the code by the reinstitution of adoption in 1921.[37] The 1919 decree of free food distribution in practice had no substantial results because during the War Communism era, 1918 to early 1921, most of the institutions that provided care for children were not in operation.[38] It is also virtually impossible to believe that during warfare and economic collapse, children's playgrounds could feed children, whereas no playgrounds existed in the countryside where the majority of children lived. Besides that, for children who attended children's institutions, the attachment of the ration cards to these institutions had "emotional and practical disadvantages. Parents, having given up their children's ration cards, no longer could feed their children elsewhere even for money," one observer wrote. "Many parents did not trust these institutions to feed their children and refused to surrender ration cards to them. Parents could, at least in theory, feed their children in public dining rooms for money once a day."[39] Later, the state itself admitted that it had no idea of the number of hungry and needy children, an awareness that would have been necessary, in order to provide them with free food rations, a matter, which will be discussed in Chapter 4.

In any case, the intentions of the mew government to create an ideal socialist childhood met serious challenges, which the government itself created by implementing policies based on unrealistic goals and all too realistic *realpolitik* methods. Why were certain policies of the government so unrealistic and what can explain the too realistic methods for their realization?

Psychotic Realities: Revolutionary Maniacs and "Defective" Children

In psychiatry, there is a condition called bipolar disorder where patients experience alternating phases of depression and mania. It seems that the Bolshevik government almost always experienced mania, a state of excitement and high spirits.[40] During a state of mania, people feel abnormally energetic—have little need for sleep, are happy or irritable, and usually make impulsive decisions regardless of the consequences.[41] Contemporary descriptions of early Bolshevik leaders may indicate some mental health dysfunctions. For example, the Commissar of Education Lunacharsky described Felix Dzerzhinsky's face as changeable: "and then the same agitated, as if angry face, flaring nostrils, as if breathing in the breath of a storm, the same burning eyes." In another description of Dzerzhinsky by Lunacharsky, we read: "and in his eyes, familiar to all of us, a somewhat feverish fire of excited energy immediately lit up." Of note is that Dzerzhinsky headed several key offices in the early Bolshevik government. Of course, the purpose of this book is not to make diagnoses, but rather to note an aspect that has been relatively little studied by historians. Maybe a professional psychiatrist will find interest in the question of mental health of Bolshevik leaders: these have vast opportunities for research.

Most of the government policies and legislative initiatives discussed here that disregarded consequences can be viewed from this psychiatric perspective. But there were even more rules and laws to consider. For example, as mentioned earlier, despite the emerging problem of street and starving children, coupled with the collapse of the schooling and childcare system, the government eliminated the entire private and public donation system and banned adoption. As a direct consequence of this and other policies and laws, thousands of starving and homeless children roamed the streets of Moscow, Petrograd, and other urban centers trying to survive. In 1918, most of these children were orphans and inmates of the tsarist orphanages, which were closed by government decision. The conditions of existing or newly created public childcare facilities were appalling.

It seems that the psychotic condition of officials made it impossible for the government to see the social reality, or perhaps this reality triggered some impulsive reaction due to the same psychological disorder. An assessment of the main contemporary periodicals of the Bolshevik Party and the Soviet government shows that children's homelessness in 1918–19 was hardly mentioned; perhaps it seemed less worrisome than other issues, since it did not see this as an acute problem. The reality of street children was of little concern to the government back then. The words "street children" rarely appeared in major newspapers during 1918–19, as opposed to late 1920–2. As mentioned above, the communications between the Commissar for Enlightenment Lunacharsky and the head of government Lenin had no reference to street children or children's starvation in 1918. During its early years, the government was vigorously working on the elimination of the old tsarist methods of bringing up and educating children and the introduction of new, socialist ways. The government was also intensely concerned about Bolshevik propaganda. Likewise, none of the Bolsheviks' early legislation policies about children differentiated between homeless, starving, or other children and, in some terms, tended to be more demonstrative of an imaginary idealist future than relevant to the present. In the presence of numerous homeless and starving children in 1918–19, the concrete legal and political activities of the government regarding children and childhood tended to exist in a separate realm from the challenging reality. For example, at a congress on children's vocational education that gathered in May 1919, speaking delegates, including V. I. Lenin and N. K. Krupskaya, made no mention of homeless and starving children, although these problems were becoming more and more acute by the day. Instead, the congress discussed vague ideas about socialist upbringing and education.[42] It seems that the Bolshevik authorities simply did not see or, perhaps, refused to see street children as an issue, regardless of the challenging reality. This perhaps explains why most studies on this subject begin their discussion with late 1920, whereas the issues of starvation and homelessness among children had already existed during 1918–19.

No Bourgeois Element in Children's Upbringing

Nonetheless, starving and homeless children first came to the attention of at least some public figures and members of professional intelligentsia already in 1918. As the state faced starvation in cities and industrial centers, what particularly harmed children both in families and in existing children's institutions was the slow response to this severe and growing problem; in fact, the first initiative came from an independent public organization. On the initiative of V. G. Korolenko, a group of concerned public activists in Moscow created the League for the Rescue of Children, headed by E. D. Kuskova, N. M. Kishkin, L. A. Tarasevich, E. Peshkova, and other representatives of the Russian intelligentsia in the fall of 1918. The League became a legal organization approved by the Council of People's Commissars.[43] During the first year of its activities, the League established fourteen children's homes, a children's sanatorium in Moscow, and several kindergartens and clubs. During this time, the organizations helped 3,500 children. The League's children's institutions usually occupied small apartments of two to three rooms and accepted no more than twenty-five to thirty children, usually of the same age for each premises. The league's main focus was the individual approach to upbringing and educating the child.[44]

In light of unprecedented children's starvation, the League suggested that the government should ask for help from foreign countries, including the United States, which irritated the Bolshevik government at the time. At first, the League was a completely legal organization approved by the Council of People's Commissars; even so, its links with overseas charities began to raise suspicions. In March 1919, the League addressed the Council of People's Commissars with a request to send a delegation abroad to purchase goods for children. Lenin directed this proposal to Cheka's head Dzerzhinsky with the note: "I think there is a catch to this." F. E. Dzerzhinsky replied that he considered letting Kuskova, Saltykov, and others go abroad harmful, since "there is not a single one of them who honestly recognizes Soviet power." At the end of his letter Dzerzhinsky stated bluntly that "the abroad will not feed our children."[45] As a result, the trip did not take place.

Acting in accordance with its ideology of expropriation and, most likely, due to the psychotic state of its staff, the People's Commissariat for Food vetoed almost all the League's food received from the Russian, American, and Danish Red Cross branches. By the beginning of January 1921, all children's institutions of the League for the Rescue of Children were transferred to the authority of the Moscow Department of People's Education,[46] whose leaders let slip the real reasons for the closure of this organization: "We cannot allow the Kishkins and Kuskovas to bring up proletarian children or even street children."[47] Approaches to the education and upbringing of children of "bourgeois elements" were hardly consistent with the early Soviet regime's concepts of upbringing and caring for children, which involved placing children in a new socialist environment. Of course, the Bolshevik state did not trust the Russian educated society, which remained essentially bourgeois and did not fit into the new ideal of the socialist society that the state wanted to create.

Red Cross and American Relief Administration

Despite the reluctance to use bourgeois aid, alien to Soviet ideology, in the end the government turned to the United States for help. The emergence of the Red Cross and the American Relief Administration in the Soviet state occurred after Maxim Gorky's request for help to starving Russia and the subsequent signing in Riga of an agreement on assistance with the People's Commissar for Foreign Affairs, Maxim Litvinov. Also in March 1919, the Central Collegium of the Russian Red Cross Society proposed applying to the North American Red Cross for help in the fight against hunger. Faced with challenges, the Bolshevik government welcomed the idea, and the American relief agencies then became involved in helping feed the hungry. The Americans created then 120 kitchens in post-revolutionary Petrograd, which made it possible to feed 42,000 hungry children under the age of 14 who first underwent a medical examination and had a special card—an admission ticket issued by a local authority. Initially providing hot meals for the hungry, ARA also began bringing in cotton and wool clothing. Citizens of other countries, including the United States, helped starving Soviet citizens with food parcels. They purchased a $10 food voucher at an American bank or ARA office and went to the nearest ARA warehouse, where they exchanged vouchers for parcels with food of about 53 kg. By the end of 1921, ARA aided 565,000 children—in Samara, Kazan, Saratov, and other provinces.

It should be noted that, as a result of Cheka counter-intelligence activities, it became known that the ARA was not only involved in organizing assistance to children but was also used by American intelligence to establish contacts with the remnants of the white underground and to collect information about the early Soviet regime.[48] The US aid administration was also caught smuggling jewelry and art out of Russia. For example, in December 1922, at the Moscow customs, in the presence of official representatives of the ARA, the diplomatic mail of this organization was opened. In the parcels, the customs found:

> one amethyst, bordered with small pearls, in a gold frame with a platinum chain; one gold ring with three large diamonds sprinkled with a rose; a pendant with eleven large diamonds and a large pear-shaped pearl in the form of a pendant in a platinum setting with a platinum chain with pearls; 88 assay gold round box with enamel and in it one gold ring with two large pearls and small diamonds, one string of medium-sized pearls of 66 pieces, one platinum ring with a pearl (separately from the ring), one gold ring with a large emerald studded with diamonds; a checkbook with forms from No. A001558 to No. A001573 inclusive, obligations of the RSFSR in 1921 in the amount of one hundred million [rubles].[49]

In a review of the political and economic state of the RSFSR as of May–June 1922, the GPU noted that the ARA was "a very significant center for spy organizations," the entire composition of which consisted of former officers and police officials—a significant proportion of them had taken a direct part in the intervention during the period 1917–21.[50] In the opinion of the GPU, the American officers of the ARA, if necessary, could become first-class instructors in counter-revolutionary uprisings. All ARA employees (which was repeatedly revealed by agents and confirmed by documentary data) were "anti-Soviet minded" persons. On March 29, 1923, at a meeting of the Politburo of the Central Committee of the RCP (b), a resolution was adopted to eliminate the activities of the ARA on Soviet territory. It was decided "to begin the liquidation of the ARA after current ARA cargoes in transit or in the ports, have been transported to local bases, i.e., from June." In 1923, the ARA transferred its functions to the "Swiss Committee for Helping Children."[51]

Nevertheless, during its activities the ARA distributed 1,019,169,839 children's and 795,765,480 adults' meals. This food was provided to the population free of charge. Along with food aid, according to the agreement of October 22, 1922, the ARA provided the needy with manufactured goods, including shoes and other items. For example, 1,929,805 meters of fabric and 602,292 pairs of shoes were given to the population. Medical assistance was provided to 1 million patients. In rural areas, the ARA also supplied the population with agricultural implements and varietal seeds.[52]

Children Evacuated

Faced with the growing problem of starving children in the "red capitols" (Moscow and Petrograd), during the second half of 1918 the government began evacuating children (whether homeless or not) from the starving cities' children's homes to the southeast and to the Volga provinces on the assumption that it would be easier to feed them in grain-producing areas. For this purpose, the government began to set up summer camps and homes in those areas. These camps were under the authority of various commissariats, including the Commissariat of Enlightenment, which had primary responsibility. Unfortunately, funding for this commissariat was far from adequate to fulfill the task. Regardless, local agencies of the commissariat vigorously evacuated homeless children and the children of "former children's homes" (those that had been closed in Moscow and Petrograd) to the countryside: to Pskov, Tula, Kaluga, and other provinces. The evacuation was the only practical measure, the government itself undertook to relieve starving children in 1918 or to remove street children from cities. It might have made sense to move children out of starving cities into the countryside, but the evacuation methods were frequently ineffective and dangerous. One must assume that the state was simply trying to rid itself of these starving children. Indeed, originally aimed at relieving homeless and starving children, the practice of evacuating them turned out to produce the opposite result. For example, in 1919 the Commissariat of Enlightenment opened and operated a summer camp for Moscow's children to keep them out of starving Moscow. As later became clear, the camp had been set up in a disease-ridden area.[53] Regardless, the government evacuated about 4,500 Moscow children to this camp and to other destinations in 1919.[54] In 1919, at the All-Russian Congress for the Protection of Childhood, a delegate from Voronezh province announced:

> The experiment of the past year of putting children on trains and sending them to Voronezh or Saratov province has not worked. Practice shows that these children live much worse than those in the Moscow area ... Children were evacuated too hastily ... This was done frequently by just sending them away, without even knowing where.[55]

Even so, the most incomprehensible aspect of the government's actions was that it involved evacuating children to the very rural areas which were experiencing acute famine because of forced grain and foodstuffs procurement. About 20 to 30 percent of children perished or disappeared on their way to these "relief" areas. What happened to the rest is unrecorded. Some children tried to return to Moscow or to go further south. In a telegram to the chairman of VTsIK M. I. Kalinin, dated December 17, 1921, one government official reported that evacuation of starving children led to "mass mortality" among them and called for urgent measures to remedy the situation.[56]

Nevertheless, the government continued its evacuation policy and even extended it to other starving cities. Even though this practice magnified starvation and homelessness among the republic's children, the government viewed these evacuations as the only possible way to ease the catastrophe. Later, however, in the early 1920s, children were moved out of the countryside back into cities. Evacuations in either direction were placed mainly in the hands of the underfunded Commissariat of Enlightenment. Unfortunately, children's institutions where the evacuees could be placed were already in critical condition. The commissariat had insufficient funds for childcare and lacked experienced workers to perform the work properly. Not surprisingly, the uncoordinated nature of the activities of responsible organizations led to terrible results. In Chelyabinsk province, for example, there were 270,000 officially registered starving children who needed relief in 1921. Within five months only 1,100 children were evacuated. The local agency of the Commissariat for the Enlightenment was supposed to supply the evacuated children with clothes and foodstuffs during transportation. However, the local branch of the Commissariat of Food Supply refused to provide the expedition with food. As a result, about 20 percent of the children died on the way.[57] Of course, most children throughout the country were not evacuated. Only 800,000 children were placed in children's homes.[58] These figures and facts were published in governmental documents and official newspapers. The government knew that its evacuation policy had failed; nevertheless, for the time being, this chaotic and deadly policy *remained* the main government program for solving children's starvation. In fact, during these years children themselves were moving to Moscow or southern areas on their own: they believed those environments were safe and that they could find better opportunities to survive. In response, the government began blocking population movement, including street children, to the south and placed a "blockade" of armed detachments in the path of people on the move. These detachments often faced armed resistance from the population, including children. According to one contemporary, *besprizornye,* organized in groups, used any possible means, even weapons, "to break this blockade."[59]

Besides evacuation, the government used various types of reception centers and temporary orphanages for evacuated children. The circular path of most street children, followed by the armed detachments, was usually as follows: street—reception center—evacuation—orphanage—street. The police and the Cheka busily tried removing street children from the streets, train stations, and markets. Before being placed in childcare facilities, children were sent to reception and distribution centers to receive assistance and be prepared for a meeting with an organized team. Then the children were transferred to stationary establishments: directly to orphanages, labor communes, colonies, or to institutions for special instructions for "morally handicapped children." While orphanages accepted children from twelve to fourteen years old, labor communes accepted older children. From the age of 14, inmates of orphanages were admitted to factory schools, from the age of 16—to a permanent job or to individual and brigade apprenticeships. Children often run away from orphanages and labor communes since the latter were usually inappropriate for living or heavily exploitative.

Evacuations and the placement of children in shelters were, by definition, related to starving homeless children, although in practice these policies had little effect on these problems, except to worsen them. Moreover, evacuations and re-evacuations often led to dangerous consequences for the evacuees. Later, on June 20, 1924, when, it might be added, it was far too late, the Council of People's Commissars of the RSFSR issued a special decree categorically prohibiting the mass evacuation of children and their transfer from one area to another.[60] Nevertheless, the initial measures to improve conditions for children in 1918–21, as they were performed, were chaotic, disorganized, and even dangerous to the health and life of children. Neither the declaration that all children were to be under state guardianship, nor the evacuations, nor the distribution of free food could even begin to solve children's starvation and *besprizornost'*. The government either did not recognize the full seriousness of the problem or, preoccupied with other issues [civil conflict, peasant uprisings], did not care about children's starvation and homelessness.

Figure 8 Homeless children play cards on the street. Moscow. 1918. Source: Open public domain https://fishki.net/1577961-20-vek-v-fotografii-luchshie-snimki-iz-arhiva-agentstva-tass/gallery-2149880-1918-god-deti-besprizorniki-igrajut-v-karty-na-ulice-photo.html?

Early Bolshevik Childcare Institutions

As noted in previous chapters, all Soviet children were under the care of the state, as were all children's institutions. Despite an acute increase in the number of children in need, many viable childcare facilities were closed, and newly created ones were often completely unsuitable for children. Moreover, as the republic faced severe food shortages and hunger, inhabitants of existing orphanages and shelters were starving. For example, the bread ration in Moscow's best-funded children's homes declined to ½–¼ *funt* (about 1- ½ pound) a day.[61] Most institutions were overcrowded and suffered not only from food shortages but also from the lack of basic everyday necessities, such as soap, mattresses, clothes, and shoes, not to mention medicines. Several children shared one bed. Often, they slept on the floor.[62] In children's homes, wrote an observer:

> The condition of these children does not much differ from those without homes. Children's homes, experiencing shortages of fuel, food, and clothes, are a source of high mortality. What could be the condition of street children? ... The children's population is dying out catastrophically and the measures the central government employs are completely unable to stop it.[63]

Another report described the following:

> In some orphanages, wooden blocks were installed to wrap rags around a child's feet, but this is a happy exception. In other regions, as in Astrakhan, Kursk, Saratov (materials of the children's protection department of the NKP), there is literally nothing to wrap up, there are no rags, and the children run barefoot, their hands and feet are freezing. From chills, the child's body is covered with ulcers. To this it must be added that everywhere children get scabies, and on the child's body there is a continuous ulcer, continuous scabs, completely covered with lice. The child rots and decomposes alive. It is terribly cold in orphanages; children's rooms are not heated anywhere in Simbirsk, Saratov, Tsaritsyn, and other provinces. There are whole snowdrifts in the rooms' corners.[64]

In Akhtubinsk, Astrakhan region, the department asked to be allowed to discharge children from orphanages and send them "around the world for alms," as "there is nothing to eat." In Atkarsk, Saratov region, responsible officials said that

> it is better to take the children out of the orphanages out of town and shoot them there than to torture them as is happening. It is a shame to even talk about any educational work amid such horror and nightmares. Children absolutely do nothing, the elders have fun, play cards, smoke, drink "Nikolaevskaya" [vodka], girls 16–17 years old are up for sale.[65]

Children's homes provided no education for their inhabitants and had no control over them. For example, the inhabitants of the well-known Podkopievskii children's home in Moscow played cards, drank alcohol, used drugs, and engaged in "perversive sexual activities." Conditions in this home became so critical that in December 1921 it was finally closed.⁶⁶

Unfortunately, what is said about children's homes during this time equally applies to the late 1920s and 1930s, as will be described in the following chapters. Certainly, this suggests not only incompetence and disorganization on the part of the responsible officials, but their failure to act responsibly and professionally. Again, the psychotic disorder of those in charge of policy may explain this failure but cannot justify it. Measures to cope with children's homelessness and starvation were not only ineffective but often aggravated the problems. In many instances, homeless children used children's homes as shelters for the night. Most children preferred to try to survive on their own. To survive, starving street children turned to crime, a development that deeply alarmed the state. But, in the end, who was responsible?

Council for Children's Defense and Appeals for Public Support

On February 2–8, 1919, the First All-Russian Congress of Workers in Defense of Children was held in Moscow, convened at the initiative of the People's Commissariat for Social Protection. Opening the work of the congress with an address that welcomed the audience, People's Commissar for Social Protection A. Vinokurov outlined his goal—"to exchange views, share experiences and develop a better plan for the socialist protection of children." In fulfilling the intended goal, the delegates (about 300 in number) discussed the priority tasks in all areas, including protection of children. Special attention was paid to urgent measures to save children, as well as to improving the functioning of orphanages and using orphanages as the basis for educating the younger generation in the spirit of communism.⁶⁷

In pursuance of the congress's resolutions, on the initiative of the Chairman of the Council of People's Commissars V. I. Lenin, the government established the State Council for the Defense of Children, "taking into account the difficult living conditions in the country and the obligation of the revolutionary government to protect the younger generation during a dangerous transition period." The Children's Defense Council was instructed "to deploy a special inspection for the safety of children, to protect them from exploitation, abuse, homelessness and to include them in the circle of school, preschool and general social care." Other tasks of the council were control, coordination, and locating funds in order to support children's institutions and to evacuate children to grain-growing areas—which starving children had already been doing on their own,—as well as creating children's summer camps, and agree on plans for organizing public catering as well as providing various materials and food supplies for children. The council had several ambulances designed to transport street children being picked up at train stations. The council included representatives of the people's commissariats for enlightenment, health, labor, state charity, and food. Representative from the Enlightenment Commissariat A. V. Lunacharsky became the council's head.⁶⁸ The council was given the right to veto a document if it violated the rights of children. The initiative to create this council came from Lunacharsky, who was among the few state officials displaying a real interest in protecting children from abuses and starvation. However, this attempt was not successful; as Lunacharsky later noted, "nothing came of it,"[69] more likely because Lunacharsky possessed no executive power in the government, which delegated most administrative powers and several key commissariats to Cheka head Dzerzhinsky. Furthermore, as mentioned earlier, Sovnarkom and its head Lenin wanted Lunacharsky to concentrate on propaganda activities in urban centers. Of note is that street children never became a subject of discussion between Lunacharsky and Lenin during 1918–19. Despite its weak efficiency, the activities of the Council were nevertheless more humane and useful than the use of barrage detachments against street children migrating by rail, as was the case in the North Caucasus and in several other provinces in 1920.

Worth mentioning is that the state council for children's defense relied not on the state but on public and private donations of food and received food supplies from various agricultural producing regions. Despite the acute risk of their own starvation, peasants seemed to be very enthusiastic about supporting starving children in cities. Peasant local bodies gathered everywhere to make decisions to support children. At the beginning of 1919, the Council for the Protection of Starving Children of the Red Capitals was formed in Saratov on the initiative of local party organizations. One of the first activities of the council was the collection of food gifts for Moscow and Petrograd children.[70] In most instances, food donations were sent to Moscow. It seems that the council concentrated its activities on Moscow. Available data reveals that in the twelve days after its formation, the Council received 105 poods (3,792 Lb, 1,720 kg) of grain, 60 poods (2,167 Lb, 982 kg) of flour and and 14 poods (506 Lb, 229 kg) of crackers from the Voskresensk region of the Novouzensk district of Saratov province; and 4180 poods (150,951 Lb, 68,470 kg) of selected wheat flour from Tokmak of Tauride province. Peasants from the Bolshaya Aleksandrovka village of the Kherson district, Kherson province decided to send 1,200 poods (43,335 Lb, 19,657 kg) of foodstuffs to the Council's fund and offered to receive 300 starving children from Moscow "whom they would undertake to feed free of charge." Red Army soldiers of units stationed in Samara informed Krupskaya that they had sent flour and crackers to Moscow to distribute to orphans. Many people and organizations throughout the country responded to the needs of Moscow children and shared perhaps their last piece of bread. Children of the Novouzensky district of Samara province wrote:

> Greetings to the children of Moscow. We, the children of workers and employees of the Valuisko-Kostychevskaya Experimental Station, are sending you a present—8 parcels of crackers. [We] could send them monthly, but we don't have any packing boards. In the spring we will have vegetable gardens, come to visit us.[71]

The parcels with food came from various places across the Soviet Republic—from the students of the unified labor school in the village of Pokrovka (near Stary Oskol, province), from the Komsomol members of the village of Novoukrainka of Mykolaiv province, etc. During the year since its organization, the Council for the Protection of Children received more than 35,000 poods (1,263,948 Lb, 573,317 kg) of food donations.[72]

Nevertheless, although the Bolshevik government had eliminated the old professional childcare foundations and institutions and replaced them with inefficient ones, taking the matter in its hands so to speak, in the end, it relied on public and private institutions and individuals for support of starving children. Obviously, the government realized that it could not handle the problem alone and that a call for public help was necessary. This perhaps was the first step back on the part of the state from its earlier proclaimed ideals and a precursor of the 1922 New Economic Policy.

The Children's Week Campaign: "Children Are Flowers of Life"

Perhaps encouraged by generous food donations from rural areas, the government organized a "children's week" campaign to collect some food supplies for starving children of Moscow and Petrograd. The story of this campaign deserves some detail because its expectations met somewhat unexpected results. The initiative for the campaign came earlier, but the government was very slow to respond. In January 1919, the interdepartmental commission of the People's Commissariat of Education turned to Lenin with a proposal to hold an "Aid Week" for hungry children, during which industrial goods would be exchanged for food in the countryside.[73] It took over a year for the government to announce and organize "a week of aid" for urban children by means of a special resolution. Thus, the first all-Russian "children's week" was organized in November 1920 by a resolution of the All-Russian Central Soviet Executive Committee and the People's Commissariat of Enlightenment. This campaign pursued two goals—(1) propaganda and agitation aimed at helping children in need in the institutions of the People's Commissariat of Education and the People's Commissariat of Health and (2) collecting bread and foodstuffs for starving children in Moscow and Petrograd.

Rules and instructions for organizing a "children's week" in localities were sent out in advance from the center to all cities and arrived everywhere at the same time. A trip to the southern and southeastern cities was organized to conduct on the spot agitation campaigns and to collect bread. Three instructors were sent from the People's Commissariat of Education, nine students of the All-Russian courses for workers in orphanages, from the People's Commissariat of Health (a doctor-correspondent), nine women agitators from the *Zhenotdel* MK VKP (b) and the Central Commissariat, the Committee of the All-Union Communist Party (Bolsheviks), a locksmith who showed film *Children—Flowers of Life*, and a secretary-typist. A total of twenty-five people took part in the trip. They were provided with a separate campaign vehicle.

The local population reacted with understanding of the children's week's purpose, and, despite their own hardship, gave everything they could. In cities, these were mainly manufactured goods, in villages—food (someone even gave a large carpet and a crystal vase). Collectors had subscription lists and a receipt was issued for each item. The collected items were carefully recorded and distributed. A total of 6,249,319 rubles were donated in cash. Besides all other tasks, they did not forget to hold children's parties. Local drama companies, schoolchildren, and government officials took part in the performances and concerts.

As mentioned, this campaign led to somewhat unexpected results. As part of the first "week of the child," children's institutions in Vladimir, Tula, Kharkov, Rostov-on-Don, Tsaritsyn, and Krasnodar were examined. The situation and the general conditions of children's institutions in the observed cities were deplorable: many institutions faced hunger, cold, complete absence of bedding, linens, clothing, and footwear; there were also reports of epidemic diseases. In orphanages and schools, there was a complete lack of teaching aids; the teaching staff in many institutions was casual and did not have special education in the field of pedagogy. These were workers "against their will for a piece of bread," as many of them openly stated.[74]

Upon the return of the propaganda train, the People's Commissariat of Education and individual participants in the trip kept in touch with the localities for an extended period, corresponding with them and helping by sending educational literature and various materials from Moscow. Based on the collected materials, a general protocol was drawn up, which was personally handed over to Cheka head F. E. Dzerzhinsky. The report reportedly made a strong impression on him. Among these who traveled with the Children's Week group was a Commissariat of Enlightenment official, a deputy of the Moscow City Council and Chairman of the Council for the Defense of Children, Asia Kalinina. She inspected the Volga region, where the food procurement campaign had been most actively carried out. Kalinina reported that:

> the number of unattended children is growing with dreadful speed ... *Besprizornost'* has approached an appalling extent in recent times. In an unorganized and chaotic mass, the children moved to the south where it was warm and well supplied .... This flow of children is growing day by day and took on a threatening character ... In search of a way out of the current situation, the head of the evacuation point of the Caucasian Front issued a completely unacceptable order: to put up a barrier and not let any such children into the Caucasus. Children on the Don and in other places met the same obstacles. The child here falls into a trap, and wherever he turns, weapons are everywhere. He runs wild, becomes like a young animal looking for ways to break through this network in any way, even with the help of weapons.[75]

In a letter dated March 4, 1920, an observer wrote that children's homelessness had not been eliminated but "the opposite, it deepens and takes ever new victims and homeless children are not only orphans but also those who have parents."[76] Obviously, the "new victims" did not come from the First World War, but from *realpolitik* of the government, namely from the violent food appropriations, the obligatory revolutionary tax, and war communism. As shown in the previous chapter, numerous hungry children were moving south. In order to survive, children committed all kinds of crimes and were themselves often victims of adult criminals.

"Defective Children": The Moral Inferiority Turn

In any society there is a category of children with developmental disabilities and a field of science dealing with these children—children's "defectology," or study of children's disabilities. In Russia, pediatric defectology began to develop widely in the middle of the nineteenth century. A small number of institutions appeared that provided this category of children with treatment, education, upbringing, and rehabilitation. Modern researchers note that social policy and practice in pre-revolutionary Russia had very similar features with European pedagogical, organizational, and managerial views.[77] Until 1917, however, the term "disabled child" referred mainly to children with physical or mental disabilities. After 1917 it took a new turn. Assuming that "disability" is constructed to a great extent by social expectations and institutions, rather than biological differences, the new government associated social deviance with disability and introduced a new term "moral inferiority." Homelessness as a social phenomenon was closely associated with juvenile delinquency, which rose sharply after 1917. Juvenile delinquency and homelessness were increasingly defined as social disobedience and associated with moral inferiority.

It seems that there was no single criterion for identifying "handicapped" and "morally handicapped" children. In practice, these terms were often used as interchangeably. During this period, retarded children with delayed developmental abilities were often placed in the same group with socially dangerous ones, the so-called "spoiled" or "criminal" children. In particular, in accordance with the classification developed by the Department for Handicapped Minors of the Moscow Department of Social Security, "defective" children were divided into three groups: mentally retarded, morally defective, and an intermediate group of children "combining mental retardation with moral depravity." Morally defective children, in turn, were subdivided, according to the "degree of defectiveness," into three main stages. The first stage included children "spoiled" ("thievish, deceitful, cruel and fighters"), but "accessible to correction"; the second stage—"socially dangerous" (previously convicted of committing a crime), but still "correctable" minors; and a third—"criminal," "completely uncorrectable." According to historian T. M. Smirnova, children who committed criminal offenses automatically fell into the category of minors of the second and third stages of "moral defectiveness."[78] Given starving children's tendency to "commit" crimes to survive, this policy would have dire consequences.

The very word "besprizorniki" spurred alarm for people on the streets and was a huge headache for the police. There had been a catastrophic increase in the number of criminal cases against street children-adolescents: a total of 12,500 and 32,635 criminal cases were already initiated in 1920 and 1925, respectively. Homeless children became enemies and were viewed as a dangerous social evil. Those who asked for bread were told "leave me alone," and "get out!" Child thieves, if caught, were brutally beaten up or tortured even to death. Children answered with dignity, even with their anger, hunger, orphanhood: "Try, to live my life!" Many were gloomy and spiteful, thieves and prostitutes, semi-wild animals, and others were also "children, gentle children who never knew fairy tales about the snow queen or the sparkling Christmas star, but real dreamers and eccentrics … but where? What pity for these visions of a merciless night?" The very circumstances of their threatened deaths by starvation forced the children to resort to crimes. Theft was the predominant crime of the homeless; more than 90 percent of homeless children were guilty of this crime. Also, prostitution, begging, peddling, and human trafficking, all defined as crimes by the state, were widespread among street children. As mentioned, all street children who committed crimes came under the authority of the Commissariat of State Charity's commissions for juvenile affairs.

The focus of these commissions was not the offense itself, but the personality of defendants, their upbringing, and education. At this point, the commissions followed ideas of some late imperial Russian lawyers, for example, M. N. Gernet, who continued his activities after the Revolution.[79] The materials of the commissions included statements of victims, protocols of detention, and interrogation of minors, as well as decisions of investigators from criminal investigation agencies. In the course of investigations, members of commissions kept records in the form of questionnaires and statistic sheets, in which they described juvenile offenders and their offenses. These documents varied in form. If in the questionnaire the answer was entered in free columns, then in the statistical sheet it was necessary to choose the appropriate option for the ready answer or briefly enter the missing information. The purpose of these sheets was, first of all, to establish the circumstances that were important for the study of the personality of the minor and his living conditions. The instructions for filling out the sheets stated that they served as material for acquaintance with the activities of the Commission on Juvenile Affairs. The questions recorded in the questionnaires can be combined into semantic groups: the path of a juvenile offender to deviant (asocial) behavior; the influence of family and school on his/her behavior; gender and age characteristics, physical condition, and appearance of the child; range of interests; appropriate ways and means of correcting juvenile offenders. In general, this type of document allows us to define in general terms the social image of the juvenile offenders. Most were street children.

As mentioned, government officials had begun linking child homelessness with crime and "moral inferiority" and called for drastic measures to tackle the problem. In the summer (June–July) of 1920, the First All-Russian Congress of "Morally Inferior Children" was held in Moscow. The congress discussed the "moral inferiority" and criminality of children and defined the categories of "child inferiority." Obviously, most of the Congress did not view street children as hungry victims of government policy, as they really were, but instead displayed more concern about finding explanations for the phenomena in psychology and behavioral science. More than half of the members of this congress did not have any educational, pedagogical, or medical experience, which was the direct result of a radical collapse and reorganization of the entire school system, exacerbated by other government policies toward the population. Although some schools were still operational and new schools were opened, many former teachers were fired and replaced by completely untrained and inexperienced staff. Senior professionals—who some contemporaries might call the "old school"—simply did not meet the new Bolshevik criteria for being a suitable teacher.

The materials of the congress testify to the ongoing conflict between the commissariats of justice and education about children's deviant and criminal activities. Educators and lawyers advocated educational approaches and rehabilitation, while the People's Commissariat of Justice, staffed mostly with revolutionaries, pursued a tough policy against children who committed crimes. An employee of the Moscow Criminal Investigation Department complained that crimes committed by street children flourished for a "known" reason, but

> admitting its existence, we must say that it is extremely difficult to fight these criminals. The situation is as follows: child criminals cannot be kept in prisons; they

must be kept in special homes for the so-called morally inferior children. There are no such houses, and where there are, they are also worthless: no educators, no guards. Children run away, become impudent, feel their complete impunity and act with might and main, sometimes more sharply than adults. Now it is even accepted as a rule that one adult "leader" goes into "business" as an experienced person, and the rest—as small bipods. And so, we catch them, send minors to the commission, and a day later they are free again and again do their dark deeds. We can safely say that 40–50% of all thefts are committed by them.

The officials of the Commissariat of Justice blamed growing children's criminality on the inadequate activities of the Commissions for the Affairs of Minors and saw the solution in the revival of regular courts for juveniles.[80] Already in December 1919, the Justice Commissariat introduced an act of reinstalling criminal courts and imprisonment for adolescents between the ages 14 and 18, in cases where "medical and pedagogical methods" were ineffective.[81] The draft of the new Criminal Code immediately found its opponents within the Commissariat of Education. Pedagogues did not share the position of the Commissariat of Justice on the problem of children's growing criminality. A Commissariat of Education official wrote that:

> One should not blame the growth of children's criminality on ... the commissions for the affairs of minors ... one should remind oneself of the period we are enduring and the moral stresses through which Russia has gone, which primarily affect the impressionable and unstable minds of the children.[82]

The author warned about the harsh consequences of the proposed draft toward children and emphasized the hope that Sovnarkom would not share the point of view of the Commissariat of Justice. However, the Commissariat of Education was unsuccessful in influencing Sovnarkom's decision. On March 4, 1920, Sovnarkom issued a decree that affirmed that court trials and imprisonment for minors remained restricted. Criminal cases involving minors at the age of 14–18 were still to be heard by the Commissions on Minors.

Since the government began to define children's criminality and besprizornost' as "the moral inferiority" of children, some government officials considered moral inferiority to be the main source of homeless children crime. Nevertheless, homelessness by its nature promoted children's theft, begging, peddling, and prostitution. These actions, which by state definition were crimes, were the only way for most of starving homeless children to survive. According to the new decree, the state began to consider child homelessness as a moral inferiority. The commissions had to recognize homeless children as morally inferior and send them to certain institutions of the People's Commissariat of Health for special treatment. But if the commission found it impossible to apply medical and pedagogical treatment in a specific case, the person would be transferred to a court of general jurisdiction.

In April 1920, the State Council for the Defense of Children created the Children's Guard Militia (later called the Children's Inspectorate), a special agency for children that hoped to replace the regular police agency for children. To provide the newly established agencies with experienced staff, the council organized training for social workers. These social workers were supposed to monitor children at train stations, squares, markets, and other places where children gathered so that they would not be taken to the regular police authorities.[83] If the departments of the Children's Defense Council were more engaged in office work and holding meetings, then social workers carried out inspections of street children, studied the conditions of children in orphanages, and were on duty in places where the children's contingent gathered. Obviously, the Commissariat of Education, which had failed to influence the Sovnarkom in March, was trying to mitigate the negative consequences of the new decree and the new approach. However, according to some scarce archival sources, there were juvenile detainees in prisons and detention centers for adults, a matter what will be discussed in the following chapters.[84]

Conclusions

It was during this time that the Bolshevik government began to realize the urgency and magnitude of the problem presented by street children. What turned the street children phenomenon into such a serious problem that the government began to view it as a security threat and demand emergent measures in late 1920? What alarmed the government the most was the extremely large number of homeless children roaming the streets, markets, and train stations, and, most importantly, their involvement in activities the government considered criminal and counter-revolutionary. The head of the department of legal defense of the People's Commissariat of Education N. V. Kommodov, in his report for June 1921, wrote that it is surprising that the government "had not previously noticed the growth of homelessness and crime among children. It is surprising that people could not understand that children's homelessness would take on the character of a national catastrophe."[85] Another factor was that criminality among street children also changed and began to take an organized shape. Starving children joined into gangs and committed armed robbery of supply wagons and food storehouses; often, they cooperated with adult criminals.[86] This association of street children with a serious public threat alarmed the government, resulting in the involvement of punitive government agencies and eventually helped shape government approaches to the phenomenon. As will be shown in the following chapters, the state gradually criminalized homelessness and begging, introduced severe penalties for vagrancy, and harshened policies against juvenile crimes in general.

4

New Economic Policy: Cheka Comes to Play

I don't know why I feel love for children like for no one else. When I meet with them, my bad mood immediately disappears. I could never love a woman as much as I love them, and I think that I could never love my own children more than I love them. It often seems to me that even a mother does not love her children as passionately as I do.

F. E. Dzerzhinsky, 1902[1]

The most expedient measure to prevent the growth of crime is to take care of street children – this is where all compassion and will should be directed, and the broad public opinion of the masses should be attracted to the fight against crimes and criminals.

F. E. Dzerzhinsky, 1924[2]

By the end of 1920, the Soviet authorities realized that children's homelessness, starvation, and criminality had magnified exponentially. In addition, the early Soviet state faced a serious financial crisis. One can blame revolutionary circumstances, but the activities of the new government and its responsibility for children's starvation and homelessness cannot be discounted. Immediately after the Revolution, the government closed many children's institutions and, even worse, confiscated their buildings for state and party needs. In return, many children's institutions received unsuitable premises or were relocated to uninhabitable rural areas and, in most cases, were either underfunded or received no funds at all.[3] In fact, affected by the financial and institutional crisis, most institutions and children had to survive on their own, without any state support. The state had liquidated all charitable foundations, without creating any alternative for pressing humanitarian issues. Paradoxically, the problems of children's starvation and homelessness—essentially humanitarian problems—began to be viewed by the government primarily as political ones, and the fight against them was deemed a fight against counter-revolution and against threats to state security and public order.

Not surprisingly, almost all measures to reduce children's starvation and homelessness proved ineffective. As shown in the previous chapter, for example, the evacuation of children to the countryside in 1918–19 backfired. The state of children's institutions was catastrophic and unbearable. Institutions for the care of homeless and

Figure 9 Escorted street children in Moscow, 1924, by K. Kuznetsov. Source: Open public domain.

other children often displayed criminal negligence, indifference and did not fulfill the functions assigned to them. At the same time, the Soviet state quickly changed its attitude toward street children. As their numbers grew, in the overwhelming majority of cases the attitude of the state toward them changed dramatically: from viewing them as hungry homeless children with low morale and mental imbalances authorities now saw them as socially dangerous vagrants. The Bolshevik administration believed that homelessness caused mental disorders, which in fact was true in most instances. Regardless, some authorities later began to believe that it was mental disorders that made children homeless vagrants. The latter perception shaped the attitude of key government agencies and institutions about these children for decades to come.

It is also necessary to consider the fact that this period was highly unstable for Bolshevik power. A wave of anti-Bolshevik protests swept across the country. Within the government itself there were rivalries and intrigues. By the end of 1920, the Bolshevik Party was able to finally seize full power in all or most Soviets and bend them to their will. This caused serious political and social protest. To continue to stay in power, the party relied on *realpolitik*—that is, on punitive institutions and measures, namely the Cheka and repression. Often, as the Bolsheviks seized power in the Soviets, the Cheka, in turn, took over local Bolshevik party organizations. Thus, the Cheka assumed real political, economic, and executive power and controlled almost all state authorities.

The chairman of the Cheka, Polish revolutionary Felix Dzerzhinsky, "Iron Felix—the knight of the revolution," headed several other key people's commissariats and departments all at the same time.[4] Dzerzhinsky, in his letters, always showed a strong love for children, as evidenced above by his letter to his sister. Whether this love for children had a disinterested character, historians will perhaps never know.

Nevertheless, the Bolshevik state appointed Dzerzhinsky as head of the Children's commission. Thus, the Cheka and its successors state security agencies, the GPU (Main Political Directorate) of the NKVD and later the OGPU (Unified State Political Directorate), became fully involved in the problem of street children and were fully responsible for children, orphanages, as well as for commercial companies that used child labor.

The laws concerning street children and childcare facilities underwent pronounced changes during the New Economic Policy, which restored some market relations. According to the new perspectives, assistance to children in need became commercialized; children had to engage in productive work and earn money to support themselves and their institutions. This was exactly in line with the Bolshevik ideas about raising children through productive labor that Krupskaya emphasized in her numerous speeches and works. Most orphanages and children's homes turned into labor colonies and productive units. In all children's labor camps, the state created production enterprises which used their inmates' labor. The Cheka's Children's Commission created and headed the joint-stock company "Larek" and the postal service "Univerpocht," both of which widely used the labor of children and adolescents. (Neither Larek nor Univerpocht has been mentioned in existing historical analyses.) One way or another, it was the Cheka and later the GPU and OGPU, which came to be in charge of eliminating the street children problem. This chapter will review the government's efforts to combat child hunger, homelessness, and crime during the New Economic Policy period. It will consider changing perspectives on street children and juvenile delinquency, as well as the dynamics of policy toward these children.

Unattended Street Children: Victims or Criminals?

As noted in the previous chapter, the Soviet state became seriously concerned about the increase of children's criminality and the uncontrolled chaotic movement of large numbers of unattended children across the country by 1920. The sharp rise in children's crimes resulted from starvation and the attending homelessness went hand in hand with these ailments. Apparently, most unattended children were hungry and sick obviously, in desperate need of food, shelter, and care. But since the state, which took formal responsibility for all children, could not fulfill its obligations, children had to rely on themselves to survive—they had to look out for their own livelihood and food. It is obvious that all these circumstances pushed street children into various crimes, including petty trade, prostitution, and even making counterfeit money. In a few cases, street children formed criminal associations—gangs—united by strict discipline and the authority of a leader. As historian Svetlana Gladysh observed, "the word *besprizorniki* alone aroused anxious abject fear in the man on the street and was a headache for the police."[5] According to Commissariat of Enlightenment official Asia Kalinina, "dozens of hungry and frozen children beg for alms, learn perversions, rob, terrorize and cause panic in cities and villages."[6] In the end, however, street children were defenseless and vulnerable, and were themselves victims of pedophiles and traffickers. They were easy prey for adult criminals who actively involved teenagers in their adult criminal underworld. Children often assisted adult criminals.

In the urban environment of Russia, different categories of homeless people were known to be engaged in one or another activity to survive. Almost all street children were known to be "piecers" or beggars. Compared with pre-revolutionary data, begging in Petrograd in 1920–2 increased five to seven times. "Piecers" begged for money or food. "Children, blue-skinned from the cold, starving, came running from the street in rags," Baroness M. D. Wrangell described her post-revolutionary days in St. Petersburg.

> They licked our table and, looking with dead, white eyes greedily into your mouth, whispered: "Aunty, aunty, leave the spoon," and as soon as you moved the plate away, they, like jackals, pounced on it, tearing it out of each other's mouths, licked it clean.[7]

Usually, from the age of 14–16, street children moved into the category of thieves and formed gangs. Every homeless thief had one or another thieving "profession." Child thieves who specialized in stealing from apartments or shops were known as "skokari." They earned from 2 to 10 rubles a day and immediately spent them on sex, wine, gambling, and expensive things. Thieves were sometimes simply called "screens" and "suitcases." "Shirmachi" "cleaned" the pockets of citizens, what brought them from 1 to 3 rubles a day. The income of the "suitcase" was completely dependent on the contents of stolen suitcases.

According to M. Gernet, among the criminals detained for theft and held in the pre-trial detention center of the government's Cheka division, adolescents from sixteen to twenty years old were the majority: it should be borne in mind that young people under 14 were not usually held there.[8] By 1920, criminal activities among children more than doubled compared with 1913, and since 1916—by 38.5 percent.[9] The number of criminal cases against street children and adolescents increased extraordinarily: in 1920, there were 12,500 and in 1925—32,635 registered crimes committed by children.[10] Most crimes committed by children were recorded in 1921–2, which reflected the results of the state policy of appropriating surpluses and imposing various mandatory taxes on peasants. However, these figures are likely an underestimate because they only reflect cases that had gone through juvenile commissions. So, in 1921, there were about 55,000 registered children who committed crimes, and in 1922 this number dropped to 53,374. In 1924, the weekly periodical *Yunyy proletariy* (Young Proletarian) cited the following figures: if in 1913–16 in Saint Petersburg/Petrograd, about 9,000 cases were initiated against persons under the age of 18, then in 1919–22 this figure more than doubled and approached 23,000.[11]

Most of the convicts were homeless. According to local education authorities, 81 out of 100 street children committed crime over the years. Street children were mainly involved in property offenses. The overwhelming majority of crimes were theft (up to 91 percent), but children also committed more serious crimes, including robbery, rape, and murder. The penalties were various and depended on the severity of the offense, the record of previous offenses, and the presence or absence of a family. For example, some children were given bail to parents or relatives, others were placed in foster care, and some were given jobs or factory schools. But the orphanage was still considered the main method of re-education.

In the eyes of the state authorities, as noted in Chapter 3, these children were mentally handicapped and therefore needed special corrective institutions. According to a document of the Samara interdepartmental meeting of the Provincial Executive Committee of February 22, 1920,

> Many children commit theft, and these children are mostly from houses for the defective [institutions for children with physically or mentally handicapped children], but they are looked at through the fingers ... No supervision from the Department of Public Education is taken, nor are any measures taken to isolate or correct them. Many of the defective children have passed up to 50 times through criminal investigations.[12]

The government created special corrective labor homes for delinquent children. They were called institutions for "mentally handicapped" children. In his report about the state of crime dated May 20, 1921, the head of the Moscow Criminal Investigation Department, Iosif Yakovlevich Freiman, stated:

> As regards the flourishing of children's crimes, the causes are well known, but, admitting its presence, we have to say that the fight against these criminals is extremely difficult. The situation is as follows: child-criminals cannot be kept in prisons—they are isolated in special homes for so-called mentally handicapped children. There are no [special] homes, and where there are, they are also worthless: there are no educators and no guards. Children run around, become impudent, feel their complete impunity and rule with might and main, sometimes better than adults. Nowadays it is even accepted as a rule that one adult "leader" goes to the "business" as an experienced person, and the rest are small fry. And thus, we catch them, send minors to the commission, and a day later they are free again, and again do their dark deeds. We can safely say that 40–50% of thefts are committed by them, here are the numbers ... [The archival document contains no numbers.][13]

These unresolved problems of children's institutions created new problems. For instance, he authorities of the provincial reception centers and homes for handicapped children began to refuse to detain or accept juvenile offenders.[14] State authorities were facing a dilemma about measures to cope with underage offenders. Earlier, as mentioned, the government abolished criminal courts and imprisonment for minors of both sexes under 17 and introduced juvenile commissions. This normative act had a retroactive effect: court cases about children, even completed ones, were subject to review. They, like new cases, were transferred to extrajudicial bodies—commissions on juvenile affairs, which were under the jurisdiction of the People's Commissariat of State Charity and included representatives of three commissariats: state charity, education, and justice. The guiding principles of 1919, however, reduced this age to 14.[15] The decree of March 4, 1920, granted the commissions on juvenile affairs the right to take cases of minors over fourteen years old to court, "if the commission establishes the impossibility of applying medical and educational influence on a minor"—in other words: for minors over fourteen years old. The instruction of June 12, 1920, provided for the obligatory presence of a judge in these commissions, but gradually the judicial element outweighed the pedagogical and medical elements in them.[16] On May 2, 1925, the state formed a central commission for minors, which combined the activities of all commissions; and, although it was a part of the Commissariat of Education, the representatives of the Commissariats of Internal Affairs and Justice also appeared on equal terms.[17]

In 1922, a repressive punitive criminal policy was introduced against minors between the ages of 16 and 17.[18] The Criminal Code of the RSFSR of 1922 established criminal liability on the general basis of sanity from the age of 16, and in certain cases, at the discretion of the commission on juvenile affairs, from the age of 14.[19] Article 56 of the code allowed the extension of stay in correctional institutions of minors who did not display sufficient improvement by the end of the sentence imposed by the court.[20] The 1922 code also introduced mandatory mitigation of punishment for minors from fourteen to sixteen years old by half and from sixteen to eighteen years old—by a third. In July 1922, the government added an amendment to Article 22, according to which the death penalty was not applied to persons under the age of 18 (at the time of the offense). It is difficult to judge, however, whether the death penalty was actually applied to underage children due to the lack of data during of these lawless times.

The guiding principles of the Criminal Code in the edition of 1924 gave the Union's republics the right to establish the age of criminal responsibility for minors. The Criminal Code of the RSFSR of 1926 initially excluded criminal liability from the age of 14, but later this provision was canceled. The decree of the All-Russian Central Executive Committee and the Council of People's Commissars of the RSFSR of October 30, 1929, changed the wording of Article 12 of the Criminal Code, establishing the age of criminal responsibility from sixteen on. The amended Criminal Code of the RSFSR of October 16, 1924 stated that measures against a juvenile offender should be without torture and of a "medical and pedagogical character," which was proclaimed as one of the most important features of Soviet correctional labor.[21] The purpose of placing minors in institutions created for the implementation of such measures was to teach children qualified types of work, for which special workshops were created on the grounds, expanding the horizons of prisoners through general and vocational education, as well as physical development, for the purpose of bringing up a full-fledged citizen of the new country.

Later, in 1926, Article 12 of the Criminal Code of the RSFSR allowed criminal trials of children starting at the age of 14 for "grave crimes" such as theft, violence, murder, etc. However, despite this tightening, the prohibition on the death penalty for minors under 18, and the mandatory mitigation of punishment for children and adolescents aged 14 to 16 years—by half, and at the age from 16 to 18 years—by a third remained.[22] All these provisions would survive until 1935, when the Stalinist government introduced amendments that allowed the possibility of applying capital punishment (execution) to children from 12 years of age, a matter that will be explored in the next chapter.

Children in Prisons

Although the Soviet state made many claims about child protection, as discussed in Chapter 3, the reality was different: the state abused children everywhere. Paradoxically, the consequences of Bolshevik *realpolitik* affected all children, whether they were homeless or not. Although the state abolished juvenile imprisonment, this abolition remained largely on paper. In practice, despite laws prohibiting the imprisonment of children, the local Cheka and later GPU and NKVD agents took young offenders and sent them to regular prisons, where they often remained in cells with adult prisoners for months and years. Such actions of the Cheka authorities were arbitrary and illegal.

In his memoirs, a pen-named author "Nadezhdin," who spent a year in the Cheka's Butyrka jail, wrote with bitterness: "… 'dangerous spies'— children of 16, 14, 10 and even 8 years old —spent months isolated in male holding cells."[23] Nadezhdin recalled:

> Particularly amusing was the 8-year-old spy, unusually small, even for his age— citizen Pyotr Osipovich Pokalnis. His story is interesting. Somewhere at the front, in the battle zone, there was a small section of a peasant potato field. It's time to dig potatoes, winter is coming, and, with it, hunger. The elders do not risk going into the field: they will have to shoot or be shot. [They] send Petya [Pyotr]. The Whites come, find Petya, flog [him] and chase him home. The next day he no longer wants to go. He receives a bribe from his father and goes on to continue digging potatoes. The Red Army appears. First, Petya's potatoes are confiscated … They beat him properly and drag him to the Special Department, from where, in pants and without a hat, with the title of "spy", they bring him to Moscow to the Butyrki and put him in "strict solitary confinement." And for four months the prison made fun of the little spy, who walked importantly in prison cells and a dressing gown on a quarter-hour walk. Then, under Zakharov, he was transferred, along with other children, to a juvenile colony. Where are you now, Petya? Did you even manage to get home before the next harvest, or, corrupted by prison and colony, are you now selling matches in the Sukharevka market?[24]

Nadezhdin became an emigrant, and his story may not seem entirely reliable, but there are many other available sources to foster his recollections. As the criminal activity of children increased, the state abandoned its moderate policy and reinstated courts and imprisonment for minors. According to contemporary officials, juveniles who committed a criminal offense were taken into custody and then transferred to the People's Court and even to the Revolutionary Tribunal. The Cheka authorities continued to arrest children, most of them homeless, despite the ban and fears of the People's Commissariat of Enlightenment. In his report for the first half of 1920, the head of the Moscow Cheka, Stanislav Messing, noted that during this time, 1,119 boys and 604 girls under the age of 17 were detained in the Cheka jail of the Sukharevka district (department of the Cheka of Moscow).[25] In the Sukharevka district of Moscow, there was one of the largest markets in the city, always filled with street children who engaged in petty trade or were committing petty crimes. Therefore, such many children in this Cheka prison might not reflect the situation in other prisons.

Nevertheless, the Cheka usually imprisoned entire families, including children, and often the children were held hostage. Many children were arrested along with their parents who had participated in peasant uprisings during the surplus appropriation campaign. The children of "enemies of the people" went to prison with their parents, as well. For example, on March 16, 1925, political prisoner of the Chelyabinsk prison, Elena Goncharova, who was imprisoned with her preschool daughter, turned to the Political Red Cross for help with food and clothing. Goncharova asked for oatmeal, barley coffee (with a state administration stamp), two pairs of children's stockings, a children's book, and a dozen of colored pencils.[26]

It sounds absurd, but there had been cases where children were accused under the political articles of the criminal law. A letter dated December 19, 1929, to the Political Red Cross from Leningrad reports that in early September 1929 six children from a middle school were arrested. All were charged under Articles 58-10 and 58-11 (counter-revolutionary and anti-Soviet activities) on December 8, 1929, and sentenced to two years in the Solovetsky "Special Purpose Prison" on the Solovetsky Islands in the White Sea. The oldest child had just turned sixteen years. The acts that incriminated to them, according to the letter, referred to 1927, that is, to the period of time when each of them was—twelve to thirteen years old. So, in practice, five boys of the age not subject to liability under the law ended up on the Solovetsky convict island. In this and many other cases, the state ignored its own laws. In the letter, pointing out that a possible mistake might have occurred, the petitioners asked for help, which in the end never came.[27]

Of particular interest is a letter dated January 2021 to the head of the Cheka, Felix Dzerzhinsky, which it is reported a three-year-old boy in the Moscow prison, Butyrka, with his imprisoned mother, who turned out to be a member of the Socialist Revolutionary Party and a political prisoner, the famous Eugenia Ratner. The letter was written in a bitterly sarcastic manner. Ratner called Dzerzhinsky a "great educator" and noted that

> the difficulty of the government's position is growing. The fatherland is in danger, and the interests of communist politics imperiously demand the most severe repressive measures be taken against Shura [her 3 years-old son]. For this purpose, at first, it is proposed to send Shura to one of the provincial convict centers to deprive him of the possibility of being a harmful influence on the outside world. One fine night, armed to the teeth, Chekists flood the prison premises, pull half-naked women almost from their beds by force, push, beat, drag them by the arms and legs along the iron and stone stairs to no one knows where, no one knows why. They also burst into our cell, pounce on a frightened, screaming child that is not a child's cry ... Don't you remember, citizen Dzerzhinsky, the nightmarish pictures of tsarist hard labor, in the same Butyrka walls? But then the children's cells were not locked, they had preferential treatment, they always received educational programs. So, your first educational experience was a success. Shurka [her son] sits under lock and key and has resigned himself to this. I hope that this pedagogical system, applied to all children of the RSFSR, will yield no less brilliant results. I only regret that the state of the press in Russia makes it impossible for

me to advertise this instructive experience sufficiently, but I have no doubt that history will fully reward me for it.[28]

It is not known what happened to Shurka, Alexander Lvovich Ratner-Elkind; his mother, Eugenia Ratner, who was sentenced first to death and then to five years in prison, died of cancer in the Moscow's Butyrka prison clinic in 1931.[29] Dzerzhinsky's reaction to her letter is also unknown, but it is clear that the death penalty was commuted to a five-year prison sentence, which may indicate Dzerzhinsky's role in a radical softening of the original sentence. It should be noted here, however, that this radical change in the original verdict indicates the impulsiveness of the decision making of the Soviet criminal justice system, which may reflect the aforementioned bipolar disorder among officials who passed such verdicts and decisions according to their mood or whim. Following the policies of *realpolitik*, the state involved coercive institutions in clearly humanitarian matters.

Cheka—Educator of Homeless and Hungry Children

The Soviet authorities who daily dealt with street children had to admit that "the ideals proclaimed in the first year of the Revolution, which determined the new position of the child in a new society and the state, encountered huge obstacles in their implementation."[30] The government needed to put an end to the continuing influx of children to Moscow, because all means of aid were exhausted and the city could no longer accept homeless children from all over Russia. The continued influx of children led to hunger, death, and crime. The authorities, fearing that the children would turn into organized gangs, asked people not to provide any help to street children.

Meanwhile, it turned out that children escaped orphanages and connected workshops, preferring street begging, petty trade, prostitution, and crime. During the New Economic Policy, children quickly mastered market opportunities and learned how to earn easy money. Earning 50–70 million rubles a day by various ploys, the teenage vagrant never wanted to return to work in the orphanage. To prevent this from happening, the government urged people not to buy anything from children in order to wean them from easy money. The government urged people not to take children's tears at face value, insisting that the tears were fake and that the children manipulated people by counting on the public's sympathy to raise more funds.

The situation was gradually becoming chaotic. As noted earlier, the new government had no knowledge about how many street and needy children there were and little understanding of children's institutions. The Bolshevik government, seriously concerned about the "growing masses" of street children moving to Moscow and to the South, predictably resorted to *realpolitik* policies by appointing the infamous Cheka (All-Russian Extraordinary Commission for Combating Counter-Revolution, Sabotage and Profiteering) to track and trap them. The government organized Children's Commissions and appointed Felix Dzerzhinsky as its chairman. Let us remind the reader that the Cheka was an institution of coercion and the main predecessor of the Soviet Union's repressive organs, OGPU, NKVD, and then the KGB. Although the Children's Commission was formally affiliated with VTsIK, the Cheka dominated it. Thus, the Cheka came to be in charge of dealing with street children.

Almighty Knight of the Revolution Dzerzhinsky

The Cheka's leader, Felix Dzerzhinsky, also maintained several other important positions in the government and directed several key departments in 1918–26, including the commissariat for railroads. Obviously, this signified a key role for Dzerzhinsky and the Cheka in Russia at that time in carrying out Bolshevik policies (through *realpolitik*). Officials argued that the creation of the Children's Commission was intended to facilitate the work of organizations that were responsible for street children's relief, but the commission in fact also took responsibility for the provision, education, and protection of the interests of children on a national scale. The commission quickly took charge of most institutions for street children. Education Commissar Lunacharsky later recalled that

> Felix Edmundovich [Dzerzhinsky] approached me, as always, heated, and hasty. Whoever met him knows his manner: he always spoke as if in a hurry, as if in the consciousness that not enough time had been allowed so that everything was being done in a hurry. Words caught up with other words in waves, as if they were all in a hurry to turn into action. — "I want to throw some part of my personal forces, and most importantly the forces of the Cheka, to fight against children's homelessness," Dzerzhinsky told me, and in his eyes so familiar to all of us, a somewhat feverish fire of excited energy immediately lit up ... "I came to this conclusion based on two considerations. First, it is a terrible calamity. After all, when you look at children, you can't help but thinking everything is for them! And yet, how many of them have been crippled by struggle and need ... It is necessary to create a wide commission under the All-Russian Central Executive Committee, of course, with the direct participation of the People's Commissariat of Education, which would include all departments and all organizations that may be useful in this matter. I've already talked to someone; I myself would like to head this commission; I really want to include the Cheka apparatus in the work. The second consideration pushes me to this: I believe that our apparatus is one of the most effectively working. Its ramifications are everywhere. People reckon with it, are afraid of it. Meanwhile, even in such a matter as saving and providing for children, there is negligence and even predation."[31]

Thus, Dzerzhinsky proposed to involve the resources of the Cheka in solving the problem of homeless children. Prime Minister Vladimir Ilyich Ulyanov (Lenin) unconditionally welcomed Dzerzhinsky's initiative. Later, in January 1921, the Presidium of the All-Russian Central Executive Committee created a Commission for the Improvement of Children's Lives, also known as the Children's Commission (or *Detkomissia*).

The Cheka's *Detkomissia*

The fact that the Children's Commission was created under the Cheka was, perhaps, inevitable. As mentioned above, in practice, the local Cheka authorities had already participated in the "solution" of the problem of street children; however, this participation had not been formally authorized. Dzerzhinsky influenced the decision of the All-Russian Central Executive Committee and the Council of People's Commissars to organize the commission and his own appointment as its chair.[32] Undoubtedly, the "knight of the revolution", the Polish revolutionary Dzerzhinsky, instilled in Lenin confidence in the implementation of Lenin's realpolitik: Lenin admired Dzerzhinsky both for his decisiveness and his ruthlessness toward the enemies of the Revolution. In addition to Dzerzhinsky, the Children's Commission also included representatives of the food, education, and health commissariats, the worker-peasant inspection, trade unions, and the Cheka.[33]

The Presidium of the All-Russian Central Executive Committee each approved members of the Commission personally. It should be noted that, although the *Detkomissia* formally related to the All-Russian Central Executive Committee, the Cheka played the dominant role in its decisions and activities. The commission included three members from the Cheka: Felix Dzerzhinsky as chairman, assistant to the chairman of the Cheka Vasilii Stepanovich Kornev (who also headed the armed forces of the Cheka and, later, NKVD's militia) as a member (he actually acted on behalf of Dzerzhinsky in this commission), and the secretary of the commission, an employee of the Cheka D. Nazarov. In 1921–2, most of the commission's meetings were chaired by Kornev. He oversaw and carried out the day-to-day work of the commission. During the first few years of its existence, the administrative apparatus of the *Detkomissia* was in the building of the Cheka's armed forces. This clearly reflected the controlling position of the Cheka in the policy and activities of the *Detkomissia*. Contemporaries often called the Children's Commission the "Extraordinary Commission for Children," a turn of phrase that emphasized the role of the Cheka. The leaders of the provincial and local children's commissions at that time were also officers of the Cheka, including such well-known Chekists as F. P. Fomin, A. F. Martynov, R. A. Pillar, I. P. Pavlunovsky, G. S. Syroezhkin, and T. D. Deribas. A. F. Martynov, for example, headed the Odessa Provincial Children's Commission, I. P. Pavlunovsky—Omsk, and T. D. Deribas—Samara. Clearly, the appointment of the Cheka to lead the organization of aid to children was in line with Bolshevik *realpolitik*.

The commission developed a strategy for combating homelessness, but in parallel with the formation of local commissions, urgent measures were taken for general children's relief. On January 27, 1921, Dzerzhinsky issued a circular letter to all local bodies of the Cheka to take immediate measures for the relief of street children. Dzerzhinsky wrote:

> The situation of children, especially street children, is difficult … Three years of intense struggle on the fronts (of the Civil War) did not make it possible, however, to do everything necessary to provide and supply children and surround them with exhaustive care … And the Extraordinary Commissions cannot remain aloof

from this concern. They must help the Soviet authorities in every way they can in the work of protecting and supplying children.[34]

Dzerzhinsky identified children's homelessness with counter-revolution and emphasized that his colleagues "working in the Cheka should have seen the importance and urgency of taking care of the children ... Care for the children is the best way to exterminate the counterrevolution."[35] Local Cheka bodies simultaneously began to function as local branches of the Children's Commission. One member of the Cheka staff recalled:

> As regards the struggle with children's homelessness, F.E. Dzerzhinsky required leaders of the local Cheka agencies to participate in this [struggle] every day. And we always considered the struggle with children's homelessness as a main Cheka task.[36]

From that moment on, all measures to eliminate child homelessness were carried out under the vigilant supervision of the Cheka Children's Commission. For the Cheka, the key to solving the problem of the presence of homeless children in the cities and on the railways was their removal and resettlement. Removing homeless children from the streets became the most important task for the Cheka and took on the character of a war, in which employees of the Cheka, the police, and the criminal investigation department took part. To search for children, special patrols and task forces were used, which, among other things, were sent to unguarded railway stations. The staff of the Paramilitary Guard on the railway included teacher, educators who carried out their activities in railcars or receiving rooms.

The commission examined orphanages, set up reception centers, monitored distribution centers, looked for sources of funds, and conducted an extensive propaganda campaign. The propaganda was aimed at society and called for broad mass material and financial support for the state's efforts to combat homelessness. The commission confirmed that now the main task should be not to improve the lives of children or to provide them with any additional benefits, but literally to "save the younger generation from extinction." The task of the moment was to provide all the children of the Republic with food.[37]

The commission's agents found that the existing institutions "exhibited criminal negligence, slowness and indifference to the needs of children."[38] Dzerzhinsky required that

> All cases of theft, abuse, or criminal attitude towards children—and slovenliness—the Extraordinary Commission must bring to the attention of its Executive Committee ... and all cases requiring punishment must be transferred to the Revolutionary Tribunal or the People's Court according to the importance of the case—for the publicity of the proceedings.[39]

A survey of one of the labor communes in Moscow showed that boys "from the age of 6–7 years old smoke 25–30 cigarettes a day, occasionally drink 1–2 bottles of moonshine, everyone sniffs cocaine in large doses."[40]

According to Dzerzhinsky, "the care for children is the best means for exterminating counter-revolution. Having put the matter of providing and supplying children at the right level, the Soviet government acquires its supporters and defenders in every working and peasant family, and at the same time inspires broad support in the fight against counter-revolution." Within two weeks, the Cheka ordered all subordinate agencies to report about "what has been done on this issue, as well as to plan for future work in this direction."[41]

Even though the attempts to solve this problem at the state level had already been undertaken earlier—the Bolshevik government had officially proclaimed free food and state care for all children—there was practically no state nutrition for children, which was discovered by the commission's own inspections. As noted, the Children's Commission's reports, by 1921 "nutrition for children was not established positively anywhere and children lead a half-starved existence." In the report of the Children's Commission to the Presidium of the All-Russian Central Executive Committee on April 15, 1921, it was stated that in some places the children ate only bread and cabbage or frozen potatoes. The reports also stated that until now, no information had been collected on the number of children in the republic as a whole and in individual provinces, which made it impossible to supply the provinces with children's food rations on a planned basis.[42] It should be noted here that the registration of homeless and starving children was in fact not carried out, according to the Cheka commission itself. Therefore, first, the Children's Commission tried to establish the number of children in various regions in order to organize the supply of them with the appropriate number of rations according to a specially developed norm. As mentioned, before the creation of the Children's Commission, the number of street children and children in need of placement in children's institutions was unknown, but also the number of children's homes, schools, and other children's institutions, as well as the number of their students. The supply of childcare facilities was random.[43] At this point, one may assume that all the Bolsheviks' work on free food for children was a fiction from the very beginning.

Thus, only in mid-1921 did the government establish children's daily rations depending on local conditions. On average, each inmate of a secure children's institution was entitled to 200–300 g of bread, about 100 g of meat or fish and the same quantity of cereals, 300–400 g of potatoes, 12 g of salt and sugar per day. In some provinces, the diet also included eggs (20 per month), milk (a glass per day), and vegetables (about 200 g).[44] However, in practice, this established daily ration was issued only in some "exemplary" children's institutions (e.g., in the "Experimental House" of the State Pedagogical Service of the People's Commissariat for Education), where basically "children of communists were allowed"; for "children of the Comintern" there were specially allocated twenty-five places. Most children's institutions did not provide vegetables and white bread at all and very rarely provided butter, meat, and sugar.[45] One may conclude that adequate norms were for children of Communists only.

The Children's Commission often worked on and supposedly corrected problems on the spot. For example, as mentioned earlier, many of the tsarist children's institutions' buildings were occupied by new Soviet institutions. In a telegram to the chairman of the Tambov Regional Extraordinary Commission A. Levin "On measures to improve the lives of children" dated April 14, 2021, Dzerzhinsky insisted:

> Immediately take all measures to fully aid and find fund to help the provincial commissioner for improving the lives of children. The renovated house, in which the special force department is located, must be transferred to the children's hospital, as well as the allotted vegetable gardens. The issue of improving the lives of children is one of the important issues of the republic, and the Cheka should meet the need halfway, and not create obstacles.[46]

Nevertheless, the Cheka was still a repressive and punitive institution, not entirely suitable to work with children. Apart from any humanitarian considerations, the Cheka's involvement as a state political police reflected the government's need for an effective state institution to deal with a problem the government considered important to national security. Thus, the Cheka, as "the most efficiently functioning organization" with its "threatening chairman," was the logical institution for the state to control the 7.5 million "child mass."

Local bodies of the Children's Commission of the Cheka—under the provincial (regional, regional), county (district, district), and city executive committees of the Soviets—were also organized under the local bodies of the Cheka. The commission and its local bodies carried out: the issuance of binding regulations concerning the protection of the life and health of children and the coordination of measures to combat homelessness, which were undertaken by the people's commissariats of internal affairs, education and communications, trade unions and organizations of the RCP (b)—VKP (b). Children's commissions collected food and items for children, distributed rations and funds allocated by the state among children's institutions, and assisted in organizing and supplying children's institutions (reception and distribution centers, boarding schools, etc.). That is, Children's Commissions, which depended mainly on the punitive Cheka and later the GPU, performed functions that before the Revolution were considered charity and were performed by state, public, and private charitable organizations. The effectiveness of the work of the Bolshevik Children's Commissions was tested soon enough—child hunger and homelessness did not decrease.

In the meantime, not all government's officials agreed with the Cheka involvement. The Commissariat of Enlightenment displayed anxiety about Cheka involvement in the Children's Commission. Despite his general agreement with the participation of the Cheka as "the country's most effectively functioning organization," Commissar for Enlightenment Lunacharsky at the same time expressed strong concern about measures the Cheka-led commission would undertake to deal with homeless children. In a February 1921 letter to *Izvestia*, Lunacharsky hinted that the Cheka was an investigatory and punitive apparatus and its "well known" methods could lead only to negative results.[47] Lunacharsky, as mentioned earlier, possessed neither authority nor power in the government and was not able to influence the government's decision: the *Sovnarkom* remained firm in its position.

Government "soft liners" attempted to mitigate the dire consequences of the Cheka's intervention and organized several alternative child protection agencies. In 1921-2, a new unified system of bodies and institutions for the social and legal protection of minors was created. The social education sector of the People's Commissariat of Education of the RSFSR was transformed into the Main Directorate of Social Education and Polytechnic Education of Children, which initially included a department for the legal protection of minors. From April 1922, this department was reorganized into the department of legal protection of minors and the education of disabled children. The department dealt with homelessness and delinquency of children and worked together with the children's inspection, reception, and distribution centers, the commission on juvenile affairs, and enforcement agencies.

Later, at the beginning of 1922, the commission of the Council of People's Commissars suggested that the All-Russian Central Executive Committee abolish the Children's Commission for its overly militant activities in relation to helping street children. In February 1922, the Cheka itself was reorganized into GPU (Chief Political Office) of the NKVD and Dzerzhinsky retained his powerful position as the head of GPU. In March 1922, during the absence of Dzerzhinsky, the presidium of VTsIK abolished the *Detkomissia*.[48] This action was not accidental; obviously the Sovnarkom commission and VTsIK disapproved of the activities of the *Detkomissia* (i.e., the Cheka). On March 25, Dzerzhinsky, having learned about the VTsIK decision, sent the chairman of VTsIK Michael Kalinin a letter protesting "categorically" the VTsIK decision and demanding the presidium of VTsIK to cancel it. Also, Dzerzhinsky emphasized that there was no other institution which would be able to manage the problem.[49] The protest was effective: the *Detkomissia* was revived, thus preserving the Cheka/GPU's role in the matter. This confirmed the perception of the problem of homeless and starving children as political, not humanitarian, which in fact reflected its scale and essence. It became essentially a political problem caused by Bolshevik *realpolitik*. The Bolshevik government seemed to be subconsciously aware of its responsibility for deepening the problem of child homelessness and starvation.

During 1921–2, the government created various commissions, called dozens of conferences and councils, and involved various commissariats and agencies in attempting to solve the problem; in reality, Dzerzhinsky's argument was correct: not one of the institutions was effective. The commission organized donations and collected money and gifts for homeless children. It received and distributed aid from the American Relief Administration. During these years the problem of street children was openly recognized. Already in 1921, articles and notes about street children began to appear in the leading state and party periodicals. *Izvestia, Pravda,* and other newspapers published articles about homeless and starving children. Beginning in 1923, more or less serious literature on children's homelessness began to appear.

NEP and New Market Opportunities

Meanwhile, with the introduction of NEP (New Economic Policy), the Children's Commission began to explore commercial opportunities. In 1921, the process of transformation of children's homes into manufacturing establishments, as the means to make them self-supporting intensified and virtually all children's homes became labor communes. The initiative to create labor communes for homeless children again came from the Cheka's head Dzerzhinsky. Dzerzhinsky believed that all orphanages should be "self-sufficient" labor communes, a matter that will be discussed in this chapter. In March 1921, on Dzerzhinsky's initiative, the Children's Commission organized a stock company "Larek" (Shack), which carried out retail and trading activities. The ostensible purpose was a humanitarian one: to accumulate finances for the relief of homeless children and take under control the already existing involvement of homeless children in petty street trade. In addition, the Children's Commission established a brush manufacturing operation, a cosmetic laboratory, a pawn stores, a cotton wiping cloth manufacturer, a junk bureau, and numerous casinos. In 1925, the government organized another commercial enterprise under the auspices of the same *Detkomissia*. This was the postal parcel service, named Univerpocht (Universal Postal Service), to facilitate logistical, manufacturing, and commercial activities of children's labor homes. All these institutions—labor communes, the share company Larek, the postal company Univerpocht, and other enterprises were under the patronage of the *Detkomissia*. In 1926, to increase the budget, the Children's Commission organized a lottery. The number of issued lottery tickets was 4 million at 0.5 rubles per ticket for the amount of 2 million rubles. Twenty thousand prizes were drawn from among items confiscated by the Cheka. Among the main prizes was a gold Faberge box, weighing almost 16 pounds and studded with precious stones.[50]

As background to these issues, we should note that in order to survive, homeless children engaged in virtually all kinds of activities that could earn food or money; street trade was one of them. Tobacco products were the most popular commodity of the children's street trade. Street children were quick to realize that tobacco goods were in constant demand. They sold cigarettes, cigars, tobacco, and perhaps other handy items of that type. Thus, Larek was aimed at regulating children's involvement in street trade, as well as taking children's street trade under its control. The creation of Larek also reflected a general policy to take control of individual vendors and to regulate their activities. Meanwhile, Dzerzhinsky also headed the Higher Council of People's Economy of the USSR (VSNKh); in 1921, he revealed an interest in the free-market economy and in share stock companies.[51]

Larek was organized as a stock company with several specified shareholders: the *Detkomissia*, the Agricultural Department (Glavsel'prom), Mossel'prom (Moscow's agency of rural manufacturing), GUM (State Universal Store—a super department store), Gosbank (the State Bank), and other agencies. The Children's commission received 25 percent of the company's shares free (without investment of its funds).[52] The Children's Commission drafted a business plan for the company, which was directed to Dzerzhinsky. The Children's Commission's associate chair, Kornev, expected the company to earn about 400 billion rubles. This sum in late 1921 to early 1922 would account for about 220,000 dollars. In addition to the 25 percent of the free shares, the commission was expected to purchase 25 percent more, thus becoming the major shareholder.[53] Kornev confirmed the usefulness of the stock company.

In April 1922, the Children's Commission appointed L. G. Reznikov as empowered representative for organizing manufacturing, commercial, and procuring enterprises on a free market basis throughout the republic. The commission authorized Reznikov to act as an intermediary in all commercial transactions including manufacturing and sales and with guaranteed access to financing. It also exempted these enterprises from taxation. The Children's Commission hoped to devote the enterprises' profits to children's relief in starving provinces.[54] It seems that Reznikov acted on behalf of the Children's Commission organizing local Larek companies and other local children's commissions enterprises in addition to Larek.

Larek consisted of a wide network of small retail stores as well as individual retailers, many of whom were simply homeless children. Larek stores and retailers sold tobacco, cigarettes, matches, playing cards, and later even furs, caviar, smoked beluga, sturgeon, and other luxury goods. Larek also sold commodities produced in the children's labor communes. Suppliers of Larek were variable: they stretched from tobacco companies to the local militia (police). In a telegram to the Children's Commission, dated October 21, 1922, the Larek management requested that, since the Moscow police (militia) was actively involved in raids against non-licensed tobacco dealers, it transferred all confiscated tobacco goods to Larek, if the commodity was in satisfactory condition.[55] By this time, the Cheka's warehouses were full of goods confiscated during 1918–20. These goods were also sold by Larek stores.

In addition, Larek and the Children's Commission itself, as well as its regional structures, operated casinos, and organized lotteries. In May 1926, the central Children's Commission allowed local children's commissions to conduct commodity lottery and arrange a casino, and gambling houses.[56] Furthermore, Larek and Univerpocht distributed publications and played a very important role in distributing party and government periodicals, newspapers, and propaganda stamps and posters throughout the USSR and particularly in regional industrial towns and in the countryside.[57]

In December 1923, Soviet newspaper *Izvestia* praised Larek activities. "The Larek unitary partnership, whose shareholders are Mossovet, GUM, Makhorosindikat, Petrotabaktrest, and other organizations, is engaged mainly in the retail trade of tobacco products and partly in the products of the Fat Trust (soap and perfumery) and confectionery. The partnership began its activity a little over a year ago, with a fixed capital of only 90,000 rubles in gold. Trade is carried out exclusively through street kiosks, the network of which has developed very quickly and now reaches 158 kiosks. In addition, recently "Larek" has begun to carry out its activities in the provinces. Now two kiosks are already functioning in Serpukhov, and will soon be opened in Bogorodsk, Orekhovo-Zuev, Pavlovsky Posad, and Podolsk. These provincial kiosks will already have a wider range of products. In addition, "Larek" intends to develop its activities in the near future by entering large village bazaars. Currently, an average of 1,500 tons of smoking units, up to 25 boxes of shag and the same number of matches are sold daily through the kiosks. For the period April–October, the turnover of "Larek" was expressed in the amount of 1,829,000 rubles. The overhead costs of "Larek" for the maintenance of the administration and taxes do not exceed 15 percent. In the warehouses of the partnership there are significant stocks of goods, at their cost several times the main supply."[58] Paradoxically, the newspaper article kept silent about how the enterprise actually helped homeless children.

A document of February 3, 1923, issued by RKI (Worker-Peasant Inspectorate) audited the activities of Larek and suggested closing it down. The Inspectorate found shortcomings in the company's accounting records, as well as the absence of financial reporting. The company earned profits but did not allocate in a timely manner a part of it to the *Detkomissia*. Its report caused debates; most agreed to revisit the relations between the *Detkomissia* and the share company. The report stated that "since we cannot close Larek," instead of having it allocate 25 percent of its profit, it should pay the Children's Commission a variable progressive monthly rent.[59] Larek, Univerpocht, and all other businesses of the Children's Commission did not shut down but continued to exist for years thereafter.

A Stall with Embezzlers and the Casket Just Opened

This was precisely established, finally, by the latest survey of the activities of the board of the Moscow share partnership of the state retail company "Larek," carried out by the RKI. As a result of this survey, the RKI found that

> the apparatus of the state retail store Larek stole and plundered hundreds of thousands of rubles within 10 months (from October 1, 1924, to August 1, 1925). There were extremely favorable conditions for Lark's trading activities: 60 percent of its turnover was made up of transactions with commission goods, which give a guaranteed profit in the form of a solid percentage of sales. Under such conditions, Larek would live, but live, if not for … waste, appropriation, mismanagement, etc. With a turnover of 15 million rubles, million was spent only on the maintenance of the apparatus. The embezzlement was made for more than 327 thousand rubles. Out of 432 "embezzlement" cases, only 4 were transferred (before August 1, 1925) to the court, when the same persons made from 2 to 4 waste, and the board of Larek was limited to the fact that …. transferred them from one trade unit to another.[60]

In addition to embezzlement, there were also unauthorized expenses and overruns incurred by store managers, which were recorded in the balance sheet at the expense of "unreliable debtors." According to this account, up to 300,000 rubles flowed from the cash desk of Larek. In addition, 1,500 documents were not recorded in the records and, therefore, were not reflected in the balance sheet. Larek had neither statistical accounting, nor calculations, nor verification of estimates approved by shareholders, but there were unprecedentedly chaotic, confusing, and neglected accounting and reporting; unsystematic accounting records; and unacceptable negligence of managers and "friction" between board members, which subsequently resulted in a major skirmish. According to the report,

> the state lost several hundred thousand rubles (exact figures were specified). The composition of the "leading" "responsible" employees of the Larek, as well as persons from its audit commission, will have to answer for their actions in court, and many of them will undoubtedly have to "go to jail", but this should already be attributed to profit, and not to the loss of the Larek.[61]

During 1926–8, there was another audit of Children's Commission enterprises. Once again, the reports revealed unsatisfactory keeping of financial records and reports. Financial reports came usually with six-month delays. One of the resorts stated that the regional children's commissions pursuit of funding took "unhealthy forms." Children's commissions prioritized casinos and lotteries. The number of casinos increased by 30 percent between 1926 and 1927. In some instances, local children's commissions received 75–95 percent of their funds from running casinos. Children's Commission casinos heavily located in areas populated by workers.[62]

The report also revealed that some regional children's commissions maintained heavy overhead costs: up to 74 percent of their profit was spent on the distribution of post stamps and lotteries, whereas some reported no overhead costs on the same activity.[63] Obviously, dishonest employees of the local commissions used the commercial enterprises as an opportunity to benefit themselves and their families. (The examples when managers of children's communes employed their relatives and allowed their own children to use colonies' cafeterias exist in archives.)[64]

Cheka's and GPU's Children's Homes

A feature of the first decades' orphanages and labor colonies was the extremely weak state support, expressed by food, material, technical, organizational, and methodological needs, on the one hand, and almost complete freedom from control or oversight, on the other. Initially, these institutions were under the patronage of various state bodies, which created great organizational chaos, but later the forced labor camps and correctional institutions were transferred to the Cheka and the OGPU. In conditions of weak organizational and methodological control, the administration of children's institutions received a degree of freedom as regards pedagogical, educational, and administrative creativity that was unthinkable either before 1917 or after the mid-1930s. According to contemporary accounts and reports, the state and party authorities were least of all interested in the situation of children. Children's homes received no supplies. "Children from children's homes collected garbage in weed boxes to satisfy their hunger, begged and quarreled over every piece of bread."[65] It is obvious that for some administrators saw the colonies as opportunities to appropriate their funds, food, and even their pupils for their own selfish purposes. Ironically, the appointment of the "almighty Cheka", as already mentioned, had had as a main goal the reduction of administrative abuses.

The commission discovered that in many instances children's homes administrations consisted of relatives; orphanage managers hired their non-professional relatives for the sole purpose of receiving benefits and free meals, or to arrange for their own children food and clothing at the orphanage's expense. For example, in Tsaritsyn province, a survey of the conditions and work of orphanages revealed twenty-five such cases; in Astrakhan—twenty. An inspection of Tsaritsyn orphanage No. 38 found that its manager, E. Kobyakov, "widely practiced the beating of children and that one boy fell ill after one such beatings. Kobyakov employed his wife and daughter in law in the orphanage and their treatment of children was very rude."[66] According to another report, "the children witnessed how this group of employees steals their bread, jam, soup in buckets, etc."[67] The commission found that such cases were common in most regions. Obviously, the authorities of many orphanages found it difficult to resist the temptation to use their position, especially in light of the overwhelming hunger that gripped the country.

As earlier on, reception centers and orphanages remained the main institutions for dealing with street children and adolescents. Children were taken from the street and sent to the children's reception center, and then to the orphanage or to correctional institutions. The policy of removing children from the streets led to overcrowding in orphanages; orphanages, required to take in all children, did not have the means to support them. The state also could not support these houses financially. Conditions in these centers were catastrophic. Medical doctor V. Nazarov visited children's reception center organized by the People's Commissariat for Education in October 1921. The center had the capacity to host forty children but had 400. According to Nazarov, children's

> reception centers tuned out to be dumping places where children were crammed without counting and without measures of support. Children were literally piled up in the same rags they came in with from the street. When I first visited the central reception center, I could not stay in it for more than three minutes, my head was spinning, and I was sick from the stench. In one large room, on the bunk and on the floor, on the pianos, on the windowsills, about two hundred children were swarming with hunger, raving in typhus, agonizing and already dead (according to the staff, corpses were removed out only once a day). The children's psyche was so depressed that corpses served as headboards for those who, perhaps, tomorrow expected the same fate; children put bread on the corpses: corpses served as tables.[68]

Nevertheless, with the assistance of the "effective" Cheka, the government's chief measure was the removal children from the streets and the placement of them into these children's colonies and homes. According to the official statistics, by 1922, there were 125,000 children in these institutions.[69] About 150,000 children were evacuated from starving areas to Siberia, Ukraine, Caucasus, and other regions and placed in children's homes. As mentioned, the practice of taking children from streets and placing them in children's homes led to extreme overcrowding. When in 1923, the government transferred children's institutions from the government's budget to local budgets, this led to a sharp reduction in the numbers of these institutions and of children in them. Boguslavsky wrote in the journal *Krasnaya Nov* that

> at the present time, the local executive committees continue to have a tendency to reduce the network of orphanages and the number of children in them; in recent times, this reduction has not only not decreased, but, on the contrary, has increase. So, in the period from June 1, 1924, to June 1, 1925, the number of children's homes has decreased by 26.6%, and the number of children in them by 16.2%. In the period from June 1, 1925, to June 1, 1926, the number of institutions fell by 20.3%, but the number of children increased by 25.9%.[70]

The figure of 6,063 children's homes in 1922 was reduced to 3,971 in 1923 and the number of their children from 540,000 to 253,237. In the next five years, the numbers fell again by half.[71] In 1925, 2,811 orphanages boarding 21,136 and in 1927-8, 1,430 children's institutions with 92,007 pupils. For the sake of reducing expenses, orphanages were often transferred to remote villages and monasteries, where they, in the words of Nadezhda Krupskaya, "do not bother anyone." The evacuation of children continued despite the prohibition of this practice in 1924, as discussed in Chapter 3.

As mentioned, with the introduction of NEP (New Economic Policy), which represented sharply different economic policies and facing serious financial problems, the head of the Cheka Dzerzhinsky wanted to make children's homes financially self-supporting. In a telephone text addressed to VTsIK, Zhenotdel (Women's Section), the Central Committee of Komsomol, the Central Committee of Labor Unions, and other state agencies, Dzerzhinsky stated that the "aim is to establish a labor regime in [children's homes] and bring about self-sufficiency as regards repairs of premises, equipment, clothing, shoes, and so on." He suggested that children's labor communes should have "production, organized in workshops" and should sell their products through the stock company, Larek. According to the Cheka's head, this would create "a source of self-financing" for these children's institutions. Dzerzhinsky also called on all the government institutions for help.[72]

Although this is not the subject of this book, it's worthwhile noting that in early documents regarding children's labor communes, there was no mention of institutions' educational goals. During the early 1920s, children's labor communes were coercive institutions.[73] Documents from the mid- and late 1920s did begin to reflect some idea of education and correction of children in the communes. Another shift occurred later: documents from the 1930s once again considered the children's labor communes as a means of correction and punishment through productive labor rather than education, a matter that will be explored in the next chapter.

In any case, during the early 1920s, children's homes became manufacturing "self-supporting" workshops, which included a broad spectrum of handicrafts and trades: book binderies, sewing shops, locksmiths, and carpentries. Children produced toys, paper products, cardboard articles, shoes, garments, and so on.[74] Ironically, what Tsarist Russia tried to regulate and reduce—child labor—the new Soviet government was quickly reintroducing. The 1923-4 internal audits reveal the reality of early Soviet children's exploitation, which to this day has never been fully recognized or acknowledged publicly. A 1924 report from Orel city and province informed the central *Detkomissia* that most children's labor communes had workshops or manufacturing establishments (artels). Some labor communes were under the patronage of the Charitable Association "Friend of Children" (*Drug detei*), which had been created in 1923 but most operated under the *Detkomissia*. The report from Orel province stated that children usually knew nothing about their earnings, nor how much money their workshops made, nor about the overall volume of their production.[75] They did the work, presumably had something to eat and basic shelter. Not surprisingly, these children often fled children's labor communes for the streets, where they believed they could better survive.

Nevertheless, the question of what was to be done with the growing juvenile delinquency still remained. Dzerzhinsky closely related children's criminality with homelessness. In February 1924, in his letter "On the Punitive Policy of the Soviet State" to the Central Control Commission of the Communist Party of Bolsheviks Dzerzhinsky wrote:

> The most appropriate measure to prevent the growth of crime is to take care of street children, to which all compassion and will should be directed, and broad public opinion of the masses should be involved in the fight against crime and criminals.[76]

Unfortunately, such expressions of good will remained largely on paper.

Since the state related children's criminality with "moral defectiveness," juvenile delinquents were usually sent to institutions for morally defective children under the authority of the Commissariat for Enlightenment. At the collegium of the OGPU (a special body of state security of the USSR), it was decided to create a special type of institutions for young criminals. The state began to transform orphanages into closed labor-correctional colonies. Their main task was to reeducate and socialize juvenile delinquents through labor and strict discipline. By 1925, there were 258 such institutions with 16,000 pupils.[77] The most famous of them were the Bolshevo labor commune near Moscow and Maxim Gorky's labor commune near Kharkov.

The history of these communes is covered in darkness because contemporaries apparently wanted to hide controversial points. Thus, primary sources are either unavailable or nonexistent. As the official sources reveal, by OGPU order of August 18, 1924 N 185, a children's labor colony at the OGPU for fifty people was organized to fight against violators of the law between the ages of 13 and 17. The Bolshevo labor commune was, in fact, headed by Matvey Samoylovich Pogrebinsky, employee of the Cheka-OGPU-NKVD of the USSR.[78] In 1933, the commune was given the name "Yagoda" in honor of the NKVD head. The commune hosted only young men aged 16 to 21 years. The length of stay in the commune was two to three years. These young men were convicts serving their sentences in the Butyrskaya and Taganskaya prisons, concentration camps, or other prisons. They had an average of seven to eight convictions behind them (i.e., they were mostly recidivists), the main age was 17–18 years, but there were also 13-year-olds and 25-year-olds.[79] "They are mostly socially ill, but they still cannot be called socially dangerous, although they could easily become so,"[80] as Pogrebinsky described his words. The number of communards steadily increased and grew from eighteen in 1924 to 5,000 in 1936. Productive labor was at the heart of education.[81] In theory, the work of the labor commune and education were based on the principles of trusting relationships between pupils and teachers, which supposedly made it possible to form a sense of responsibility among former criminals. As conditions for admission, teens were required to break off all contacts with former criminal friends; give up alcohol, drugs, and card games; and be ready to work and obey the decisions of self-government bodies. Initially, children and adolescents of the commune worked for a state farm of the OGPU, where the commune was located. Later, the commune organized carpentry and shoemaker's workshops. Both workshops used manual labor.

In 1926, the commune established a shoe factory and knitwear production, and in 1929, a sports equipment production. According to contemporaries, the commune almost ignored education for its child residents. Although, the workday for children lasted eight hours, the colony, according to the accounting books, was unprofitable.[82] In addition to work and study, the colony's pupils engaged in sports, music, and art. Numerous sections operated in the colony: music (choir, wind, string), drama, radio circle, art studio, and sports. The commune could be proud of its athletes who reached the all-Union level in football (soccer), hockey, skiing, gymnastics, speed skating, tennis, athletics, and rugby. Many famous people graduated from the commune. We can name the poets P. Zheleznov and V. Derzhavin (translator of Persian poetry); the artist V. Maslov, who had personal exhibitions and was repressed in 1937; the football player M. Sviridovsky, a participant in the legendary "death match," in which the Dynamo (Kiev) team played against the Nazi Germany Air Force team. A library was formed, which by 1928 had up to a thousand volumes, newspapers were subscribed to at the occupants' expense. In 1930, a technical school was opened in the commune.[83] This commune gave a "start in life" to homeless children who accepted the new government, but what would their lives have been like if they had not become homeless children in the first place.

Makarenko's System

Makarenko's labor commune for children was founded earlier, in 1920 and received a new impetus in 1924. This institution, intended for the re-education of juvenile delinquents, was organized outside the city on the territory of a former colony for juvenile delinquents. This highly publicized commune was led by pedagogue Anton Semenovich Makarenko, who was and is considered an outstanding educator of troubled teenagers. For his achievements in the field of education and rehabilitation of young people (both from among the former homeless children and from families) and preparation for their further successful socialization, Makarenko became a well-known figure of Russian and world pedagogical literature. According to a widely publicized opinion, the author of the famous *Pedagogical Poem* had a simple method of reforming juvenile delinquent colonist. His first and inviolable rule was neglect of the past. This meant that the colonists had to forget their past life. Makarenko did not correct these children, mostly boys, rather he taught them to live differently. His main tool was honest joint creative work that would leave no time for anything else. The colony created its own controlled democracy; it possessed a design which he described in his *Pedagogical Poem*. In the colony, Makarenko introduced the wearing of uniforms. From April through September, colonists were required to wear boxers with two front spacious pockets, and a belt and a T-shirt, regardless of the weather outside. Makarenko explained this as the best hygienic clothing for boys.[84]

The personality and methods of Makarenko, however, received rather contradictory responses from both contemporaries and researchers. Some reproached Makarenko for child abuse, pointing that his method was based on harsh discipline, violence, and the suppression of the individual. Krupskaya criticized his methods, and, after her devastating article, Makarenko was dismissed from the leadership of the colony he organized. Thanks to his patrons from the NKVD, he was transferred to other activities related to children. Historian and philosopher Boris Paramonov suspected Makarenko of homosexual pedophilia, although without citing any documentary facts. His conclusions were based on the psycholinguistic analysis of Makarenko's *Pedagogical Poem*. Paramonov stressed that in his book, Makarenko described only boys and used sensual terms for their characteristics. Paramonov writes:

> And [Makarenko does] so dozens of times: all those beautiful eyes of Korotkov, slender legs of Vanya Zaichenko, beautiful lips of Pyotr Ivanovich, sensitive fingers of boys, shameless boys, and their uncomplicated clothes, Spiridon's big and smart mouth, boyish waists, elbows and stomachs, lovely kids—misogynists, colonists, compared with elves and Mercury, who has wings on his feet; even about the enemy of the colony, ... the author will not hesitate to say that he was a handsome brunette ...[85]

In his analysis, Paramonov even went further to conclude that he would not rule out the possibility that "Makarenko not only beat children, but also killed them. No wonder he had a revolver." The situation in the colony, according to Paramonov, was terrorist, with penalties that appeared later. Paramonov stated that during the years of the Civil War, in 1918–20, no one noticed or paid attention to violations and abuses. The colony was created in an atmosphere of general confusion and disorder when it was easy to cover up tracks. The author concludes that Makarenko was not a teacher, but a godfather of a prison, and his colony was a den of thieves. "Of course, he put an iron order so that he could fool any commission." Paramonov viewed as "very suspicious" the story of Makarenko's dismissal from the colony, because Makarenko spoke about it "very sparingly." Paramonov is especially struck by one Makarenko's phrase, in which Makarenko wrote: "It was necessary to withdraw my friends from the colony as soon as possible." Paramonov is perplexed: "What kind of friends are these?" and continues:

> I believe that we are talking about the so-called assets, Makarenko's detachment commanders. These were criminals whom Makarenko used: after all, it was not for nothing that Zadorov grinned showing his teeth cutely and for some reason clung to Shelaputin's blooming face. And Makarenko selected the appropriate educators, appointed by the state: almost all of them were from the category of single eccentrics (this is again a euphemism), deprived, as Makarenko says, of family selfishness.[86]

As mentioned above, the organizers and leaders of children's colonies had uncontrolled authority at this time. This opened up a possibility for various abuses of children. Beatings and corporal punishment in the colonies were not uncommon and children's colonies could have been an object of interest for pedophiles. Nevertheless, it is very difficult to unequivocally state anything about Makarenko's methods due to the lack of evidence. All that historians have are the official sources and some memoirs. Some memoirs mentioned rather awkward episodes from the life of Makarenko's colony.

Figure 10 At the Makarenko Orphanage. Source: open public domain.

For example, Nadezhda Feliksovna Ostromentskaya (1893–1968), who worked in the Gorky colony in the summer of 1926 as a club worker, then as an educator-teacher and later became a Ukrainian children's writer, left a memoir. She related the "story with sticks and clubs," which, according to Ostromentskaya, the pupils themselves had to bring from the forest (after which they were used for their own corporal punishment). Nadezhda Krupskaya refused a personal meeting with Makarenko because of his educational methods of physical abuse of children.[87]

Apparently, abuse of children, including corporal punishment, was widespread in many childcare institutions. State newspaper *Izvestia* reported in 1928 that in Barnaul, the case of fourteen teachers was heard (the head of the district department of public education, his deputy, inspectors, heads of orphanages, schools, and educators), and were accused of "the widespread use of corporal punishment—in children's homes there was a police torture chamber."[88]

"We think about it little and do less to resolve it"

Children's homelessness and starvation became a continuous and pervasive issue throughout the 1920s. Despite all that had been done, in December 1922, at one of its meetings, the member of the *Detkomissia* made a decision to ask Felix Dzerzhinsky to report to "the high party and soviet institutions about the terrible state of the underage population of the republic and, particularly, on the catastrophic growth of children's homelessness."[89] This move can only testify to the fact that even the participation of the

Cheka was incapable of solving the problem, because the Cheka itself was the political instrument that created the problem. By 1923, some state officials finally realized that the entire government's approach to the problem of *besprizornost'* was ineffective. Paradoxically, some state officials were still "discovering" street children as a serious issue. In March 1923, Nadezhda Krupskaya wrote in her article in *Pravda* that

> actually, we have only the vaguest notion of how many *besprizornye* we have and what a plague it is. We think about it little and do less to resolve it ... We have seven million registered homeless children (and how many might have not been registered!)[90]

The statements of Dzerzhinsky and Krupskaya fully reflected the fact that from the very beginning the state did not take care of children, despite the deep irony that it declared its intention to take all children under state protection.

In January 1924, the Second Congress of Soviets of the USSR created a special Lenin Fund in the amount of 100 million rubles to help street children. Of these, 50 million rubles were provided by the Soviet government and were inviolable, that is, only the interest on this capital was subject to spending. The remaining 50 million rubles were republican funds and other collections made on the basis of special decrees. The Central Commission had its own local bodies in the form of local commissions for fund management, which were organized in a year, in January 1925. The money could be spent on ongoing activities to "fight" against the homelessness of minors in accordance with the decisions of the Central Commission, which oversaw local Leninist funds.[91] It is difficult to judge how effective the fund's activity was. No doubt the foundation helped some starving street children. But in the context of the general policy of the state, based on *realpolitik*, the situation of Soviet children did not improve, and the situation of homeless children even worsened.

In February 1924, the government called a conference to work out a plan to reform "the existing system of struggle with *besprizornost*." The participants of the conference discussed the social aspects of the problem, the policies of the existing institutions, and the methods used. The conference criticized the idea of considering homeless children as morally defective.[92] Krupskaya, who was actively involved in the development of official state propaganda, in her speech, again blamed the old regime and the war and recognized the role of "organization of society" in the elimination of homelessness. Krupskaya wrote that

> we must understand that the elimination of homelessness, caused by the war, caused by the destruction of old relationships, old ties, is possible only through an organized society. Those forms of eliminating homelessness that are practiced in bourgeois countries are unsuitable for eliminating homelessness in our country.

Propagandist Krupskaya's assertion that homeless teenagers were fleeing old-fashioned orphanages was sly. In late imperial orphanages, there were almost no problems with runaway children, while, in orphanages of the Bolshevik type, cases of runaways were constant. Krupskaya wrote that the government had to "beat with a wedge," that is, destroy the social relations that gave rise to homelessness. But here the question arises about the expediency of evicting children's institutions from their old and solid mansions. Was such a confiscation justified by the need to break old ties? Krupskaya was cunning again. Nevertheless, despite everything, she expressed the idea of involving the "organized public" in the elimination of child homelessness.

A. Kalinina, the chair of the children's extraordinary commission of the Commissariat of Education and a delegate to the conference, recalled in her interview in *Pravda* that "meanwhile our first goal is to improve our approaches to the *besprizornye*, [so that we consider them] as physically and morally normal, which the majority of *besprizornye* are. These children require special sensitive pedagogues who can understand them."[93] Several days later, she wrote in *Pravda*: "We have to acknowledge openly that the old methods are all 100 percent unacceptable and have to be eliminated."[94] Such conclusions from an official who had worked with homeless children during all these years were also a recognition that the government had been completely unable to deal with the social problem. An official document from April 16, 1924, acknowledged that children's homelessness "has reached an extent that can threaten public security."[95]

In 1924, the government introduced some measures against arbitrary and chaotic evacuations by setting strict rules for re-evacuation. The latter was allowed only in cases where it was established that parents or relatives lived in the area where the child was sent, and there was an opportunity for these persons to accept children as dependents.[96] In 1924, there was a change in regard to the so-called "morally defective children." As discussed earlier, the state considered all street children to be morally flawed. The Second All-Russian Congress of the Social and Legal Protection of Minors, held in November 1924, finally abandoned the term "morally defective" in relation to street children. This had a positive impact on approaches to the upbringing and re-education of street children and adolescents.[97] Even so, it did not end the problem.

During 1924, the government carried out wide propaganda to involve society in relief for homeless children and in solving *besprizornost'*. The official state newspapers began to publish daily reports and articles calling on society to respond. The state officials and concerned people offered their ideas. Nadezhda Krupskaya wrote in her article in *Pravda*:

[Children of] different ages require different approaches. The age of homeless children varies from the youngest all the way to 17–18 ... The problem of children's homelessness requires great thoughtfulness, great organization, and great patience.[98]

Even at this point, some ideas suggested by officials tended to be unreasonable and were used rather for propagandistic goals than for practical ones. State leaders often intermixed ideological elements with the social problem. A certain "A. G-n" wrote in *Pravda*: "I think that any factory or plant could undertake to provide for a group of *besprizornye*. We should hand over *besprizornye* to working families."[99]

In fact, none of these ideas came about in 1924. Although some government officials had changed their opinion about homeless children, having recognized mistakes in considering them as morally defective, the government still had no meaningful program to relieve homeless children. Even in 1925, a reader of *Pravda* could see such statements as: "the question of children's homelessness has begun to attract the attention of our ruling organs and the proletarian community."[100] One wonders where its attention had been all this time.

Again, in 1926, an official document reported that there were no statistics or accurate record of homeless children in the provinces and made an inquiry to gather such data.[101] Nevertheless, the state, having taken childcare in its hands, was not able to fulfill its commitment and responsibility, and was not willing to turn this matter over to public or private hands. The state also failed in its commitment to improve economic conditions of families—the children's immediate environment,—but in most cases made these conditions worse.

In early March 1926, the Children's Commission, the Commissariats of Education and Health, and the Central Committee of the Komsomol appealed to the Presidium of the Regional Congress of Trade Unions. The Children's Commission stated that child homelessness, a "legacy of wars, devastation, and famine," remains a serious social disaster. The commission called for the broad worker-peasant community to be involved in this cause. The appeal said that the working people of the Soviet country, organized in trade unions, should play a big role in this great and difficult undertaking. The appeal was published in the *Izvestia* newspaper. It is noteworthy that the authorities, who had destroyed public charity, took the care of children into their own hands, and failed to cope with the problem, now called for a worker-peasant community "organized" through trade unions to deal with it. This was an indirect confirmation of the failure of the state charity proposed by the Bolsheviks earlier on. Bolshevik *realpolitik* had in reality exacerbated the problem.

The unavoidable conclusion is that the state did not really know how to overcome homelessness and acted impulsively and reactively, a conclusion based on measures and actions undertaken. In March 1926, the government adopted Regulations on the Fight against Homelessness, and in September approved a three-year plan for the actions. In April 1926, the Presidium of the Moscow Council of Workers', Peasants', and Soldiers' Deputes announced that Moscow became "the center of concentration of homeless children who are coming from other provinces, which makes the struggle with homelessness particularly difficult."[102] (In other words, nothing had changed since 1918-19.) A 1926 decree called for immediate measures to combat children's homelessness on railroads.[103] As noted, earlier the state transferred children's homes funding to local budgets. However, this worsened the situation of orphanages and led to mass flight of children. From the mid-1920s, the government loading children's homes and orphanages. In April 1926, the government introduced "procedures and conditions" for the transfer of street children to peasant families to prepare them for agricultural work.[104] Thus, the Bolshevik government once again turned to the population for help and again returned to the institution of patronage, which it had liquidated immediately after the Revolution.

On May 12, 1926, the central Children's Commission instructed its local commissions to take measures to combat child homelessness in the near future. The Children's Commission required the transfer of 19,000 teenagers from orphanages to peasant families, handicraftsmen, artisans, and production. The state allocated to each teenager a one-time assistance in the amount of 50 rubles (950,000 rubles in total).[105] Children's social inspectors identified families who were willing and able to accept street children and children from orphanages for registration of guardianship, patronage, or adoption. In addition, the central commission made an order for the return of children who were able to restore ties with their families to their families.

In general, peasants and handicraftsmen were interested in taking children from orphanages because this provided them with an additional land plot for each child they take, and an exemption from paying a single tax for three years. Moreover, peasants enjoyed the right to free education of a foster child at school and received a one-time allowance for it. The original, early ways of arranging the lives of teenagers were to marry them off or send them to the army or military schools. The distribution of children to artisans and peasants, not backed up by protective measures, often led to abuse of children by "guardians." This "philanthropy" very soon turned into a new type of trade, and when the state stopped paying money for children or famine set in, they were simply thrown out into the street. As a result, foster children often became street children again. The fate of homeless children deprived of a family depended on attention from society, but Bolshevized society turned out to be indifferent and cruel. Nevertheless, the measures to transfer children to foster families might had the potential to eradicate child homelessness if the state did not subsequently carry out expropriatory policies, collectivization, and land seizures as regards the very families and localities involved, policies which gave rise to new waves of children's homelessness.

In early 1928, the government launched mass seizures of homeless children and adolescents from the streets, railway stations, and other habitats and their placement in temporary detention centers, orphanages, and shelters—once again repeating past failed measures. In a circular of the People's Commissariat of Education, dated March 19, 1928, the work to eliminate street homelessness was equated to a "combat mission." On April 5, 1928, the Central Committee of the All-Union Communist Party issued an order to eliminate child homelessness in one or two years. According to A. N. Krivonosov, this work "resembled a large-scale military KGB operation" with a clearly planned concentration of the main forces and means, a certain direction of the main "strike," the strictest secrecy of the operation, coordination of joint actions, and thorough intelligence collecting. A mass action to "remove" homeless children from the streets began all over the country, at the same hour, on the night of April 12–13, 1928. Only employees of the OGPU, the police, and the criminal investigation department were involved in the operation, plus, in rare cases—employees of the children's inspection and Komsomol workers.[106]

The process of removing children from the streets and their habitats was initially carried out only in large cities and at junction railway stations and then with further advancement into the interior of the country. For these purposes, railway children's reception centers were created in advance. All detained children during the operation were escorted to an orphanage, accompanied by an armed guard. In order to prevent the movement of homeless children from region to region, armed barrage detachments were deployed at the junction railway stations. Homeless children desperately resisted: they made single and mass escapes, disobeyed police officers, broke the glass and bars on windows, called themselves by false names, and tried in every possible way to show physical resistance. According to G. Rauch, when groups of homeless children put up particularly stubborn resistance, troops were called in to help the police, who suppressed the riot with machine-gun fire. The treatment of detainees was not much different from the treatment of prisoners, as evidenced by an excerpt from the order of the head of one of the reception centers:

> The dispatch of homeless teenagers will be carried out on the morning of May 3. Those to be sent must be awakened at 4 o'clock in the morning. At 4:30 am, an escort will arrive to escort them to the station. The transfer should be made according to the lists by roll call ... The surrender of people to the convoy must be carried out without delay. Being late is unacceptable.[107]

The government once again set itself the task of eliminating child homelessness as soon as possible by means of hastily drawn up operational plans for the elimination of street homelessness. The main goal was to empty out orphanages and reception centers from children as soon as possible. Gradually, children's homes began to be "unloaded," and homeless children were provided with rooming houses and day workshops. From orphanages and children's homes, children were either sent to their homeland; given to their parents if they were found; or were handed out to peasant families, families of handicraftsmen, and/or collective and state farms.

Nevertheless, despite all these harsh measures, the flow of homeless children never ended. Historian Rozhkov rightly pointed out that the contemporary periodicals refute the conclusion about the complete elimination of street homelessness.[108] For example, the June 11, 1928, issue of the Moscow newspaper *Vechernyaya Moskva* reported: "Recently, the influx of homeless children from the provinces to Moscow has increased tremendously ... Homeless children arrive with every train that comes to Moscow." On September 21, 1928, newspaper *Trud* reported that in August up to 1,500,000 homeless children arrived in Moscow. *Izvestia* wrote in February 1929 that in 1928 more than 21,000 homeless children were seized from the streets.

Moreover, by the spring of 1929, the state, now firmly under the control of Stalin, planned to completely eradicate street homelessness, a phenomenon which represented "a sharp contrast with the rising economic well-being of the country and its growing cultural level." These immediate measures emphasized involving the broad public in the issue but in practice the old Bolshevik *realpolitik* methods prevailed. The government relied on mass removal of children from big cities to the countryside to either newly created children's homes or to foster families.

Conclusion

As the above discussion suggests, over the entire 1920s, the state reported on issues of children's homelessness and starvation as the growing and pervasive ones and always called for urgent measures to deal with them. The state measures to relief the issue always turned out to be virtually ineffective. Over the entire decade, government officials reported on increasing numbers of street children. Street children were feared by many and often hated and shunned. Even some children who lived with their families suggested "destroying the homeless children, otherwise you can't walk in the evening."[109] By the end of the 1920s, such sentiments became completely aligned with the plans of the country's leadership, well reflected in the Stalin's words when he visited Leningrad and saw many street children. Stalin noted to the city's authority: "you have littered the city with homeless children, homeless children are lying on all the streets, and you need to clear the city of this garbage."[110] This attitude would set in motion a new page in the history of Soviet children's tragedy during Stalin's reign.

5

A "Happy Soviet Childhood": Stalinist Childhood Revisited

Our state differs from all other states in that it does not spare money for good childcare and good upbringing of young people ... I think that nowhere else is there such care for a child, about its upbringing and development, as in our country, the Soviet Union.

Joseph Stalin[1]

not subject to disclosure
Lately, there has been beggary among children and adolescents, which is growing on a massive scale in certain cities, like Omsk, Novosibirsk, and Tomsk.

Official report, 1931[2]

Only persistent and hard work poisons the youth of unfortunate children, and vice versa: sycophancy, lies, slander, squabbles, gossip, and other evils flourish. And why? Is it because the people are evil? No. It is because a bunch of scoundrels, holding power in their hands, are evil.

Vladimir Moroz, 14 y.o., 1937[3]

On May 31, 1935, the Soviet government introduced a special decree "On the elimination of children's homelessness and neglect." The decree stated that mass homelessness had in fact been eliminated in the country and the new task was to toughen legislation against underage offenders. A month earlier, in April 1935, a decree "On measures to combat juvenile delinquency" introduced criminal liability of minors from the age of 12 for vagrancy, theft, causing violent bodily harm, mutilation, or murder "with all of applicable criminal punishments" employed for adults, including the death penalty. The decree also strengthened responsibility of parents and guardians and introduced material and criminal liability for their children's actions. This marked the triumph of coercion over pedagogy and education, and the legalization of Stalin's repressions against street children. The government no longer viewed street children as homeless, in need of help and rehabilitation, but as vagrants in need of isolation and coercion. However, despite the repressive laws, children's homelessness persisted throughout the 1930s and beyond. Children's starvation contended.

As we have seen earlier, since the beginning of Soviet power, various departments and organizations became involved in dealing with street children—the People's Commissariats of Charity, Health, and Education; the Cheka and its successors; the GPU and OGPU; the NKVD; trade unions; the Komsomol; local party bodies; women's departments; etc. Stalin personally pointed out the urgent need to eliminate children's homelessness.[4] Regardless of all that, the history of childhood tragedies continued throughout the 1930s and spawned huge new waves of hungry and homeless children. For the entire period of the early Soviet power, from the Bolshevik takeover to the outbreak of the Second World War and beyond, the state could not eliminate starvation and homelessness among children.

As previous chapters illustrated, the constant suffering of Soviet children was rooted mainly in the government's economic and demographic policies, summarized under the rubric, *realpolitik*. The policies were usually extortionate and ineffective, and the government relied on coercion, force, and violence to implement them. Historian Sheila Fitzpatrick noted that during the 1930s there was the second generation of street children in the Soviet Union, as direct results of collectivization, migration, dekulakization, and hunger (and I would add repression and imprisonment).[5] In the 1930s, children from expropriated families whose parents were arrested or expelled from villages deprived of their property, and/or subjected to other forms of repression, constituted a separate category of children: children-enemies of the state. Some children were processed through courts for high treason and counter-revolutionary activities. The Soviet state encouraged a hostile attitude toward the children of kulaks and the children of other "enemies of the people." But were the other kids better off?

As explored in Chapter 2, during the 1930s the geography of Soviet children's tragedy changed: during the 1930s, homeless and starving children troubled the Soviet authorities primarily in the Arctic regions and Siberia. Nevertheless, the village actually continued to be the main source of children's tragedies. As collectivization and dekulakization continued, the living conditions of large numbers of peasant children and their families deteriorated. During the pre-war decade, confidential and classified letters and telegrams informed central authorities in no uncertain terms that homelessness and beggary among children had taken on a mass character.[6] These letters were numerous and each of these letters contained an urgent appeal for help in dealing with the growing problem.

Despite the government's calls in the late 1920s and early 1930s to eradicate children's homelessness and to take decisive action to relieve the plight of homeless and starving children, the problems still persisted unceasingly. The government could or would not cope with the problems it constantly created. Due to the endless growth of homeless children's numbers, children's labor colonies did not have the means to provide for their child inmates. The norm of food products was far from meeting the needs of a 12–18-year-old teenager. In order not to die of hunger, children ran away and stole. According to a contemporary, children "will definitely not starve, but will go to steal and eat their fill."[7]

In 1935, the Stalinist government decided to eliminate the problem by the mentioned decrees and introduced coercion as the only way to cope with street children. Homeless children began to be regarded as vagrants, entailing administrative and criminal liability. The state introduced a passport system, registration, and strict regulation of the population's territorial mobility. Were the new measures capable of addressing the issue? This chapter will investigate children's conditions during the collectivization campaign and explore the years before and immediately after the outbreak of the Second World War.

Drawbacks of Stalin's Collectivization: A 'de'Classified Reality

Contrary to the official Soviet declaration of a "happy childhood," early Soviet childhood was gloomy and unhappy for most Soviet children, regardless of whether they were orphans, street children, living with or without their parents, or whether they were children of kulaks, or children of other social groups: officially proclaimed "happy childhood" was restricted to the elites, until Stalinist purges ruptured that bubble too. During the late 1920s and 1930s, most Soviet children continued to experience extraordinary hardship, as they had since the Bolshevik Revolution. Mortality rates among children remained astonishingly high. Bolsheviks and later Stalin's *realpolitik* policy brought the population to prolonged hunger and despair. Many families were subjected to repression, arrests, and forced resettlement to Siberia and other areas with completely absent livelihood infrastructure. Children's hunger and homelessness continued throughout the 1930s, combined with political repressions and terror against elements of the population during the Great Purges. The tragedy of Soviet childhood took on acute forms; children were traumatized not only physically and emotionally: the policy of the state traumatized them psychologically. Children were stigmatized as "children of enemies of the people," "kulak children," and "children-enemies." Naturally, this tragedy was hardly the result of a war or some inevitable emergency that the government could not avoid. Many children were not orphans and had one or both living parents, but the state forcibly separated them from their families. What principles did Stalin's regime follow, if not *Realpolitik*?

The anthologies *Children of the Gulag* and *Silence Was Salvation: Children Surviving the Stalinist Terror* provide excellent primary sources of information about the Siberian special settlements where families of "enemies of the people" were resettled in the 1930s along with their children.[8] The editor of *Silence Was Salvation*, historian Cathy Frierson, writes that the children's population of the GULAG suffered from state oppression and lived in miserable conditions, a version that seriously disputes the official Soviet notion of a "happy childhood." Nevertheless, state oppression began long before Stalin took power. Under Stalin, children's tragedy continued and received an even uglier impetus.

As previous chapters illustrated, in 1928 the government began collectivization of agriculture and the attending expropriation (dekulakization or *raskulachivanie*) campaign. Both violent and repressive campaigns hit children in the rural areas hard. Both campaigns involved arrests, deportations, and executions without trial; affected numerous peasant families; and sparked significant popular protest that involved children. Conditions in collective and state farms' villages were often life-threatening. Collectivization led to widespread famine in virtually all rural areas it affected.[9]

Local intelligence agencies from most rural areas of the Soviet Union reported widespread famine, children's homelessness, and poverty from the late 1920s throughout the 1930s. It should be noted that these reports were classified as secret or top secret and prohibited from public circulation. No one could publicly discuss or mention the issues of children's homelessness and starvation. The deterioration of material conditions of most of the population prompted the state to scrutinize the data gathering system. All negative information about economic and social conditions and the living standards of the population, including data on wages and nutrition, as well as the level of supplies of basic necessities, housing, etc., became "top" secret and closed to the public. The Statistics Records Committee directives of 1927 and 1928 listed as top secret and secret much data and proposed "drastic measures to combat all forms of negligence" of the maintenance of confidential information.[10] Thus, for researchers of the Stalinist period, there is an obstacle to an objective assessment of the period, since the balance of primary sources is upset in favor of those that are in the public domain, and many top secret classified documents still remain unavailable.

The authors of the available confidential letters were local OGPU—United State Political Office—agents and the reports were addressed to the regional and central organs of the OGPU and NKVD, in fact, punitive and coercive institutions. What requires an emphasis here is that these local Soviet security services primarily looked for potential threats to the state security and public order. Here, to provide an historical and comparative context, we must remind the reader that during the imperial times, hunger and homelessness were in fact viewed as humanitarian issues and areas of responsibility and concern of the government, of the community, and of church charities, as explored in Chapter 1. After all, the tsarist secret police never dealt with starving and homeless children. It seems that the Stalinist state continued to view these problems instead as political and cared more about the implications for state security and how to keep the problems under the control of the state than about the people in need themselves, continuing its repressive and expropriatory policies. Of note here is that close examination of both late imperial and Stalinist social practices will put into question some recent assumptions or outright assertions about neo traditionalism during the latter period.

Starvation and Diseases

Children's misery continued during Stalin's reign. Stalin's collectivization led to a humanitarian catastrophe that Russia had not seen even in 1920–1. According to a classified report from 1933,

> Over the last May, June, and July months, in cities and in several districts of our region, there is a large increase in children's homelessness. As a result of the removal of street children from the street, existing orphanages are overcrowded ... The flow of street children to the cities continues. Children are coming from the regions of the Lower Volga, Ukraine, and Central Asia. Most of the incoming children are extremely malnourished; among them there are deaths due to malnutrition. Further admission of children to orphanages is completely impossible.[11]

As an urgent solution to this issue, the government demanded that village councils and collective farms support all former street children and orphans sent to them earlier.[12] This was required, of course, unreasonably, for the starving villagers could hardly feed themselves. Not only were people subjected to humiliation, starvation, and dispossession, they suffered from numerous diseases, of which children were the most susceptible group.

Starvation during the 1930s caused severe health issues, especially mental disorders, a matter that deserves more attention than it has received. In medicine, starvation is defined as a severe deficit in caloric energy, below the level necessary to sustain the body's activity. This is an extreme form of malnutrition. For humans, prolonged starvation can cause permanent organ damage and, ultimately, death. In addition to physical pathologies, starvation causes acute psychological disorders. The initial stages of starvation can affect mental health and behavior. The symptoms consist of an irritable mood, fatigue, trouble concentrating, and preoccupation with thoughts about food. People with these symptoms are easily distracted and lose energy. As starvation progresses, physical symptoms appear. The timing of these symptoms depends on age, weight, and general health conditions. One of the notable signs in infants and children is bloating. Thus, starving rural families could hardly perform their labor duties on collective and state farms.

Numerous classified reports informed central authorities about starvation and health conditions in the countryside. A secret memorandum of February 20, 1932, from a local OGPU agent reported to the central office about the living and health conditions of peasant families in the Volga region.[13] People had not had "a piece of bread for over a month" and developed related illnesses due to malnutrition. For example, a poor peasant woman, a candidate for the Communist Party of the Bolsheviks, and her two children were swollen from malnutrition. The peasant Ivan Semenovich Kamaev, "a candidate for the Communist Party of Bolsheviks, did not eat bread for a month and on January 5, 1932, to feed his family, he slaughtered his last cow." Poor peasant woman Fedosya Gavrilovna Alekseeva and her five children were swollen from malnutrition. The memorandum continued that in these villages some collective farmers quit their jobs and, despite being tied to livestock, left, while other collective farmers stayed, "indicating that if 'we leave here our families will starve to death'." The "members of the collective farm board and even party members are in a panic over this situation." Kolkhoz chairman Andrei Dmitrievich Sukhorukov, a party member, convened a general meeting of collective farmers on January 1, 1932, where he helped the latter choose a delegation and send to the local government petitions for the allocation of bread. In the village of Orlovskoye, "due to a lack of food in schools, the distribution of hot breakfasts to schoolchildren has stopped; in connection with this, many schoolchildren dropped out." In the same village, according to the memorandum,

> several agricultural workers and laborers worked all year round for the collective farm, did not retain any food for themselves, but instead handed it all over to the communal dining room. Now due to the absence of food, the diner was closed for more than a week, and these collective farmers were left without any food and had literally not a piece of bread.[14]

The memorandum also stated that recently, "due to the lack of food," the number of beggars asking for a piece of bread increased significantly. Many peasant families were surviving on surrogates and consumed rotten vegetables and meats that caused serious illnesses.[15] According to a letter to a local health department of the Volga region, "the mass of the people ate all kinds of garbage, not excluding carrion of animals, birds, etc."[16]

Similar facts about the absence of foodstuffs and widespread diseases were reported from numerous collective farms and regions. According to a March 1932 "special message" of the OGPU about the food situation in the Brodokalmak district of the Urals region, food shortages "were becoming even more aggravated." Due to starvation and malnutrition, as well as the consumption of hay, chaff, and other surrogates, a growing number of peasants suffer stomach diseases, tumors, etc. In some collective farms, the food shortage was so serious that collective farmers began to eat carrion, quinoa, spoiled food, and unsuitable bread substitutes. There was "no bread in the Potapov collective farm for three weeks," stated one message. Cases of tumors due to hunger were reported. On the collective farm of the village of Kirdy, the collective farmers ate oat bread, which caused a massive disease and tumors. "By now, the supply of oat bread has also run out, therefore the collective farmers, including schoolchildren, are starving."[17] Another top confidential OGPU report, dated March 9, 1932, informed about conditions in the Tatar Republic:

> Cases of illness, edema and, in some cases, death from hunger have been recorded. In the Alkeevsky district, a child died of hunger. The whole family of the collective farmer Khabibullin (three children and a wife) swelled from hunger. In the Aktash district in the village of Novoye Gireyevo, a collective farmer and his two children are starving; the children were swollen from malnutrition. In the Alkeevsky district in the village of Kargopol, collective farmer Bizhbov brought his child bloated from malnutrition to the village council, demanding bread. Bizhbov himself was also bloated.[18]

There were numerous extreme and extraordinary incidents. Desperate teenagers and adults killed small children for food. Cases of infanticide and cannibalism were recorded in many regions. The following shocking incident is described in a secret document of the chairman of the district committee of the Bolshevik Party, dated March 1933.

> In the village of Novopetrovskaya, two teenagers killed a neighbor boy of 8 years old, cooked, and intended to eat him. The mother collective farmer, having come home from work, caught them doing this. These teenagers had also intended to slaughter their younger brothers and sisters, according to their confession. While the slaughtered boy was being cooked, they consumed fresh meat from his corpse.[19]

In one memorandum, the authorized representative of the OGPU for the Central Black Earth Region of Russia informed the regional committee of the All-Union Communist Party of Bolsheviks about a case of cannibalism in the village of Bogoslovka on June 20, 1933.

Top secret. In the first days of June, in the village of Bogoslovka, Rasskazovsky district, a poor collective farm woman, Zh.M.I., for the purpose of eating, killed her daughter Antonina at the age of 1 year 6 months, which she ate for 6 days ... Zh. was arrested, and the OGPU district apparatus is investigating the case.[20]

It is generally assumed that the most acute starvation happened in Stalin's USSR during 1932–3, but in fact it seems starvation continued throughout the entire decade of the 1930s and became endemic. Many classified reports to the central intelligence and party authorities came throughout the 1930s and the government did not respond to people's needs. According to a classified report from March 1934, in the Chelyabinsk region, in some places, the food shortages and starvation aggravated. The report informed about facts of illness, swelling, and death from hunger.

In the Singul collective farm of the Yalutorovsk region in November-December 1933, 12 people died of starvation; in January 1934, 10 people died. Similar facts have been noted in several other collective farms in the region.[21]

Members of collective farms "Krasny Putilovets," "Krasnye Eagles," "Progress," "Peredovik," "Young grain grower," "Bolshevik," and others of Mokrousovsky district eat exclusively surrogates. Over thirty cases of stomach diseases and eleven cases of death due to hunger were recorded. The facts of eating surrogates and the growth of diseases on this basis were also noted in Shumikhinsky, Dolmatovsky, Uporovsky, Kopeysky, Nagaybaksky, and other regions.[22] A 1937 top secret report from a head of the 5th department of the 4th department of the State Security Agency informs that in the Mordovian Autonomous Republic, in the Kochkurovsky, Tengushevsky, Zubovo-Polyansky, Insarsky, Torbeevsky, Ruzaevsky, Atyashevsky, and Chamzinsky districts, there were more than 135 families of collective farmers (from three to eleven people per family), who were surviving exclusively on surrogates and meat from animal corpses. In these families, twenty-nine people were swollen. In the Chelyabinsk region, in the village of Verkhniy Zhukovsky, children of collective farmer Krivoshchekova were swollen from malnutrition, and Krivoshchekova died. In the collective farm "Krasnaya Zarya" of the Shmakovsky village council of the Mostovsky district, the family of the collective farmer Krashakov of six people were swollen from malnutrition. Some collective farmers of the collective farm Rodina, Kurtamysh district, ate the meat of fallen dogs.[23]

As mentioned, famine severely damaged the health of many peasants, both adults and children. Since most rural people starved during Stalin's collectivization, one may assume that many peasants suffered mental or physical disorders. Most of these peasants could hardly perform their required labor errands on collective farms. Local NKVD agents reported numerous facts of "categorical refusals of collective farmers to go to work on the grounds that they are hungry, exhausted, and unable to perform any physical work." The reports spoke about massive absenteeism (60–70 percent of the total number of collective farmers) in Chelyabinsk province. On the "Put' Oktyabrya" (October's Road) collective farm in the Urals region, a group of collective farmers categorically refused to work, demanding the distribution of grain. Poor peasant Balandina from the Zverinogolovsky district complained that

> It's unbearable to continue living. There is not only no bread, but even no chaff. In a week I'll hang my children, then they'll put me in prison and that's better. In prison, at least 400 grams of bread will still be given. There is nothing else to do, it's a pity to look at the children, how they suffer.

Classified reports from local GPU and NKVD agents revealed seemingly decadent sentiments and dissatisfaction with soviet power and ascribed it to the ill influence and agitation of the kulaks and other and anti-Soviet elements.[24] A classified local NKVD report stated in 1936 that group of kulaks on the collective farm "The Way of the Peasant" of the Kolyvan Village Council, composed of Stepanov, Likhanov—the latter was previously expelled from the ranks of the CPSU (b)—systematically conducted anti-Soviet agitation, persuading the collective farmers not to go to work, saying:

> "Is it possible to work without bread and stripped naked, let's quit work," "The Soviet government with these collective farms is going to ensure that we die of hunger, look, we worked in the spring and autumn, and the result—our bread was taken from us, and they themselves were forced to sit hungry, we must leave the collective farm."[25]

Documents reveal facts that the kolkhoz regime treated its members harshly. The authorities paid no attention to health issues and had no sympathy with the sick peasants since they considered as anti-Soviet anyone who refused to work for medical reasons. Regardless of their health condition, most collective farmers were forced to work in order to get a workday, known as *"trudoden"* that would guarantee them some food. Those who could not work received no *"trudoden"* and, therefore, no compensation from their collective farms which further exacerbated their situation.

Regardless of starvation in the countryside and facing the problem of overcrowding in children's homes, the government required village councils and collective farms to provide care of all orphans brought up on the territory of collective farms at the expense of the collective farms and their mutual aid funds to prevent the children from leaving for cities and the streets.[26]

Child Labor Instead of Schooling

As noted earlier, Krupskaya justified child labor as a means for proper socialist upbringing, necessary for education. In the same spirit, local rural and kolkhoz authorities required children to work. Just as children worked in labor camps, they worked in kolkhozes and state farms. Sources and documents illustrate that kolkhozes exploited child labor. The communist children organization's (Pioneers) newspaper *"Pionerskaya Pravda"* was full of letters similar to the one sent to the newspaper by pioneer Dmitriev:

We, guys 12–15 years old, work 13 hours a day on a par with adults. We often must do a lot of work and the pay is unequal. We are paid half or even a third for the same work as adults.[27]

The general prosecutor's office received reports from several regions and territories. The reports reported widespread use of labor of children under 14 in collective farms. At the same time, the length of children's workdays, as a rule, was equal to the length of the adult workday. In some cases, children worked at night. Many children who constantly worked on collective farms did not attend schools.[28]

Children were used in difficult and hazardous jobs. For example, in the Belgorod district of Kursk region, in 1938, 473 minors worked on twenty-eight collective farms and ninety-six working children were under 12. The children worked on a par with adults, cleaning tractor trailers, transporting grain, stacking, and at night. There were many reported cases of work-related injuries among children. In most cases, minors worked ten to twelve hours a day. In this district, forty-five children did not attend school. In the Gryazinsky district of the Voronezh region, 685 children under the age of 14 worked. In the Ivanovsky district of the Dnepropetrovsk region, 247 children worked in nineteen collective farms. Their workday was ten to twelve hours; 114 children between the ages of 10 and 14 did not attend school. In the Koloyarsky district of the Georgian Soviet Socialist Republic, 117 teenagers worked in thirteen collective farms. The duration of their workday was from seven to ten hours. Some reports noted that "parents of 27 adolescents lead a parasitic lifestyle at the expense of the labor of their children." They themselves worked a little and write down the workdays worked out by their children.[29]

The same facts were reported in other regions. The practice of calculating the workdays of adolescents and children varied in collective farms. In some collective farms, workdays were counted for minors and in others, for their parents. In the instructions, the attorney generals considered it necessary to prohibit the use of child labor at night and work harmful to their health, as well as to establish regulations for hiring children (in their free time from school), the length of the workday, and the procedure for paying children.[30]

It is doubtful that the initiative to use child labor in farms came from below. Bolshevik theorists justified child labor by insisting that under the Soviet system— "under workers' rule,"—any exploitation was completely ruled out, since workers' power did not exploit labor. For them, under the workers' government, the work is joyful and rewarding. Therefore, even in the Soviet constitution there was an article on labor: labor is the right and honorable duty of every citizen of the country. Krupskaya, in her speech at the VII Congress of the RLKSM, "Four directions of pioneer work," expressed the view that "under serfdom [children] worked uncontrollably, under capitalism they worked out of fear of hunger, now it is necessary that the work be conscious, cohesive, cooperative." Thus, the Soviet government wanted to regulate child labor, but not to eliminate it. Meanwhile, some rural children fled to cities and urban areas trying to escape exploitation, starvation, deportations, or repressions.

The highly publicized slogan "education for the masses" that the Bolsheviks used since 1918 proved to be a fiction. By analogy with the early 1920s, many children were not able to complete school because they were starving. Faced with a shortage of basic foodstuffs, rural children were often forced to interrupt school attendance—as testified to by well-informed reports from various primary sources. For example, in a letter from the Opochetsk rural district, Pskov province (February 27, 1929), peasants wrote to a Leningrad newspaper, *Krestyanskaya Gazeta,* that "many thousands of residents of our Opochetsk district are starving. School-age children drop out of school because of the lack of bread …"[31]

Despite the introduction of universal education, which everywhere met the approval of all sections of the collectivized and non-collective peasantry, in reality many parents could not send their children to schools due to hunger and other factors. According to one classified report, "peasants complained about the lack of shoes and clothes, which deprived their own and foster-care children of the physical opportunity to study in schools." Especially great dissatisfaction was caused by fines for parents of children who could not attend school due to hunger and lack of shoes and clothes. Paradoxically, the Soviet government fined the poorest social segments for problems the government caused. Examples of such a relationship are numerous: a classified NKVD memo from village Kalinovka of the Proskurovsky district of the Central Black-earth region of Russia reported that

> a kolkhoz member, a poor man, brought a half-dressed child to the village council and said: 'Here is my student, see if he can go to school like that. Take these 2 rubles. Well, and when you find yourself in my position, buy yourself a rope with this money and hang yourself.'[32]

The same is noted in the settlement of Zarud'e, where most parents did not want to send their children to school. They stated, "If we are not given clothes and shoes, we will not send our children to school."[33]

Kulak Children

The situation of kulak children was one of the most discussed topics in the letters and complaints from expropriated peasants to the authorities. For example, in a memorandum of the Council of People's Commissars of April 3, 1930, summarizing the peasant complaints and statements, it was noted that

> considerable attention in letters of the expropriated peasants is paid to the situation of their children, since in light of the confiscations of all property and food, they, in their opinion, are doomed to death, especially since in some areas peasants could not even shelter the dispossessed kulaks for a night because they fear falling into the category of kulaks. There are also reports that kulaks are leaving their children at village councils.[34]

In the spring of 1930, in his letter to Stalin, Oryol agronomist K. Gorodetsky painted a striking picture of the fate of children from the repressed "kulak" families in the Orel province. He wrote that "household heads often leave their families, leaving behind a bunch of children to fend for themselves, literally without any means of subsistence." The authorities classified the peasant innkeeper as a kulak and dispossessed him of all his property:

> He took his horse and left at night to no one knows where, leaving his wife, a former peasant worker, and three children from 7 to 3 years old. I am not soft, not a whiner, not mumbling, and I take this dispossession soberly as inevitable, but I cannot look at children in such a situation cold-bloodedly, they are not to blame, these hungry creatures, that their parent is a scoundrel and that everything is taken from this family, including the cow. As a spouse of a dispossessed person, his wife was denied employment and was given nothing ... Iosif Vissarionovich, urgent measures are needed to protect children, Il'ich [Lenin] would not overlook this fact in silence, I think you will not do so either.[35]

Gorodetsky's last words to Stalin reflected hope rather than faith or love for Stalin. He hoped to convince the leader and appealed to his conscience.

In addition to the economic impacts, Stalin's collectivization of agriculture and the concomitant deprivation of property from peasant families also had profound social and psychological consequences and exacerbated relations in society in general and in kulak families in particular. The social, economic, legal, and political position of kulak children depended on their loyalty to state politics. The family often came into conflict with the state system.[36]

A famous historical episode of this time comes from the shadowy story of Pavlik Morozov, a boy from eleven to fifteen years old. According to the criminal case, in the early 1930s Morozov tested in court against his father. He reported to the local OGPU that his father and other paternal relatives were kulaks, saboteurs, and enemies of the Soviet state. In response, the "enemies of the state," his paternal relatives, killed the boy along with his younger brother. His father, uncles, grandparents, and other relatives were subsequently arrested and executed or sent to labor camps. Later, according to the official and widely publicized Soviet version, the story of Pavlik Morozov represented class struggle in the countryside and the hostility of the younger generation toward the parents of their class enemies. The Soviet state declared Pavlik Morozov a hero and a role model for other Soviet children. According to another version, the illiterate boy Pavlik Morozov reported about his father, who had left the family, at his mother's direction, who hoped that this would force her husband to reunite with his family.

Historian and journalist Yuri Druzhnikov put forward one more version, namely, that Pavel Morozov was killed by the OGPU for the political purpose of toughening the fight against kulaks and accelerating collectivization.[37] But this version caused outrage from the maternal family relatives of Morozov and his teacher. Cambridge University Professor Catriona Kelly, who worked in the FSB archives, concluded that the official version of Morozov's murder was correct.[38] Kelly's findings are supported by a number of other historians and journalists.

Be that as it may, Morozov's case continues to live its own life: it arose out of hatred, and it continues to cause disagreements and conflicts. In 1999, Morozov's paternal relatives and representatives of the human rights movement Memorial filed an appeal that requested rehabilitative consideration of this case in court, but the Prosecutor General's Office concluded that the murderers had been reasonably convicted and could not be rehabilitated for political reasons. The story of Pavlik Morozov became an example of a personality cult of a Soviet pioneer hero who sacrificed his life in a struggle against the enemies of the state and in the name of a new society. Regardless, Pavlik Morozov's story suggests the abnormality of Stalinist society.

As in any religion, cults serve to strengthen beliefs: Soviet cults served to inspire heroic deeds in the name of society, the state, the party, or even Stalin himself. Nevertheless, Morozov himself fell victim to Stalinist manipulation and terror, and was likely a child who faced all the tragedies that most rural children endured during the collectivization campaign. According to historian Irina Goncharova, psychological uncertainty, the need for internal, personal choice, and the adjustment to new Stalinist values were complex and had perhaps the most dramatic consequences for children from expropriated families. If adolescents abandoned their parents and relied instead on a relationship with state authorities, the little kids, after the loss of the head of the family, were left to fend for themselves and were likely doomed to starvation.[39]

Generational Conflict

As Pavlik Morozov's case exemplifies, the Stalinist state manipulated children and used propaganda to encourage generational conflict by turning children against parents who did not fit into the Stalinist human engineering project. Propaganda and incitement to generational conflict became instruments of Stalin's *realpolitik*. The state called on Komsomol members to take an active part in all state activities, including dubious ones. The state relied on youth Komsomol detachments to carry out collectivization and dispossession. In particular, young Komsomol members were required to participate in identifying "malicious kulak" elements, to assist the relevant authorities in taking appropriate measures against them, to expel "hooligan kulak youth" from the regions, to monitor confiscated property, etc. The authorities recommended the creation of shock groups made up of the most persistent and cold-blooded Komsomol members to help district executive committees, the prosecutor's office, and GPU to carry out repressions. (One might call this class conflict run amok.)

Often, young people, Komsomol members, faced with reality, were confused and uncertain. As discussed earlier, in most cases there were no rich kulak peasants, although the state required the execution of "kulak" dispossession orders. On February 18, 1930, at a closed meeting of the Mikhailovskaya Komsomol cell, when discussing the report on dispossession of kulaks, young Komsomol members asked questions: "Why are they now dispossessed? Where to evict them? What to do with children?" It is clear that the tasks and methods of dispossession were incomprehensible to these Komsomol members. The orders of the central authorities, as a rule, consisted of general phrases, as a consequence of which specific activities were determined on the spot, depending on the mood of the performers. It got to the point that in the spring of 1930, during a meeting, to the question "What to do with the family of the evicted kulak?" a Komsomol activist replied: "Destroy to the last baby."[40]

Deported Childhood

Another dark aspect of Stalin's childhood policies were the deportations of children within the so-called campaigns for resettlement of the kulak families plus the purges that occurred during the 1930s. With or without their parents, hundreds of thousands (if not millions) of Soviet children were deported from their homes to other regions, mostly distant areas of the Soviet Russian northeast and Siberia. In fact, their numbers are difficult to calculate because of the very high mortality rate in the special settlement areas and the inadequate statistics. What can be said for sure is that the children's population in Stalin's GULAG was considerable.

Residents of the cities and regions where the exiles were sent were indignant at this depressing, nightmarish situation. "If the parents are to blame," wrote a group of Vologda residents in 1930, "punish them [the parents], but if it's not possible to leave the children, expel them [with the parents], but so that it doesn't hurt the children."

> They sent their exiles into terrible frosts—infants and pregnant women who rode in cattle cars on top of each other and right there the women gave birth to their children (isn't this a mockery); then they threw them out of the wagons like dogs, and placed them in churches and dirty, cold sheds, where there was nowhere to move. They keep them half-starved, covered in mud, lice, cold and hunger, and here are thousands of children left to the mercy of fate, like dogs that no one wants to pay attention to. It is not surprising that 50 people and more die every day (in Vologda alone) and soon the number of these innocent children will frighten people—it has now already exceeded three thousand.[41]

In a letter to M. I. Kalinin, the exiles to the Arkhangelsk region asked the head of the Soviet state if he was aware of the fact that "defenseless children from two weeks and older" were also moved with their parents and suffered in completely unsuitable barracks, because, "when we were settled in the barracks, they had five *vershkov* [almost 9 inches] of snow and ice?" The authors complained that there was "absolutely no hygiene for these very defenseless children."[42]

According to official data of the department for Special Settlers of the GULAG of the OGPU, "Information about the evicted kulaks in 1930–1931," 381,026 families for a total number of 1,803,392 people were sent to special settlements during these years. Since the kulaks were usually *edinolichniki* (individual farmers) and had a nuclear family, a typical kulak family consisted of two adults and several children. Thus, within these 381,026 families, there were 762,052 (42 percent) adults and 1,041,340 (about 58 percent) children. Other state data suggests that the eviction of the kulaks, albeit on a much smaller scale, continued in 1932–3. According to the official report, there were 1,142,084 kulaks in "kulak" special settlements in 1933. The difference between the official data for 1930–1 and 1933 is striking. What happened to other settlers, mostly children, relocated in 1931–2?

It can be assumed that the Stalinist resettlement and the GULAG affected both adults and children. Children, however, as a vulnerable and dependent social group, suffered the most from the GULAG. The following table presents the official secret report of the Siberian Regional Health Administration to the Commissariat of Health for December 1932 in the Siberian GULAG.

Table 1 Special settlers in Siberian GULAG in December 1932.[43]

SibLAG regions	Number of settlements	The number of people				Total
		Men	Women	Children to 12	Teenagers (12 to 16)	
Northern	381	34,915	39,156	51,780	16,626	142,477
Southern	119	28,362	23,906	26,287	8,046	86,601
Totals	500	63,277	63,062	78,067	24,672	229,078

According to this table, in December 1932, the Siberian branch of Stalin's GULAG hosted 229,078 settlers, of which 45 percent were children under 16 and 55 percent were adults. The data on death among children in Stalin's GULAG is fragmentary. Nevertheless, the available figures may suggest very high mortality rates. For example, in July 1932 there were 982 deaths among children under 16, and in August 1932, 529 deaths.[44] Assuming that in 1932, the average number of deaths might be as high as 755 per month, the number of deaths among children under 16 might, for that year alone, be as high as 9,060.

The Stalinist government hoped to settle the unpopulated areas of taiga and tundra but demarcated places for special settlements with considerable negligence. Many areas were located in swamps or permafrost, had no infrastructure, and were completely unsuitable for human inhabitance. It turns out that the only infrastructure that existed there were local NKVD premises with punitive, supervisory, and some medical facilities. As a result, from 1930 to 1934, at least a quarter of the families of special settlers to Western Siberia who had survived, were subjected to a new resettlement to other areas, that may also have been hostile to human living, just like the previous ones. Again, behind all these state actions, there were human destinies and tragedies of Soviet adults and children.

Documents from these regions are shocking. Most deported people suffered, but children of all ages suffered the most. Mortality rates were terrifying. As noted by the historian V. Zemskov, the first years after arrival in the special settlements were especially difficult due to climate change and harsh living conditions for everyday survival. The reader must be reminded that the resettlement was not voluntary, and it was the Stalinist state's decision to relocate adults and children from their habitual homes to areas that were uninhabitable and unsuitable for living. This fact alone led to an immense increase in morbidity and mortality.

According to the Magnitogorsk City Health Department alone, for one central village, 591 children ages 0–3 years, 174 ages 3–8, and 10 ages 8–14 (775 total) died within three months in 1930. A memorandum from the head of the Ust-Yagilyat paramedic station of the Kulay commandant's GULAG office of the Novosibirsk region of May 31, 1930, reported that kulak children of all ages were in a terrible situation.[45] This settlement was located on the territory of the Vasyugan swamps, and the area was totally unsuitable for habitation. The official stated that "settlement's children from 2 months to 7 years old are left without milk, meat, sugar, fat, and cereals. The bread and rye rations were insufficient and there occurs the complete extinction of children."

The official asked the state authorities to provide at least sugar or cereal for children who could not suckle at the mother's breast if mothers did not have milk in their breasts [because of malnutrition] and the child remained only on water. According to the official, diseases of the gastrointestinal tract were widespread among children due to maternal hunger. He had many visitors who were asking for help, but it was very difficult to reach to the responsible persons in charge of supplies. He requested urgent action on this matter:

> I think you can send 500 boxes of artificial milk and that would be good. And they arrive all the time asking to go home to their old districts, but vacation is not available for them, so then everyone is fired, but there are good reasons, such as women in labor in the snow who have already arrived on foot, and here it is freezing in the morning minus, −20 to −25 C degrees, and at least minus 10–15 C degrees during the day. I let some of them go to the nearest villages to allow for childbirth since dealing with women in labor and children is useless. Now, in some districts they have ordered building warm barracks where women give birth, and therefore we now have more or less well-being with births, although the nutrition of women in labor and children is bad.

As a result, in the summer of 1930, the punitive authorities were convinced that the Kulay commandant's settlement required immediate resettlement to other lands. Out of 9,000 originally settled settlers, adults, children, and infants, more than 6,000 had died or fled. The available materials testify to significant escapes that took place before the transfer of the economic structure of the special settlers to the jurisdiction of the OGPU. The secret review reported that

> the material and domestic disorder of the special settlers, the lack of food, the arbitrariness of the administration of economic bodies, and the prevailing opinion that they were [in fact] sent for physical destruction, to a large extent contributed to the development of escapes. An equally important factor in inducing them to escape was the separation of heads of families from their families and the lack of proper protection in special settlements.[46]

On the territory of the Urals region, in 1931, there were 128,755 families of special settlers for a total of 592,786 people. Housing construction was unsatisfactory or absent in many areas. Special settlers were placed in barracks, tents, dugouts, sheds, or housed with the local population [one wonders what the local population thought about this]. Their housing was extremely crowded and dirty, according to a classified report. The report also stated that special settlers were poorly supplied with food so that,

> in several regions, exiles are starving and eat various surrogates; there have been cases of death due to starvation. The supply of the disabled is especially bad. Medical care is not established. There is a lack of doctors, paramedics, and an almost complete absence of medicines. The existing network of medical institutions is insufficient, the construction of new ones is extremely slow.[47]

Nonetheless, despite these shocking facts, resettlement continued and there was no improvement in resettlers' conditions. According to a January 1933 classified report from Western Siberian GULAG,

> Special resettlement settlements are located exclusively in the uninhabited part of the region, mainly along the rivers originating in the Great Vasyugan swamp and flowing into the Ob River, such as: along the Vasyugan River and its tributaries, Parabel with tributaries, Chai with tributaries, etc. To the east of the Ob, special settlements are located along the Keti River with tributaries and the Chulyma River with tributaries. The Vasyugan, Parabel, Chaya, Ket, and Chulym rivers are navigable for a considerable distance, but there are no regular steamship communications; there are such only along the Ob and then every three or four days. The overwhelming majority of special settlements are located at a very remote distance not only from railway stations, but also from the piers on the Ob River. For example, in order to get to the Aipolovsky group of settlements, one has to drive 1134 km from Tomsk along the Ob and Vasyugan ... Among the settlers, 35.8 percent were children under 12.[48]

In August 1933, special settlement workers from Ampalyk (Western Siberia) wrote to the West Siberian Regional Workers' and Peasants' Inspectorate a complaint about their desperate situation and asked for protection. The complaints referred to a serious shortage of products received from the Tikheevskaya lumber office. The office provided their dependents for only 40 percent of the needed food. Non-working family members and children were given only 60 percent of the dependent ration supplemented with various herbs, "which are suitable for feeding animals, not people, for example, plantain, thistle, willow leaf, red and black currant leaves, raspberry leaves, nettles, quinoa, pity potato tops and a lot of other stuff." The workers, with irony or sarcasm, asked for clarification about "whether it is possible with the specified products to feed the flower of the future society—children, and [asserted] that such nutrition has a terrible effect on the health of children and the workers themselves." According to the complaint,

> Some children can hardly move on their feet and for the most part lie exhausted somewhere in the chill instead of playing and frolicking. Only bread and sugar are given to us. For dependents, 5 kilograms of flour and 300 grams of sugar. Current rations, we say, provides only 40 percent of what is necessary (we ask you to add at least another 5 kilograms of bread), more than that the office does not let us have. And also our working ration, due to the very large production rate required, we are all weakened from lack of nutrition, and even after having received bread (for workers without fail baked), it has to be divided into crumbs by the children, and there is bread with 60% admixture of various herbs, which is why we cannot work out the norms set, and the worker's ration goes down and down. We are already beginning to sway with the wind, as seriously ill, and because of this, the above mentioned, we have to commit crimes, go to nearby villages and carry the last things there to sell, and working in production, look somewhere on the

side of food for ourselves and the family, and by doing this, cause absenteeism, which again entails a deduction of an already meager ration for dependents and makes some special settlers decide to commit big crimes, that is, to escape from production to places where the supply of workers is better or simply where bread can be earned.[49]

The available data on mortality rates among children in special settlements is astonishing. For example, in the first quarter of 1934 in the southern (industrial) commandant's offices of the GULAG (Kuzbass coal and Kuznetsk construction) from 50 to 60 percent of children between 0 and 16 died.[50]

Special settlements also faced problems with providing education for settlers' children. In a letter to Krupskaya, the Karagai district of the Sverdlovsk region's school inspector complained that there are children of ninety-seven special settlers and these children live in various settlements at a distance of up to 40 kilometers from the center of the district. To support these children, the regional budget should receive 3,000 rubles a month or 9,000 rubles for the quarter, which was approved according to the budget, but in fact only 3,500 rubles were issued for children for the quarter. The author wrote that,

> the authorities do not send money, they do not pay attention to our needs, which causes to discontent. Our department of public education in 1937 transferred 5,000 rubles to Oblono for the manufacture of ready-made clothes; the funds belong to the children, but there are still no goods or money allocated. Meanwhile, the children have 1–2 pairs of underwear, and those are torn, and there is absolutely no way to buy anything in the area, because as soon as a store starts selling ready-made underwear that it receives, it sold out quickly; the store sells only up to ten meters per person, which for children is not enough. We [also] made a request and included an educational worker who works for us in the estimate, but the regional federal district did not fulfill our request, and educational work among the children under guardianship is not enough. This situation can no longer be tolerated, which made me write. For all the above issues, we ask you to provide us with meaningful assistance and try to influence the indicated local organizations (the district and local school boards), as well as provide clothes for children.[51]

"No person—no problem": The Stalinist Solution

"No person—no problem" can translate as "No subject—no problem," which reflects the Stalinist approach to the problem of children's homelessness and hunger. It is not at all clear whether Stalin ever uttered this phrase, but this supposedly Stalinist phrase was passed from mouth to mouth since the time of the "leader of the peoples" and reflected the public perception of Stalin. Some evidence suggests that in reality "no person—no problem" was Stalin's approach in dealing with problems. Former 2nd Deputy head of the NKVD and head of the border and internal troops of the NKVD

LVS, a member of the CPSU since 1917, Fomin Fedor Timofeevich, wrote in his letter to the central party control commission of the CPSU in November 1960:

> After inspecting the city, [of Leningrad in 1933] Stalin I.V. expressed dissatisfaction and as noted earlier, said: 'Kirov, you have littered the city with homeless children, homeless children are lying on all the streets, and you need to clear the city of this garbage.'[52] After this conversation, about seven thousand homeless children were taken out of Leningrad and sent to Siberia and other remote areas.[53]

Earlier, in August 1932, Stalin, in a letter to Kaganovich, wrote that

> outrageous things were happening on the railways. Employees along the line are raped and terrorized by hooligans and homeless children. The TO [Transportation Department of] GPU is sleeping (fact!). We can't tolerate this nonsense any longer. Call the TOGPU to establish order. Make him maintain order on the line. Give a directive to TOGPU to have armed people on the railway and shoot hooligans on the spot. Where is TOGPU? What is he doing? How can Comrade Blagonravov[54] endure all this anarchy and disgrace?[55]

It seems that the Stalinist motto—no man, no problem—was put into action. Previously, starting in the late 1920s, homeless children were collected from the streets of cities and sent out 101 kilometers. Now homeless children were subject to a legal ban. In 1935, the party and government put an end to children's homelessness with a decree officially ending the problem. The decree also suspended the activities of the Commission for the Improvement of Children's Lives.

With the introduction of this law, the state began to persecute and punish any mention or even photograph of homeless children. A very curious and tragic incident occurred in September 1937, when a certain citizen Kislova filed a complaint with the NKVD. In the complaint, Kislova stated that citizen Sapozhnikov allegedly had an ongoing relationship with foreign photojournalists and that he allegedly photographed queues at shops, as well as a group of homeless children on the street. Based on this statement, Sapozhnikov was arrested.[56]

Officially, if no children were on the streets, the problem of children's homelessness was absent. But had the issue been resolved? It definitely disappeared from official discourse, from public mention, from the media, not to mention from any type of research or investigation. Perhaps the number of street children decreased, but only because children became targets of detention, harassment, and arrests: the basic issues had not been addressed, much less resolved. Moreover, as mentioned, the Stalinist state viewed homeless children as criminal vagabonds and considered vagrancy a criminal offense. On October 26, 1935, in the Memorandum "On child homelessness, neglect, and crime" addressed to Stalin, the People's Commissar of Internal Affairs Yagoda stated that it would be wrong to pay attention, as did representatives of the People's Commissariat of Education, to the fight against homelessness. According to Yagoda, "An analysis of the materials at our disposal suggests that homelessness as a problem no longer faces the Soviet state." Yagoda emphasized that if earlier homelessness assumed enormous proportions as a result of the First World War and the Civil War, the famine in the Volga region, and the liquidation of the kulaks as a class, now there were no such conditions for mass homelessness in the country. The document stated that by that time "... unemployment has been eliminated [and] when the material security of the working people had improved significantly, there is no and cannot be an influx of homeless children." Further, the people's commissar noted that it was not a matter of homelessness, but of the poor performance of the children's institutions of the People's Commissariat of Education. They lacked proper order and control over the pupils who fled from them, joining the ranks of street criminals. The practice of combating juvenile delinquency showed that children who committed serious crimes were mostly neglected ones. The memorandum also indicated that the number of unattended, neglected children was incomparably greater than the number of homeless street children. The document noted that the established practice of combating juvenile delinquency with the help of commissions on juvenile affairs did not produce any significant results. Yagoda pointed to the need to revise the entire educational system, reorganize orphanages, and eliminate commissions for juvenile affairs. In addition, Yagoda insisted on the need to toughen punishment for minors and to create special children's courts.[57]

Stalinist Hardliners

Earlier government's documents, for internal use, reveal that these decisions resulted from the recognition that the organizations involved in solving children's homelessness and delinquency failed to achieve their mission. In a secret OGPU memorandum "On measures to combat banditry, hooliganism, and theft" of April 19, 1934, Deputy Chairman of the OGPU Heinrich Yagoda wrote to Stalin:

> The issue of combating homelessness is especially acute. Despite the huge funds spent on this goal—over 261 million [rubles] in the [Soviet] Union (more than 35 million [rubles] per year are spent in the Moscow region alone),—the issue has not yet been resolved and homelessness continues to be quite high. According to inaccurate data, in twenty territories and regions alone there are 56 thousand homeless children, of which about 60% are over 12 years old. Being essentially a negative phenomenon, homelessness serves as a constant source of replenishment of new cadres of criminal elements. Every day the police detain thousands of street children caught in the act of crime in cities and workers' settlements. However, this does not lead to anything, because, according to the law, they cannot be kept in custody, and children's homes do not accept them. Homeless children who end up in orphanages, due to the ugly state of the latter (lack of a production base and educational work, insensitive attitude towards children), run away and continue to commit crimes.[58]

Earlier, on April 7, 1934, Yagoda informed Stalin that juvenile delinquency and homelessness remained serious problems in most regions and required urgent attention.

According to Yagoda, available materials of the OGPU refer to numerous homeless children who were not removed from the street. Yagoda's statistics reveal 56,372 teenagers, including 14,000 girls, in twenty regions and territories. The predominant age was 10 and older, while 40 percent were children under 12, and 60 percent were adolescents 12 and older. In his reports to Stalin, Yagoda noted the growth of children's homelessness and criminality in 1931–4.[59] Yagoda's memorandums signaled a turning point in the state's attitude toward children's homelessness. Now the state was seriously determined to eradicate the problem in the most decisive and radical way, which in essence corresponded to Bolshevik *realpolitik*.

Earlier, in 1931, the Central Commission on Juvenile Affairs was liquidated; and in 1935, all local commissions working with juvenile offenders, as well as the Children's Commission of VTsIK, were closed. The hearings of all cases of juvenile crimes were again referred to criminal courts. At the same time, the norms of punishment for children were tightened: in accordance with the 1935 decree "On measures to combat juvenile delinquency" for theft, violence, bodily harm, mutilation, murder, or attempted murder, a criminal punishment applied only to children who at the time of the crime were 12 years or old. In the future, incitement and counter-revolutionary activities were ranked among especially grave crimes, for which immediate punishment followed. In such cases, the activities of minor children could be considered counter-revolutionary. In 1935, the Criminal Code was amended to provide for the use of the death penalty as a punishment for children who reached age 12. This new provision stated that

> Minors who have reached the age of twelve, convicted of committing theft, violence, bodily harm, mutilation, murder, or attempted murder, are brought to a criminal court with the application of all punishments. [November 25, 1935 (SU 1936, No 1, Art. 1)]

A secret note to this provision explained that the former article 22 of the Criminal Code of the Russian Republic, which prohibited the application of the death penalty to minors under the age of 18, was invalid.[60] The November 1935 provision can be considered a turning point that completed a change in course toward children: If in the 1920s, the emphasis was mainly on educational and pedagogical activities, then in the 1930s it was on arrests, imprisonment, and repression. In the 1920s, ideas and experiments with various forms of children's institutions and communes were entertained by the People's Commissariat of Education; and all sorts of ideas in the spirit of upbringing and re-education of the "new man" prevailed. To the contrary, in the 1930s even the fight against children's homelessness often turned into a war against children.

How these laws were applied is very difficult to judge because of the fragmentary sources. In his book on Stalin's secret crimes, former NKVD officer and Soviet intelligence agent, who resided in Spain, Alexander Orlov (Leyb Lazarevich Fel'dbin) writes:

> I learned that back in 1932, when hundreds of thousands of homeless children, driven by hunger, clogged railway stations and large towns, Stalin secretly issued

an order: those who were captured looting food warehouses or engaging in theft from railway cars, as well as those caught a venereal disease, were to be shot. Executions were to be carried out in secret. As a result of these mass executions and other "administrative measures" by the summer of 1934, the problem of street children was resolved in a purely Stalinist spirit.[61]

How to take Orlov's account? It may be viewed with skepticism. But, given the historical record of dealing with street children, and knowing the cruelty of the time and the "leader of the peoples," one can accept that such unwritten decrees could have existed. The author of these memoirs himself had no reason to slander Stalin's policy toward homeless children. Given his biography and merits, one can to some degree rely on the veracity of his words.[62]

The historiography of Stalinism normally distinguishes between hard and soft policies. Although I have not been able to trace any kind of soft attitude toward street children under Stalin, it is important to note that harsh policies toward homeless children depended very much on the personality and existence of Stalin himself—as soon as he was gone, this policy disappeared. An interesting fact from the history of this 1935 law: It was repealed immediately after Stalin's death (March 5, 1953) on March 27, 1953, when a decree on rehabilitation and amnesty was adopted. Criminal liability for many offenses had been mitigated. The age of criminal responsibility was raised to 16 for felony and 14 for misdemeanors.[63]

Stalin's Children's Homes

Since the mid-1930s, in connection with tightened state policy in relation to street and neglected children, the government began to create special enclosed children's institutions. The management of these children's correctional institutions also changed. Children's isolators, pre-trial detention centers, and correctional labor colonies were transferred to the jurisdiction of the NKVD. The state completed a legislative framework for these special children's penitentiary institutions. Internal affairs bodies were assigned the task of performing punitive functions in order to eliminate homelessness, neglect, and delinquency among minors. The direction of activities of children's labor colonies also changed. If in the 1920s these were children's communes of an agricultural or industrial orientation, now they were transformed into corrective labor colonies. Paradoxically, in a supposedly "workers' state," labor became a form of punishment and a means of correction. The functional focus of children's reception centers was the filtration of homeless and neglected minors with their subsequent direction to the appropriate educational institutions, medical institutions, or labor colonies of the NKVD.

Continuing from the 1920s, children's homes were in fact labor camps, where the realities were distant from widely publicized versions issued by state authorities. Conditions in children's labor camps, colonies, and other childcare institutions were usually inhumane and dangerous because of the lack of resources and simple negligence from their personal. Descriptions from classified top secret documents often point to poor sanitary conditions in these establishments.

As during the previous decade, children's homelessness never ended and often remained growing problem, according to numerous reports. A local educational official from the Middle Volga area reported that

> for the last May, June, July, in cities and in several districts of our region there is a large increase in children's homelessness. As a result of the removal of street children from the streets, the existing orphanages are overcrowded. Instead of the budgeted contingent of 7,370 children, as of July 1, 1933, there is a contingent of 9,123 pupils. There is overcrowding in orphanages of Samara, Ulyanovsk, Kuznetsk, etc. Additional funds for children's institutions for the maintenance of children in excess of the established contingent were not released. The maintenance of these children came at the expense of the worsening of the already difficult financial situation in children's institutions. The arrival of homeless children in the cities continue. Children come from the regions of the Lower Volga, Ukraine, and Central Asia. Most of the incoming children are extremely malnourished, among which there are cases of death due to malnutrition. Further admission of children to orphanages is completely impossible. Even now, children are housed in unequipped working barracks, sheds, etc. (Samara, Ulyanovsk).[64]

One report about a children's labor camp under the NKVD's jurisdiction mentioned the cold restroom "that spread the smell throughout the inmates' bedrooms." The toilets had ice on their seats, so the inmates "have set up a toilet in their bedroom right on the floor." The report continues:

> The floors were covered with dirt. Linens were changed only once a month and only once month children were taken to the bathhouse. The children were dirty and looked to be covered with lice. The camp provided no education and had no instructors to give lessons.[65]

This labor camp contained workshops that were supposed to teach children skills, but it was poorly equipped with inadequate tools. The reports usually describe the inmates of children's colonies as slovenly, with scarce clothes, and dirty faces.

Another description[66] revealed that the children's dorms were filthy dirty:

> dirt in the rooms, stoves full of soot, on floors layers of dust. The toilets were dirty. Children had lice. Too few beds: 8 children sleep in twos on beds. There are few toys and constant fights for them. There were no teaching aids, no books. There are no duvet covers on the beds. Even the nutrition of the children is insufficient. Food is given to all 3 times a day. By order of the district, breakfast for children at noon was canceled, because supposedly the children "overeat." During the inspection, the kids licked their plates with their tongues and got into fight over bread. For dinner, the children were given solid buckwheat porridge,

with almost no oils. Educational work is missing. In the evening, the guys sit in the semi-darkness – there are not enough lamps and kerosene is not always available. In this orphanage, there are 13 schoolchildren, but they do not attend school. Unsanitary conditions throughout the entire orphanage. Children are dirty, lousy, ragged, barefoot. There is dirt in the dining room. Educational work is missing. Even in children's homes, children often received no education or practical training.

In his report to Stalin, the NKND head Yagoda stated

that, the main disadvantage of the state of children's institutions is the wrong methods of organizing the upbringing of the child and youth environment, aggravated by the poor selection of workers. Frequent abuse of children by personnel and its insensitive attitude towards children lead to massive cases of children escaping from foster homes and returning to criminal activity.[67]

According to the commissar, the following examples were especially characteristic in the Saratov territory, where in the winter, several children's homes were not heated and the children in these homes got frostbite (Atkarsk, Petrovsk). Most institutions were crowded and dirty.[68]

Yagoda explained that for these reasons, homeless children fled. In the Tatar Republic, there were cases in the Laishevsky orphanage where children diagnosed with typhus did not receive hot food for two months and for seven days received no care and, as a consequence, died. In the Leningrad region, there were 2,123 children in the city's quarantine and distribution point for street children, which was designed for 800 inmates. According to a report, children sleep three people per bed. Yagoda wrote that "the state of children's institutions causes concern that with the onset of summer they may be the main source of replenishment of homeless children. All this calls for decisive action."[69] No evidence of "decisive action" exists in the records.

It seems that the government failed to improve the situation with children's labor colonies, as evidenced by numerous documents and orders. A document from 1938 reveals that according to the Department of Labor Colonies of the NKVD of the USSR, juvenile labor colonies receive numerous convicts between the ages of 12 and 16 for whom there was no precise data on their identity, place of birth, residence, and age.[70] One of the reasons may have been the very perception of these children as mentally retarded criminals, deserving nothing better. The camps were poorly funded and lacked basic necessities. All the government did was impose stricter discipline and order. For example, in October 1940, the NKVD reorganized many children's labor colonies into closed-type colonies, with a special regime for a contingent of convicted juveniles aged 12 and over to 17 years old.[71] Although the closed institutions for criminal children were supposedly independent of the NKVD-MVD of the USSR, it is almost impossible to find a separation between them and the forced labor camps of the GULAG where adult prisoners were kept.

Children—Enemies of the People

At the height of the Great Terror on August 15, 1937, the People's Commissar of Internal Affairs of the USSR N. I. Yezhov signed operational order of the NKVD of the USSR No. 00486 "On the operation to repress the wives and children of traitors to the Motherland." According to the document, the wives of those convicted of "counter-revolutionary crimes" were subject to arrest and imprisonment in camps for five to eight years, and their children aged 1.5 to 15 were sent to orphanages.[72]

In each city where the operation to repress the wives of "traitors to the Motherland" took place, children's reception centers were created, where children of the arrested were taken. The stay in the shelter could last from several days to months. Lyudmila Fedorovna Petrova from Leningrad, the daughter of repressed parents, recalls:

> They put me in a car. My mother was dropped off at the Keresty prison and we were taken to the children's reception center. I was 12 years old; my brother was eight. First of all, they cut our hair bald, hung a plate with a number around our necks, and took our fingerprints. My brother cried a lot, but we were separated and were not allowed to meet and talk. Three months later, we were brought from the children's reception center to the city of Minsk.[73]

Vladimir Grigoryevich Moroz Case

The widely publicized story of Pavlik Morozov, whose life was tragic and at the same time officially positioned as heroic, should not overshadow the stories of thousands of children who did not fit into the official version of the "pioneer-heroes" of Stalin's "happy" childhood. The duty of history is to rethink everything and put everything in its proper place. Here, the story of a non-pioneer boy, who was defined in the secret documents of the NKVD as an "enemy of the people," deserves discussion. His story did not find wide publicity and remained on the secret archive pages of interrogations and reports. His story also did not become the subject for discussion by historians, unfortunately. Obviously, the Stalinist state did everything to consign his name and his history to oblivion. The story of Vladimir Moroz came to the attention of journalist Natalia Versegova, only in 2015, after which she published an article about Moroz in the *Komsomolskaya Pravda* newspaper.[74]

A declassified confidential secret service "investigation file" introduces us to fifteen-year-old citizen, Vladimir Grigoryevich Moroz, born on November 1, 1922, in Moscow.[75] Vladimir Moroz, a Jew, the son party, GPU, and government officials, single and a pupil of the Annenkovskiy orphanage of the Kuznetsk district of the Kuibyshev region, was suspected of committing acts under Article 58-10, part 1 of the Criminal Code of the RSFSR - "counter-revolutionary activity—propaganda and agitation," which entailed the death penalty.[76] The Kuibyshev's regional NKVD office approved Moroz's arrest and detention, ruling that his being at large may adversely affect the course of the investigation. At the time this happened, on April 25, 1938, Vladimir Moroz was fifteen years old, and the local NKVD office falsified his age by adding one more year, so that "16-year-old" Moroz could be detained and sent to prison. Thus, the accused fifteen-year-old Moroz had been kept in the Kuznetsk prison since April 25, 1938. On the basis of the defendant's interrogation and testimony and without representatives for the fifteen-year-old defendant, the Stalinist repressive machine sentenced him to labor for three years in GULAG.

By this time, both his parents and his elder brother had been arrested and nine-year-old younger brother Alexander was sent to the Annenkovskiy orphanage. His father Moroz Grigori Semenovich, a member of the Bolshevik party since May 1917, the Chairman of the Central Committee of the Trade Union of State Trade Workers, was executed in 1937. His mother, Kreindel-Moroz Fanny Lvovna, as a member of the family of a "traitor to the Motherland," was sent to a labor camp. At the time of the arrests, the family lived in the famous House of Government, also known as the House on the Embankment on Moscow-river on Balchug in Moscow.[77]

The boy's story begins with misfortune, when his father was falsely accused of counter-revolutionary activities and sabotage and executed as an "enemy of the people." Of note is that his father was a revolutionary and a member of the Bolshevik party. He worked for the Cheka and GPU, and later was a member of the Central Control Commission. At the time of his arrest, he chaired the Central Committee of the Union of State Trade and Cooperative Workers. According to Stalin's laws, direct relatives of the enemies of the people were subject to repression that involved arrest and exile in the GULAG. Thus, his mother and older brother ended up in exile in the Stalinist camps. But Vladimir was sure of his father's innocence and did not understand why this injustice occurred. In an attempt to find justice, the fifteen-year-old addressed a letter to "Dear Comrade Stalin" in February 1938. In the letter, Morozov wrote that, after his father, mother, and older brother were arrested, his situation became unbearable: "Blow after blow, misfortune after misfortune [fell] on my head. I endured patiently." Moroz explained to Stalin that he was sent to a children's home in the village of Annenkovo: "Imagine my position in the children's home," he wrote, "there are only dark thoughts in my head. I have turned into some kind of misanthrope: I am alienated from people, I see a hidden enemy in everyone, I have lost all faith in people." The boy complained about his school and his loneliness in it:

> Why am I lonely? Yes, only because the general intellectual level of the pupils of the orphanage and the students at the school is much lower than mine. This is not boasting. And the school? The school is so miserable, the teachers (except for 2) are so mediocre that you don't even want to go to it. I want to get the maximum of knowledge, but here you get their minimum, and even then, incomplete.

Turning to Stalin, Vladimir asked, "Well, then how can you be satisfied. You may think that I am too soft, sentimental. No, absolutely not. I demand only happiness, real, lasting happiness." Referring to Lenin, Moroz wrote that "according to Lenin,

'There should be no destitute children in the Soviet country. Let there be young happy citizens." Writing to Stalin, Moroz revealed the essence of Soviet society:

> Am I happy? No. Who is happy? You have probably heard of the "golden youth" of the tsarist period. Such a "golden youth" now exists, unfortunately. In most cases, it consists of the children of responsible, respected people. These children do not recognize anything: they drink, whore, are rude, and so on. In most cases, they study disgustingly, although all conditions have been created for them to study. Here they are happy!"

Obviously Moroz referred to the children of the Soviet nomenklatura and bureaucracy. If their parents were loyal and escaped repressions, they lived happily and had all the benefits. "It's strange, but it's a fact," wrote the boy. Thus, the concept of "happy Soviet childhood" may certainly apply to a tiny minority of children of Soviet privileged elites. Furthermore, young Moroz asks Stalin for help: "Comrade Stalin, I am sinking lower and lower, flying at dizzying speed into some kind of dark abyss from which there is no way out. Save me, help me, don't let me die!" Stalin of course did not help. On April 25, 1938, Moroz was detained, arrested, and sentenced to three years in a GULAG labor camp, where he died in April 1939.[78]

Children's Tragedy: A Grim Reality of Stalin's *Realpolitik*

Despite the efforts of the Stalinist leadership to eliminate children's homelessness, the problem persisted. More and more waves of homeless children appeared as the state continued its *realpolitik* measures. For example, the Chelyabinsk Regional Executive Committee, as reported in a classified document,

> did not ensure the implementation of the resolution of the Council of People's Commissars of the USSR and the Central Committee of the All-Union Communist Party of Bolsheviks of May 31, 1935 "On the Elimination of Child Homelessness and Neglect", despite a special resolution on this issue by the Presidium of the All-Russian Central Executive Committee dated November 10, 1936 (Decree of the President of the All-Russian Central Executive Committee for 1936 No. 60, paragraph 17).[79]

The authorities required the regional committee to take immediate measures against underage vagrants. An April 1937 classified document obligated the chairmen of district executive committees, city councils, and village councils to wage a resolute fight against vagrancy among children, bringing to justice those guilty of allowing vagrancy.[80]

The state now equated homelessness with vagrancy. State agents detained homeless children for vagrancy, tried them before NKVD troikas, and sent them to places that were actually GULAG labor colonies. These troikas were essentially extra-judicial tribunals without due hearing or trial, and were composed of three officials, representatives of the NKVD, the party, and the prosecutor's office. Formed officially to fight anti-Soviet elements, the troikas also persecuted children. A minor could be sent to a forced labor camp for any reason, often without any reason at all. Labor colonies for children were run by the NKVD, just as was the GULAG system. Examples are numerous and terrible.

In 1938, an NKVD troika in the Gorky region had sentenced twelve-year-old Melnikov to three years in prison for "being without a definite occupation" and sent him to the Valuisk labor colony. He was an orphan, had no previous criminal record, and from the first day of his stay in the labor colony behaved and studied well. An NKVD official described the teen as a Stakhanovite and a social activist while in the labor colony. A troika of the NKVD in the Altai territory sentenced fourteen-year-old Krasnikov to five years in prison "for systematic vagrancy" and sent him to the Arkhangelsk labor colony. According to his record, he had parents, had no prior criminal record, and behaved well in the colony. A boy of the Voroshilov labor colony, Pavlov, fifteen years old, had parents, but was sentenced by an NKVD troika to three years in prison "for violating the passport regime."[81] Being "without a specific occupation" or "violating the passport regime" meant being homeless and starving, which the state considered now as vagrancy; but what occupation should a twelve-year-old have? Nevertheless, perhaps these boys were lucky, since their cases came to the attention of People's Commissar for Internal Affairs, Lavrentiy Beria. In August 1939, Beria ordered the boys released from labor colonies: Kraskikov to his parents, Melnikov to the orphanage of the People's Commissariat of Education, and now sixteen-year-old Pavlov for employment. Since they came to Beria's attention, these cases were kept in the archives, but how many cases did not reach Beria and were eliminated from the archives? Nobody will ever know. There were also cases, when prosecutors charged children 10–12 years of age with counter-revolution and political crimes, issues about which the children had no idea.[82]

Despite severe and repressive measures against street children (not to mention non-street children), the issue they presented had not been eliminated. Although there are no official data on homes and starving children, top secret NKVD reports inform about the increase of crimes committed by children and adolescents. The top secret and classified "Memorandum on Rise in Children's Crime in the Sverdlovsk region and the city of Sverdlovsk" wrote that:

> Secretary of the Sverdlovsk regional committee of the CPSU (b) Valukhin reported in a top-secret message dated May 20, 1938, that by April 1938 compared to the same months of 1937 children's crimes increased in the Sverdlovsk region and the Ural mountains.[83]

Another report from the children's isolation ward of the first police station in Sverdlovsk (now Yekaterinburg) for February 1936 describes the daily activities of the isolation ward and the measures taken against detained street children. Police, janitors, members of the public, and other agents involved in children's detention picked up 235 children in January 1936 alone in Sverdlovsk. The report stated the children "were treated appropriately." "The children's isolation ward is kept clean and in good condition, there are various games for children, but the literature," the report complained "is all old, and they don't buy a new literature due to lack of funds." The officer informed each detained child about the government decree on combating children's homelessness and neglect, and also talked with their parents and explained this decree to them and what consequences and penalties were imposed on parents for improper upbringing of their child. They also talked with children about school discipline. Most children (124) came from workers' families, seventy-two had unidentified background, eight were children of kolkhoz members, and one a kulak's child. Several children were released to their families, whereas seventy-eight were transferred to an NKVD detention center.[84]

However, the detention centers intended for keeping juvenile offenders under investigation did not receive permanent development as independent units in the NKVD system. To regulate their activities, on July 16, 1939, the NKVD adopted the "Regulations on Detention Facilities for Juvenile Offenders." According to the regulation, these facilities kept behind bars children and adolescents aged 12 to 16, who were sentenced by courts for a fixed term of imprisonment if the usual measures of re-education did not give the desired result. The permission of the prosecutor was required to make a decision to transfer the teenager to the isolation ward. The term of detention in it was limited to six months.

Regardless of numerous and supposedly vigorous efforts, the Bolshevik state was unable to eliminate children's homelessness even by the end of the 1930s. Mentions of homeless and hungry children can now be seen only in the secret documents of the NKVD and the party. As the documents reveal, the government recognized the existence of homeless children, but explained their existence by the poor work of local Soviet and party bodies, and the lack of organizational participation in the fight against the issue on the part of the Soviet public. The Bolshevik state never acknowledged its own responsibility and never discussed the social and political nature of the origins of children's homelessness and starvation.

The tragedy of Soviet childhood became even more aggravated with the beginning of the Great Patriotic War, which caused a sharp increase in the number of homeless children and juvenile delinquency. For example, the number of crimes committed by minors in 1942 increased compared to 1941 by 61 percent, and in 1944 by 181 percent. All work with juvenile delinquents during this period fell on the bodies of the NKVD.[85] Homeless children committed large-scale criminal activity and hooliganism. To counter this, the state sharply tightened laws on disorderly conduct and delinquency among children, lowering the age threshold for criminal responsibility. For certain types of crimes, it became possible for twelve-year-olds to be "tried as adults." By order of the NKVD of the USSR of June 21, 1943, a special Department was formed to combat children's homelessness and neglect. The district commissioners of this department, with their auxiliary forces of the guard network of outdoor posts, were engaged in the removal of children from the streets, markets, bazaars, squares, gardens, parks, railway station squares, stations and piers, entertainment enterprises, etc. (Readers may note the similarity with the 1920s.) Special posts and pickets composed of Komsomol members, brigadiers, teachers, and public inspectors of public education departments were set up. Special work was carried out in housing administrations with the help of residents' activists. The results of the measures taken to remove homeless and neglected children were impressive, but perhaps not in the way intended. In 1942, the police seized about 379,000 homeless and neglected children from the streets, markets, during mass raids, and detours; in 1943, more than 802,000 (respectively 277,948 and 524,497); and in 1944, more than 1,173,000 (432,898 and 740,770) respectively people. With the approval of Stalin in 1943, the NKVD created "additional labor colonies" for delinquent children, where conditions, according to descriptions, "were grim." The age of inmates in the colonies ranged from 11 to 16 years. By the end of 1943, the total number of inmates in these colonies had reached 50,000. Children's educational institutions were either abolished or abandoned and provided no education.[86]

Conclusion

As the discussion has shown, authoritarian regimes are characterized by denial and ignorance of pressing problems. The regime-controlled media wrote only what was allowed to be written about. Children's starvation and homelessness, as well as other hidden significant problems, were simply excluded from mention in all public places. And those who dared to mention them were threatened with persecution and reprisals. Most likely, the problems of child homelessness and hunger were resolved in the early USSR in a completely natural way—some children survived, grew up, and became adults, but most perished. The skeptical reader may review the statistics on mortality rates among homeless and starving children cited in this book.

Figure 11 Thanks to our dear Stalin for happy childhood. Soviet poster. Source: Open public domain.

The biggest problem for researchers of Soviet social and cultural history is that primary sources, both published and archival, can easily confuse and even mislead. Of course, one should carefully interpret published materials, always keeping in mind state censorship and propaganda intentions. Archival sources are numerous and now widely available; even so, in the Soviet Union many potentially controversial documents were classified as "secret" or "top secret" and are still closed to circulation and public access. Undoubtedly, the most controversial and revealing materials could be destroyed by the responsible authorities. Guided by the official Soviet narrative, the official histories of early Soviet children usually paint a rosy picture of a happy Soviet childhood, especially under Stalin. One cannot deny that perhaps some early Soviet children, who were able to compromise and accept the ways of the new government, moved forward to advancement, and become agents of what ultimately ended the Soviet Union. But heroes like Moroz would be reincarnated to destroy Soviet myths and lies.

Epilogue: Vanished Childhood in the Early Soviet Union

You forget, my good man, that what the artist perceives is, primarily, the difference between things. It is the vulgar who note their resemblance.

Vladimir Nabokov, *Despair*

I constantly looked for a positive moment in the history of early Soviet childhood, and instead found only the tragedy, pain, and suffering experienced by most Soviet children. The story in this book turned out to be fundamentally different from the official and widely publicized image of a happy Soviet child. The government proclaimed itself the benefactor of all children and yet the reality of Soviet childhood during the first two decades of Bolshevik power turned out to be the precise opposite for most children. The tragedy of early Soviet children and their immediate environment was real, acute, and prolonged. Child starvation, homelessness, and the accompanying high mortality remained notably and unusually high for decades: from the Bolsheviks' first rise to power in 1917 until the outbreak of the Second World War—the period discussed in this study—and beyond, as de Graffenreid's work has shown.

It was not evil providence, not the predestination of higher powers that caused protracted childhood tragedy. The phenomenon arose as a direct result of certain state policies. As this study has illustrated, before the Bolshevik Revolution, Russia had a well-established system of patronage and care for children in need, rooted in folk traditions, religion, and instituted by the state. The care for the needy had been a part of popular culture, supported by the state. Even if the ideas of the tsarist government about how to deal with orphans were insufficient, they were at least quite practical and suitable for predominantly agricultural Russia. However, these approaches were not destined to be maintained. The events of the subsequent years brought about fundamental changes to Russia. The people who came to power after October 1917 had a different worldview, different ideas, and different approaches, factors not in and of themselves evil or misguided. The new rulers, believing in new modes of approaching problems, sought to destroy the existing tradition of benevolence associated with tsarism, which, in their view, were by definition inadequate or ill-intentioned. In reality, the years of the Revolution and Civil War had a dramatic impact on the lives of numerous children, many of whom, as we have seen, were left homeless. Since the new regime closed existing institutions for the care of orphans without establishing adequate replacements, most orphans, a group that expanded exponentially, were forced to provide for themselves. Readers should stop and think: children by definition cannot care for themselves. The new government's domestic policies transformed children's starvation and homelessness, practically nonexistent prior to 1918, into ubiquitous and permanent phenomena, with some ebbs and flows, throughout the years discussed in this study. It was neither the First World War nor the Civil War that initiated and prolonged massive children's homelessness and hunger—it was grain requisitioning in the first instance and the new state's utter inability to deal with the new phenomenon its policies brought about that caused and prolonged the horrors chronicled here. Historians should have long since ceased taking seriously the government's loudly proclaimed notion of "a happy childhood" for Soviet-era children. Contrary evidence was always sufficiently available; further, for three decades archival sources provided incontrovertible evidence if only one cared to consult them.

Let us look more closely at certain realities. Having come to power, the Bolshevik government quickly imposed an official and only possible scenario according to which all social ills were assigned to the tsarist regime, bourgeois capitalism, the First World War, and the Civil War. As soon as the Bolsheviks consolidated their positions and introduced rigid censorship and official propaganda, they carefully articulated an idea of a "happy Soviet childhood." Unfortunately, until this day many researchers of early Soviet childhood have accepted this official state interpretation uncritically; in fact, they have taken it for granted as the basis for analyzing Soviet-era childhood. Nevertheless, careful study of the ongoing suffering of children throughout the 1920s and 1930s renders absurd the official scenario and concept of a happy Soviet childhood. It must be admitted that, obviously, the years of the Revolution and Civil War dramatically changed the lives of many children, making them orphans or reducing them to a state of need, but state policy and legislative initiatives aggravated the situation for all children and transformed what should have been a brief, unfortunate phenomenon into a continuous reality. Surviving orphaned or homeless children of 1917–21 became adults and could not be among the homeless and starving children of the late 1920s or early to mid-1930s. In reality, the problem of homeless and starving children remained serious, aggravated, and, in the government's own words, "a threat to public order" until the beginning of the Great Patriotic War, as evidenced by numerous archival materials.

An important aspect that this book reveals is the proprietary nature of Bolshevik rule and its reliance on *realpolitik*. Analysis of various published and unpublished primary documents in the historical context of this period of Soviet history showed that it was Bolshevik *realpolitik* that made children unhappy or, all too often, resulted in their demise. Early Soviet childhood was gloomy and tragic. As we have seen, the early Bolshevik expropriation policy, namely the requisitions of 1918–early 1920s, including aggressive food procurement, war communism, and then, later, the collectivization of agriculture and the subsequent dispossession of numerous families in the early 1930s, relied on *realpolitik* and its concomitant in this case—mass terror, and seriously shook the position of most people. This led to an acute social catastrophe, which reached unprecedented proportions and became practically unsolvable for the early Soviet state. Bolshevik *realpolitik* touched every non-elite Soviet family, but especially rural ones. Likewise, hunger, homelessness, high mortality, and chronic children's delinquency all reflected the state's reliance on *realpolitik*. Bolshevik *realpolitik*, as the major instrument in implementing policies and achieving goals, was the major cause of the misery that beset lives of millions of soviet children. During the 1920s, children's misery (homelessness, starvation, and high mortality) resulted from food requisitioning and other punitive measures used against large portions of the population. During the 1930, children suffered from the consequences of Stalinist collectivization of agriculture. Thus, most Soviet children suffered from the socio-political upheavals and dramas caused by Bolshevik rule.

While reading this book, the reader may wonder: Were the Bolsheviks really Marxist-Leninists, as they claimed to be, or were they simply usurpers of power, using ideology to cover up their lust for power? There is no unequivocal answer to this question, since after 1917 Lenin himself repeatedly changed his positions regarding the economic and social policy of the state. (In 1917, he even changed his position often on Soviet power.[1]) One thing is clear: in order to achieve their goals, the Bolsheviks always relied on *realpolitik*, which explains the catastrophic situation of the population in general and the children's population in particular throughout the period under discussion. The state proclaimed itself the guardian of all needy children, but it was clearly beyond its means to provide homeless and starving children. Instead, Bolshevik *realpolitik* became a constant source of tragedy for Soviet children.

To be clear, when the Bolsheviks came to power, they had no real tactical plan for building the new social order that they envisioned. Their strategy was simple—to create a new state in accordance with their version of Marxism-Leninism. However, when it came down to it, the Bolsheviks took the path of *realpolitik* in order to maintain their power and build a new society. Therefore, their activity in the implementation of their ideals had always been reactive, impulsive, going from one extreme to another utterly bereft of and a clear deliberate plan. The Bolsheviks considered any social or humanitarian problem to be a political one, which determined their approach to the problem. As the reader has seen, every humanitarian issue inevitably became a political "struggle" for government *in its own terminology*. Thus, the solution to numerous social problems, including children's homelessness and starvation, became a steady political struggle of the new government, always taking on a revolutionary coloration. The government created numerous "extraordinary" commissions and committees to "fight," "combat," or carry out "struggle," as reflected in the very names of these bodies. The struggle of the Bolsheviks against all the problems they faced, including children's homelessness and starvation, was always political and always relied on *Realpolitik*, that is, on coercive institutions. By 1921, when the government finally realized the magnitude of the problem of children's homelessness and criminality, it enlisted the agency of the all-powerful Cheka to fight the problem. The newly created Children's Commission was subordinate to and supervised by the Cheka. Virtually every new institution created to deal with the issues was subordinate to and run by the secret police. This alone requires note.

Among the new government's first struggles was the elimination of all imperial institutions. This struggle was reflected in laws that immediately abolished all public and private philanthropy including charitable donations of any kind, without creating any alternative and that despite the growing number of starving, homeless children. Bolshevik *realpolitik* was behind the expropriation of orphanages' buildings plus those of all schools in favor of various state, party, or military organizations, a widespread, indeed universal, policy which seriously exacerbated all problems associated with children. A serious question, without clear answer is: Why did the government abolish private and public philanthropy and take full responsibility for caring for orphans when it was sharply aware of both its financial situation and of the growing number of orphans and street children? Was it willing to sacrifice the lives of orphans and homeless children for Marxist ideology and of the allegedly socialist way of life it wanted to inculcate? If so, then the actions of the Bolshevik government were unlikely to be consonant with the ideology with which it associated itself, but rather reflected a state of mania—excitement, high spirits, and inability to foresee the consequences—all that psychiatrists associate with bipolar disorder. The unstable position of the Bolshevik government and the excessive use of violence and cruelty clearly affected the mental state of its members. Therefore, many actions of the Bolsheviks can be viewed and analyzed from the point of view of psychiatry and firmly within the context of bipolar disorder. As the reader has seen, the actions of the Bolsheviks were usually impulsive, reactive, contradictory, and always out of touch with reality on the ground. In many cases, this reality seemed threatening to the Bolshevik government which, it followed, all too often entailed strong preventive and punitive measures, that is, violence. The purpose of this book was not to pursue the study of the psychotic state of the Bolsheviks, but rather to suggest the need for more thorough study and, if necessary, the involvement of professional psychiatrists, who could provide better analysis and understanding of the early Soviet government's actions and behavior. If these actions and approaches are deemed normal than this requires new definitions of normal and abnormal.

Under these conditions, and in accordance with the principles of *realpolitik*, the state forcibly evacuated starving and homeless children from cities to the countryside, for which it created numerous dysfunctional children's institutions. As we have seen, there was no reason to evacuating starving street children into the countryside, where there were insufficient appropriate facilities; rather it was an impulsive reaction to their presence, a reality confirmed by some members of the government. The thoughtless evacuation of children led to an overflowing of inhabitants of existing institutions, which then led the state to re-evacuate children elsewhere, which only further aggravated the children's hardship. Homelessness and hunger among children did not stop, but on the contrary continued to grow rapidly, as numerous primary sources testify.

Historians generally distinguish between two opposing tendencies within the Bolshevik government regarding children: hardliners and soft-liners. Both trends, in fact, corresponded to the general line of *realpolitik*, but differed in the degree of cruelty. At times the difference was so small as to be almost imperceptible. Was it not cruel to dismantle all existing charities and place all children in need in state care in the face of state bankruptcy and economic collapse? Wasn't N. K. Krupskaya's idea of peremptory protection of children from the influence of their own parents cruel? Wasn't it cruel to take children from existing orphanages and evacuate them to the countryside where there was no vital infrastructure?

After the Civil War, when the Bolshevik state moved toward market relations, and moderate capitalism, it proposed a combination of significant economic liberalization. The Bolsheviks, however, followed *Realpolitik* methods, and maintained tight political control. During the new economic policy period, the government turned orphanages into production units—child labor colonies that used child labor. The Children's Commission, led by the Cheka, was actively involved in commercial activities, forming two joint-stock companies and supervising children's labor colonies. Analysis of primary sources in this book shows that there was practically no educational process in such colonies. At the same time, a "work for living" policy was pursued in children's labor colonies. The children worked hard, for which they could not even get normal care and food. Although the concept of a labor colony as a means of re-education of delinquent persons might be appropriate for healthy adults, what can be said and thought about its application to children, especially street children, whose plight was a direct consequence of the state grain procurement policy in 1918–20 or the collectivization and dekulakization in the 1930s? These government tendencies directly contradicted the family code of 1918, which prohibited adoptions and foster care and declared that all needy children were under state guardianship. The Bolshevik slogan "Children are the flowers of life" was devalued to meaningless words. Nevertheless, within the context of Bolshevik *realpolitik*, all this was obvious and logical.

One way or another, as we have seen, during the period between 1923 and 1928 the Cheka's Children's Commission reflected these new commercial trends in its activities. The Children's Commission launched a rather extensive commercial activity through its joint stock company "Larek" and Univerpocht. The Bolshevik government explained that the involvement of the Cheka and the creation of various children's and commercial structures were aimed at raising funds to improve childcare, considering the difficult financial situation in the country. This was logical since the financial situation in fact did not allow solving the problem of homeless and starving children. However, as primary sources and documents show, the proceeds from the casino and from Larek's activities did not reach homeless and starving children but were dissolved into the general budget through falsified financial reports and shadow bookkeeping.

Despite the involvement of the all-powerful Cheka in the problem of children's starvation and homelessness, the state that loudly proclaimed its concern for children was unable to fulfill its promises. Here it is important to understand the bipolar nature of these promises made by the government, which was well aware of the lack of its financial resources. As we have seen, during the first half of the 1920s, the state viewed starvation and homelessness among children as unresolved problems. Thus, the state had to turn to society for help. As the materials showed, the Children's Commission launched a wide propaganda campaign to involve society in solving the problem, published leaflets and articles in newspapers calling on the society to respond and take responsibility for homeless children. And the population, as the primary sources showed, responded in a heartfelt manner, despite earlier harassment during the period of the food procurement.

Regardless, in the late 1920s child homelessness and starvation remained not just an acute, but a growing problem: government officials regularly reported an increase in the number of starving street children. Juvenile delinquency also increased. The increase in the number of homeless children and their criminal activities caused outrage and hatred in society. In the late 1920s, such sentiments completely coincided with the plans of the country's leadership. This was well reflected in the words of Stalin when he visited Leningrad and saw many homeless children. Stalin noticed that the city authorities were littering their city with homeless children and demanded that the city remove this garbage. Thus, starving homeless children, as a group, witnessed the transformation of the Bolshevik state's attitude toward themselves from starving homeless children to a socially dangerous, morally defective mass, and, finally, to social scum. In truth, the state had always seen this human crisis as a political one.

Obviously, *realpolitik*, as a permanent genesis of children's tragedy, and Stalin's attitude toward homeless children as social outcasts, testified to the absence of any genuine intention to help needy children. The state aimed to solve the problem of "social dregs" and street vagabonds, but not the problem of children's misfortune. The Stalinist state did not help homeless, hungry, and disadvantaged children, but tried to get rid of them in various ways. Paradoxically, the state made millions of children unhappy, indeed desperate, on the one hand, and, on the other, wanted to eliminate them from public space. As the book explored, the Stalinist philosophy of "no man, no problem" simply excluded these children from public discussion, tightening measures against them and against anyone who dared to raise the issue of their existence.

The 1935 ordinance essentially outlawed homeless children and simply legitimized their nonexistence despite their presence. In fact, any mention of homeless children was forbidden and punished. How did child homelessness end in the USSR? The government simply stopped using the word. Stalin's government abolished the word "besprizorniki" like the word "hunger" in the context of *realpolitik*. No word—no problem. The Stalinist state transformed existing children's homelessness into the category of criminal offenses—vagrancy. Children accused of vagrancy were removed from the streets and subjected to legal sanctions, trial, and severe punishment. Regardless of this, homelessness among children was not eliminated even by the beginning of the Second World War. This unresolved problem had become eternal due to its genesis—Bolshevik *realpolitik*. In general, the issue could not be resolved because homeless children died or grew up—but their ranks were always replenished with new generations of homeless children. The genesis of children's homelessness—Bolshevik realpolitik—was tenacious.

The period of Stalinism was full of tragedy, deceit, manipulation, and contradictions, not only in historical, but also in historiographical and research terms. The contradictions and confrontations generated in this era are alive to this day and continue to generate conflicts among historians. Allegorically, one can assume that Stalin himself is alive and manipulates the consciousness of researchers and scholars of his epoch. Sometimes it is difficult to reproduce an objective picture due to the lack of sources. After all, many primary sources have been purposely destroyed, while others are still inaccessible to researchers. In the context of this book, I will allow myself to suggest that Stalinism was yet another dark page in the history of the lives of most Soviet children.

In the post-Stalinist period, homeless children caused little problems, if any, because the source of permanent homelessness—*realpolitik*—dried up. During the years of Khrushchev and Brezhnev, Soviet society achieved a certain social stability. Institutions of social support and various educational and vocational schools were widely available. Many children were given the opportunity to study at music or art schools and play sports at minimal cost to their families. Many children got the opportunity for high-quality leisure and recreation in pioneer camps in the natural and resort areas of the USSR. It was during these years that one can confidently speak of a happy Soviet childhood. Even so, for many rural children it was not yet happy, since the countryside was still impoverished and, if anything, in decline.

Since the early 1990s, there has been a new increase in the number of street children in Russia, although there are practically no official statistics on the number of street children during this period. Since street children discovered by the authorities are not released but rather are transferred back to their parents or to orphanages, no official data exist. Researchers note that economic crisis, poverty, unemployment, the weakening of family foundations, moral and psychological crisis, and the spread of mental illness all have become factors in the numbers of unattended street children. All these factors were caused by the deep socio-economic transformation of Gorbachev's perestroika and subsequent reforms, as the standard of living of many families fell sharply. Documents of the government and representative bodies of the Federation Council pointed to the destruction of state infrastructure for the socialization and upbringing of children, as well as family crises (growth of poverty, deterioration of housing conditions, destruction of the moral value and educational potential of the family) as the main reasons for the emergence and growth of homelessness. Researchers also note the general criminalization of society, including the spread of prostitution, drug abuse, human trafficking, and weak control over employers who involve children in illegal activities. Indeed, in many cases, children could engage in petty trade and earn more than their parents in the 1990s, which, of course, could not but affect the increase in street children. The illegal migration of children (often unaccompanied by adults) from the former Soviet republics caused by armed conflicts and the even worse economic situation in these countries also contributed to the rise in the numbers of street children during these years.

Even so, by the 2000s the growth in the number of homeless children gave way to a decline. According to some official data published in *Rossiyskaya Gazeta*, within the framework of the concept of the "Federal Target Program 'Children of Russia' for 2007–2010" (Decree of the Government of the Russian Federation), from 2003 to 2005 the number of homeless children decreased from 7,500 to 4,270. In the UNICEF statistical compendium, the total number of street and neglected children (delivered to medical institutions) was 64,393 in 2005 and 60,903 in 2008. The number of children identified as orphans in 2012 was 654,000 children. Most of them (523,000) were not adopted but were brought up in foster care families. A minority of orphans (106,000) remained in orphanages. Unofficially, some officials and organizations in various years estimated that the number of homeless and neglected children exceeded official data by two to three orders of magnitude. At the same time, there was an opinion that such large numbers reflected artificial "increases" that helped civil servants create jobs and increase budgets.

Acute social problems such as child homelessness give rise to various agenda myths. There are myths about millions of homeless children in post-perestroika times. These myths usually arose from unintentional substitution of definitions, when the number of orphans—children deprived of parental care—was taken and presented as the number of homeless children. In the 2000s, the number of such children in Russia fluctuated at around 700,000. All these children were in the care of the state or foster parents. However, some politicians or journalists presented them as homeless and used these estimates for political agendas.

As noted in this book, as regards Stalinism historians tend to draw various parallels among imperial Russia, the early Soviet Union, and post-Soviet Russia. Historians of the early Soviet era look for selective similarities between late tsarist and early Soviet periods, usually in terms of violence or confiscation of surplus food. Despite certain similarities, the differences were more striking. As shown in this book, they were disparate in origin, scope, and consequences. Is it advisable to look for and talk about parallels if the differences are so immediately evident? This is usually done to downplay the early Soviet crimes and to normalize Bolshevik and Stalinist brutality. In this respect, one should recall one of the characters in Vladimir Nabokov's novel *Despair*, who said that the artist perceives the difference, but the vulgar sees the resemblance. In the context of the novel, Nabokov's character was looking for similarities in order to hide his crime and lies. The problem of similarity and difference is relevant for every historian who is looking for relationships and proportions between differences and similarities. But people usually see and believe what they want to see and believe and can completely ignore everything that does not suit them or contradicts their world view. Has something like this happened to those historians of the early Soviet times who have become preoccupied with looking for certain kinds of similarities and who have consequently lost the mental ability to see obvious differences? I hope the reader has found the difference by reading this book.

Appendix One

Circular letter of the Cheka to the Extraordinary Commissions on the Adoption of Urgent Measures to Improve the Lives of Street Children

After January 27, 1921

Moscow.

To all local authorities (Cheka, OO and TChK)

The Presidium of the All-Russian Central Executive Committee at a meeting on January 27, 1921 decided to organize a commission under the All-Russian Central Executive Committee to improve the lives of children. The situation of children, especially street children, is difficult, despite the fact that the Soviet government spared no means or effort for this.

Three years of intense struggle on the external fronts, however, did not make it possible to do everything necessary in this area to provide for and supply children and surround them with exhaustive care.

Quite often it was necessary to transfer the care of children to people who turned out to be enemies of the proletarian Revolution, alien to it and to proletarian children; quite often in these children not only did these elements not develop communist ideas and feelings, but robbed these children and deprived them of what the Soviet government, under generally difficult conditions, did not spare to supply children, but left these children without supervision and worries. Now the time has come when, able to breath more easily on the external fronts, the Soviet government can take up this matter with all its energy, turn its attention primarily to caring for children, future pillars of the communist system.

And the emergency commissions, as organs of the dictatorship of the proletariat, cannot remain aloof from this concern, and they must help the Soviet government in every way they can in its work of protecting and supplying children. For this purpose, in order to involve the apparatus of the Cheka, the Presidium of the All-Russian Central Executive Committee appointed me the chairman of the above-mentioned commission under the All-Russian Central Executive Committee for improving the lives of children. Let this be an indication and a signal to all emergency commissions. Each emergency commission should consider what and how it can help children by appointing a responsible leader for this work and looking for appropriate workers both within itself and through the communist party, women's department, provincial trade union councils, etc. The work of emergency commissions in this field will, however, be fruitful only if it is carried out not in parallel with the work of the bodies in charge of providing and supplying children, but in close contact with them, in agreement with them.

To this end, provincial emergency commissions should immediately contact the relevant departments of the People's Education Department, People's Commissariat of Health, Social Security, Commissariat of Food and others and provide them with all possible assistance and support in their work, receiving assignments from them and giving them their information.

The Extraordinary Commissions in this matter should set themselves the task of:

1. A thorough and objective examination and informing local executive committees and their respective departments, as well as the Cheka, about the actual situation of children on the ground, about the state of shelters, orphanages, kindergartens, nurseries, children's hospitals, sanatoriums, about the situation and number of homeless children in need indoors in orphanages, etc.
2. Observing whether the decrees on children's food and supplies are carried out, and in finding out measures and methods for their implementation.
3. Providing permanent all-round assistance to local people's education departments, provincial health departments and food authorities in the matter of feeding and supplying children.
4. Providing strict supervision to ensure that the buildings occupied by orphanages are not illegally taken away by anyone and providing assistance in finding the best buildings.
5. Helping in the speedy repair of orphanages and in supplying them with a sufficient amount of fuel and items of their equipment.
6. The regional transport Cheka units are obliged to take under their protection street children at railway stations and on trains; to help the departments of the people's education in organizing distributors and houses for these children; if it is impossible to accept children by the departments of the people's education, find other ways to supply them with accommodation and food.
7. In all cases of theft, abuse or criminal attitude towards children, or slovenliness, the extraordinary commissions must bring to the attention of their executive committee and the corresponding department, and all cases requiring punishment and transfer the case to the Revolutionary Tribunal or to the people's court, according to the importance of the case, for a public trial.

The Extraordinary Commissions, pursuing all these tasks in their work, must remember that their goal will be achieved only when every step is directed towards the correction, improvement, and strengthening of those apparatuses of Soviet power that are in charge of caring for children, i.e. in the first place, the departments of public education. This should never be forgotten. Only under this condition the success of our efforts will not be transient and temporary. Therefore, emergency commissions should not interfere, but should help the bodies that are responsible for caring for children, should eliminate and expose criminals and seek sources of funds and forces, new workers, and help in every possible way.

By sending out the aforementioned circular letter, the Cheka hopes that the comrades working in the Cheka will understand the importance and urgency of caring for children, and therefore, as always, will be at the height of their position. Care for children is the best means of exterminating the counter-revolution. By placing the matter of providing and supplying children on the proper level, the Soviet government acquires its supporters and defenders in every working-class and peasant family, and at the same time gains broad support in the struggle against counter-revolution.

Within two weeks from the date of receipt of this period, the emergency commissions must inform the Cheka what has been done on this issue, as well as a plan for future work in this direction.

Chairman of the Cheka F. DZERZHINSKY

Source: Central Archive of the FSB of Russia.
F. 66. Op. 1-T. D. 28. L. 96–97. Copy. Typescript.

Telegram from the Deputy Head of the Politburo of the Ishim District
I.V. Nedorezov to the Tyumen Provincial Cheka

April 16, 1921

Ishim [Tyumen provincial town]
I inform you [that] telegram No. 95 from Abatsk was received today from the district police officer Korolev: "The mood of citizens is terrible because of hunger, today [in] Abatsk citizens gather in crowds: children, old people, mothers. They ask for bread. We have no way out. Citizens definitely declared: if you don't give us bread, then we'll go to the ssyppunkt ourselves and take a months ration. I ask you to act, otherwise I abdicate responsibility for what will happen not today—tomorrow. April 15". No. 495/s.
Deputy head of the Politburo Nedorezov

Source: TODAYS. F. 1. Op. 1. D. 278. L. 122. Handwritten copy.

Address of the Chairman of the All-Russian Central Executive Committee Commission on Improving the Lives of Children

March 31, 1923
EVERYTHING TO HELP CHILDREN!
TO ALL THE WORKING WORKERS OF THE USSR, THE EXECUTIVE COMMITTEE OF THE COMINTERN, THE PROFINTERN, YOUTH COMMITTEE, INTER-WORKING

Comrades!
Our young workers' republic has emerged victorious from a fierce bloody struggle against its sworn enemies, internal and external counter-revolution. With a new force,

unknown to the dying bourgeois world, the pulse of working-class social life began to beat, machine tools rattled, machines rustled, the plow moved more calmly and freely, exploding the rich earth.

But this great victory of the working people did not come without a price. As a result of the titanic struggle, deep wounds remained on the body of the country, for the final healing of which enormous efforts on the part of the workers and peasants of Soviet Russia will be required for a long time to come. One of these wounds is the still far from complete provision of the child population of the country.

The hard legacy of the tsarist system fell to the share of the first republic of labor in the world, wars and famine intensified it, and as a result of them, despite the heroic efforts shown by the Soviet government in providing all the necessary material benefits, in educating and protecting life and health, everyone on the territory of the Union of Socialist Republics, there is still an enormous number of orphans who have neither shelter nor care. Several million orphans require immediate real help.

Children's homelessness, often revealed in the most ugly, horrific forms, like juvenile delinquency ...

The Children's Commission hopes that workers abroad will respond to its appeal with their material and financial assistance and help it in the fight against child homelessness in Russia.

The Children's Commission also appeals to all foreign organizations to help the starving in Russia with a request to intensify their work to the extent possible in terms of helping children.

All to help the children!

Chairman of the All-Russian Central Executive Committee
to improve the lives of children
F. DZERZHINSKY

Source: *Izvestia*, March 31, 1923, No. 71.

Special report of the Secret Political Department of the OGPU of the USSR on the mass abandonment of children by peasants in Kiev

May 22, 1932

Top secret

Over the past few days, mass cases of abandonment of young children by peasants have been recorded in Kiev.

During the period from 6 to 10 May this year. city police districts picked up over 100 children aged from 6 months to 10 years in different parts of the city and in the bazaars, exported and abandoned by the peasants.

So, for example: Oktyabrsky district militia for the indicated time picked up 25 children aged 8 months up to 10 years old. The boulevard district of the police picked up 10 children aged 2 to 6 years. The Petrovsky district police picked up 12 children aged from 1 to 8 years. The Stalin police district picked up 24 children aged from 6 months up to 6 years old. In the rest of the districts, the selected children are of the same age.

Chief SPO OGPU G. Molchanov
Chief 2nd department Lyushkov

Source:
Central Archive of the FSB RF. F. 2. Op. 10. D. 508. L. 453.
Certified copy.

Memo from the School Sector of the People's Commissariat of Education of the RSFSR to the People's Commissariat of the Workers' and Peasants' Inspection of the RSFSR on sending homeless children to the Western Region and the Gorky Territory

May 17, 1933

On the basis of an oral statement by Comrade Karlik, Head of the School Sector of the Western District, at the end of April in Smolensk and Bryansk, 40–5 people were dropped off the train directly onto the street. Homeless children, among whom were children of preschool age, were picked up by the head of the Provincial Educational Committee.

At the same time, According to Comrade Naumova, Child Protection Inspector of the Gorky Territory, 91 children aged 16 were sent to the Gorky Detention House, whereas and the Regional Department of Education was asked to take them to an orphanage.

Such cases of unorganized sending of children without any coordination with the departments of public education and leaving children in a state that clearly threatens them with homelessness, completely coincides with the message of the inspector.

Considering such actions as criminally punishable, the School Sector of the People's Commissariat of Education asks to investigate this case, identify the perpetrators and bring them to strict accountability.

Deputy Head of the School Sector 1

Source: GARF. F. A-406. Op. 25. D. 1347. L. 8. Original.

Decree of the Presidium of the Central Volga Regional Executive Committee "On the state of child homelessness of young children"

Not earlier than June 1, 1933

1. A significant increase is noted in the region, especially in cities, of homeless children aged 1 year 2 months and up to 4 years (from January 1 to June 1, 1933, the number of foundlings increased to 600 children against 861 for the entire 1932), and in Samara—332, in Orenburg—80, in Penza—20, in Buguruslan—10 and in other cities and district centers from 3 to 5 people.
2. To note the completely insufficient network of orphanages for the reception of foundlings (only in the region there are only 6 houses with 220 beds), the huge transfer of these houses, the presence of significant mortality among foundling children due to high crowding, poor medical care, poor food supply in general and unsatisfactory work in orphanages.
3. Consider that on the part of public organizations (children's commissions, ROKK), city and district councils, attention to the fight against child homelessness and the absence of any appropriations for the maintenance of orphanages has been weakened.

Indicate to the Samara City Council and the City Health Department that they have not yet fulfilled the decision of the Presidium of the Regional Executive Committee of October 13, 1932 on the organization of an orphanage and the allocation of special funds from the budget, which forces the Regional Health Service to agree to take the children's clinical department of the OMM Institute under the receiver and liquidate the children's hospital.

In order to develop a fight against a decrease in the abandonment of children and a decisive improvement in the quality of care for children in existing orphanages, the presidium of the regional executive committee decides:

1. Personally oblige Comrade Batrachenko (Krayzdrav) by June 1 of this year. to organize children's homes for 100–50 beds each in Buzuluk and Orenburg.
2. To oblige the Orenburg City Council and the Buzuluk Regional Executive Committee to ensure the allocation of a fully adapted room for an orphanage by June 20 and to provide full assistance to the regional health in their equipment.
3. Approve the estimate of the regional health department for the deployment and maintenance of the Orenburg and Buzuluk children's homes in the amount of up to 200 thousand rubles. Instruct Zubin and Batrachenko to find sources to cover the costs of organizing and maintaining orphanages.
4. To oblige Comrade Kosterin's regional supply to pay special attention to the supply of orphanages for the placement of foundlings, first of all, to provide them with supplies, and especially milk. Tov. Kosterin, Bernul and Solomonovich and Batrachenko to develop additional measures for the deployment of decentralized procurement and a radical improvement in the supply of orphanages.

5. Considering that one of the main obstacles in the admission of children to patronage, as well as in the adoption of children by families of workers, employees and collective farmers, is the lack of provision of supplies for adopted children, instruct Tkacheva, Kosterin and Batrachenko to develop special measures for supplies for adopted children, as well as their material security.
6. To consider it necessary to provide foundling children taken for patronage with children's food cards, on an equal basis with children of working categories "A". Issue cards to those who conscientiously and accurately fulfill their obligations to raise an adopted child.
7. To oblige city councils and RIKs to conduct accurate registration of homeless and neglected children under the age of 4 by June 1 in order to ensure their immediate placement in patronages and orphanages.
8. For the operational management of the fight against child homelessness, organize a regional commission chaired by Comrade Tkacheva from representatives of the region, the children's commission, the ODD, the regional health department, the regional department of labor, the KSPS, the prosecutor's office, the Komsomol, and the police.
9. To oblige the commission to develop operational measures to combat child homelessness no later than June 15 and involve public organizations of workers, employees, and collective farmers in this work, mobilizing the funds of public organizations to the maximum (voluntary contributions, individual calls, etc.).
10. To oblige city councils, RIKs and district health departments not to send foundlings from the regions to Samara, but to distribute them to city, district houses or organize patronage.

Source: GA Orenburg region F. 980. Op. 1. D. 4. L. 20–21. Copy.

Memorandum of the head of the Middle Volga Regional Department of Public Education M. Dolinko to the Regional Committee of the All-Union Communist Party of Bolsheviks and the Regional Executive Committee on the growth of child homelessness

July 15, 1933

Secret

For the last May, June, July. in cities and in a number of districts of our region there is a large increase in child homelessness. As a result of the removal of homeless children from the streets, the existing orphanages are overcrowded. Instead of the budgeted contingent of 7,370 children, as of July 1, 1933, there is a contingent of 9,123 pupils. There are overstaffing in orphanages in the city of Samara for 340 children, in the city of Orenburg—220 children, in the city of Ulyanovsk—380 children, in the city of Kuznetsk—200 children, etc.

Additional funds for children's institutions for the maintenance of children in excess of the established contingent are not released. The maintenance of these children comes at the expense of the worsening of the already difficult financial situation of children's institutions. The arrival of homeless children in the cities continues. Children come from the regions of the Lower Volga, Ukraine and Central Asia. Most of the incoming children are extremely malnourished, among which there are cases of death due to malnutrition. Further admission of children to orphanages is completely impossible. Even now, children are housed in unequipped working barracks, sheds, etc. (Samara, Ulyanovsk).

In order to eliminate child street homelessness, begging in the region and the placement of children in children's institutions, urgent measures are required.

1. Bring the contingent of orphanages up to the contingents established by the Council of People's Commissars of the RSFSR in 9685 children. To do this, expand the existing network of orphanages for 700 children and organize new orphanages for 1045 children.
2. To oblige the village councils and collective farms to ensure the maintenance of all orphans brought up on the territory of collective farms at the expense of the funds and funds of collective farm mutual aid funds in order to stop children leaving for the cities on the street. The organization of new and expansion of existing orphanages with a contingent of 1745 children requires ... 1 thousand rubles. and children's uniforms, bedding—1745 sets.

The necessary funds can be obtained from the following sources:

1. According to the local budget of the Council of People's Commissars of the RSFSR, an amount of 4.33 million rubles was approved for the maintenance of orphanages in our region. with a contingent of 9685 children, and 7370 children were accepted in the region with a content of 3.726 million rubles. Reduction against the funds established by the Council of People's Commissars of the RSFSR for the maintenance of orphanages in our region, by 604 thousand rubles.
2. In 1932, more than 250 thousand rubles were illegally collected from the enterprises of the regional and local children's commissions, which, according to the information of the regional Federal University, can be returned back.
3. In 1932, the regional insurance fund did not complete financing of activities for work among children in the amount of up to 200 thousand rubles.

I ask the Bureau of the Regional Committee of the All-Union Communist Party of Bolsheviks to resolve this issue as a matter of urgency.

Head of the district committee M. Dolinko

Source: Samara regional GASPI. F. 1141. Op. 14. D. 7. L. 136–136v.

Script.

Appendix Two

From Criminal Case of Vladimir Moroz[1]

Letter from V. Moroz to I. V. Stalin

February 18, 1938

Dear Comrade Stalin! I have to turn to you for help. The situation forces this, I cannot do anything else. Having read your answer to Comrade Ivanov in the newspaper, I hoped that you would answer me too. What, exactly, is the unbearability of my present situation? And here's what. My father, Moroz G.S., was arrested by the NKVD, followed by his mother (who was arrested for no reason!). Blow after blow, misfortune after misfortune [fell] on my head. I endured patiently. Then I was sent to the village of Annenkovo. Imagine my position in d/d. Dark thoughts in my head. I have turned into some kind of misanthrope: I am alienated from people, I see a hidden enemy in everyone, I have lost all faith in people. Why am I lonely? Yes, only because the general intellectual level of the pupils of the kindergarten and the students at the school is much lower than mine. This is not boasting. And the school? The school is so miserable, the teachers (with the exception of 2) are so mediocre that you don't even want to attend it. I want to get the maximum of knowledge, but here you get their minimum, and even that is incomplete. Well, how then to be satisfied? You may think that I am too soft, sentimental. No, not at all. I only demand happiness, real, lasting happiness. Lenin said: "In the Soviet country there should be no destitute children. Let there be young happy citizens." Am I happy? No. Who is happy? You have probably heard of the "golden youth" of the tsarist period. So, such a "golden youth" exists now, sadly. In most cases, it consists of the children of responsible, respected people. These children do not recognize anything: they drink, they are debauched, they are rude, and so on. In most cases, they study disgustingly, although they are provided with all the conditions for study. Here they are happy! It's strange, but it's a fact. Comrade Stalin, I am sinking lower and lower, flying with dizzying speed into some kind of dark abyss, from which there is no way out. Save me, help me, don't let me die!

That's all. I hope that you will answer me soon and help me.
I look forward to an answer.
Moroz Vl.

Resolution on choosing a measure of restraint

"APPROVE"
April 23, 1938Head of the NKVD Directorate for the Kuibyshev region
State Security Captain Bocharov
Kuibyshev
04/23/1938

I, assistant to the head [of] the 2nd department of the fourth department of the State Security Directorate of the NKVD in the Kuibyshev region, state security lieutenant Timofeev, having examined the investigative material in case No. _____ in relation to citizen Vladimir Moroz, born in 1921, 1921, pupil Annenkovskogo Orphanage of the Kuznetsk district, Kuibyshev region, suspected of counter-revolutionary activities, i.e., the commission of a crime under Paragraph 58-10 part 1 of the Criminal Code of the RSFSR and taking into account that being at large may adversely affect the course of the investigation, guided by Paragraphs 145, 146 and 158 Code of Criminal Procedure of the RSFSR,

RESOLVED:
With regard to citizen Vladimir Moroz, the preventive measure for evading investigation and trial is to choose detention in the Kuznetsk prison.

Pom. Head of the 1st Department of the 4th Department of the UGB UNKVD Junior Lieutenant of State Security Timofeev

"AGREED" Head of the Fourth Division of the UGB UNKVD Senior Lieutenant of State Security Detkin

This decision was announced to me "____" _____ 193 ...

Moroz

Resolution: "The arrest was sanctioned by the Deputy Regional Prosecutor for Special Affairs"

[signature illegible]

April 23, 1938
Interrogation Protocol

April 24, 1938

On April 24, 1938, a 15-year-old detainee was interrogated in private with an NKVD officer, without a juvenile representative or a lawyer—a common Stalinist practice at the time. It might be worth looking at the transcript of the interrogation and testimony:

I, detective of the Kuznetsk regional department of the NKVD Ogorodnikov, carried out an interrogation of the accused:

1. Surname—Moroz
2. Name and patronymic—Vladimir Grigoryevich
3. Date of birth—1922 November 1
4. Place of residence—city: Moscow
5. [Current] Residence—village Annenkovo, orphanage
6. Nationality and citizenship—Jewish
7. Passport—not available
8. Occupation—a pupil of an orphanage and a student
9. Social origin—the son of employees
10. Social status (occupation and property status)
    a) before the revolution—the father is an employee
    b) after the revolution—the same

11. The composition of the family is single. Father Grigory Sem[enovich], Mother Fani Lvovna and brother Samuil were arrested. Second brother Alexander, 9 years old pupil of the Annensky orphanage.

Testimony of Accused Moroz Vladimir Grigoryevich

April 24, 1938

Question. Since when did you live in the Annensky orphanage?

Answer. I lived in the Annensky orphanage from October 23, 1937, arrived by direction of the NKVD from Moscow after the arrest of my father Grigory Semenovich and mother Fanya Lvovna.

Question. What is the circle of your close friends in Moscow and the Annensky orphanage?

Answer. The circle of my close friends is very limited. From Moscow I know well, as my friends, Kisin Ananias Abramovich; brothers Frunzik and Vladimir—sons of Emelyan Yaroslavsky; Martynov Vladimir, Kalachev Evgeny, Filler Vladimir Samuilovich, whom I know from school. Some of them, such as the Yaroslavskys, lived in the summer in a dacha next door to us, where we met. All these persons are dependent on their parents, who work in Soviet and party organizations. At the Annensky children's home, I don't have any close friends.

Question. The investigation knows that during your stay in the Annensky orphanage you carried out counter-revolutionary activities, tell us about this in detail?

Answer. I did not carry out counter[revolutionary] activities.

Question. You are not telling the truth. The investigation requires exhaustive testimony!

Answer. I repeat once again that I did not carry out counter-revolutionary activities.

Question. Letters of counter-revolutionary content found in your possession are presented to you, what can you reveal about this?

Answer. Yes! These counter-revolutionary letters belong to me, and I am the author of them. In these letters, I revealed clear hostility to the Soviet system, praising the Trotsky-Bukharin bandits, at the same time sympathizing with the convicted and executed enemies of the people and in every possible way compromised the leaders of the C[ommunist] P[arty] of the S[oviet] U[nion] (b[olsheviks]) and the Soviet government, personally Stalin.

Question. What prompted you to write these counter-revolutionary letters?

Answer. What prompted me to write these letters and embark on a counter-revolutionary path is the hostility and hatred that I have for the Soviet regime.

Question. Since when did you embark on the counter-revolutionary path and who prompted you to do so?

Answer. I embarked on a counter-revolutionary path, and then began to show my hatred for the Soviet government and the leaders of the CPSU (b) and the Soviet government as a result of the arrest of my father and mother and became even more embittered at the Soviet government after the arrest of my brother Samuil Grigoryevich Moroz.

Question. When was your brother arrested?

Answer. I do not know exactly, around January 1938.

Question. From whom did you learn about your brother's arrest?

Answer. The arrest of my brother became known from Filler Samuil Samuilovich, who informed me by letter from Moscow.

Question. The investigation has reliable data that there is a counter-revolutionary group of youth in which you were a member and organized counter-revolutionary activities. What can you say on this issue?

Answer. I know nothing about the counter-revolutionary youth group and cannot show anything about it.

Question. You speak falsely, the investigation requires truthful testimony about the existing counter-revolutionary youth organization!

Answer. I can't give any other evidence.
Written down correctly, from my words it was read to me in what and I sign
Moroz.

Ruling on the Filing of Charges

Kuznetsk

May 25, 1938I, operative officer of the district branch of the State Security Administration of the NKVD of the USSR for the Kuibyshev region, sergeant g/b Ogorodnikov, having examined the investigative material in case No. ____ and taking into account that Moroz Vladimir Grigoryevich, born in 1922, b/n, literate, a Jew by nationality, a native of Moscow, a pupil of an orphanage before his arrest, is sufficiently accused that, being hostile to the Soviet system, he carried out counter-revolutionary activities, that is, committing a crime under Art. 58-10 h. 1 of the Criminal Code of the RSFSR and guided by Article.Article. 128 and 129 Code of Criminal Procedure of the RSFSR,

RESOLVED:
Citizen Moroz Vladimir Grigoryevich to be brought as a defendant under Art. 58-10 h. 1 of the Criminal Code of the RSFSR.
P/detective of the district [district] department of the NKVD
state security sergeant Ogorodnikov
"AGREED" Head of the district department of the NKVD
lieutenant of state security [unsigned]
This resolution was announced to me on May 25, 1938.
Signature of the accused Moroz

Indictment
on charges of Mr. Moroz Vladimir Grigoryevich under
Paragraph 58-10 part 1 of the Criminal Code of the RSFSR

The indictment was drawn up in the city of Kuznetsk on June 14, 1938. The Kuznetsk Office of the NKVD received material that a pupil of the Annenkovskiy orphanage Moroz Vladimir Grigoryevich is carrying out counter-revolutionary activities among the pupils of the orphanage. The investigation carried out in this case established: That Moroz Vladimir Grigoryevich, upon his arrival at the Annenkovskiy orphanage, as being administratively expelled from Moscow after the arrest of his parents, among the youth of the orphanage was engaged in the spread of counter-revolutionary propaganda and slander against the leaders of the CPSU (b) and the Soviet government. He expounded all these counter-revolutionary views and slander in writing and read to the young people around him from among the pupils of the orphanage, praised the Trotskyist-Bukharin bandits, and at the same time sympathized with the executed enemies of the people (case sheet 8 and rev., 9 and rev., 11, 13, 15, 17).

Moroz Vladimir Grigoryevich, being interrogated on the subject of counter-revolutionary activities, pleaded guilty in full.

On the basis of the foregoing, the following are accused: Moroz Vladimir Grigoryevich, born in 1922, a native of Moscow, the son of an employee—currently arrested by the NKVD as an enemy of the people, literate, b/n, a Jew by nationality, before his arrest—a pupil of the Annensky children's home—that, being hostile to the Soviet system, he systematically carried out counter-revolutionary activities among the pupils of the orphanage, slandered the leaders of the CPSU (b) and the Soviet government, in particular Comrade. Stalin, i.e., in a crime under Art. 58-10 of part 1 of the Criminal Code of the RSFSR, and therefore—I WOULD LIKE: The case under consideration completed by the investigation and sent to the special committee for analysis. Board of the Region court, through the UNKVD in the Kuibyshev Region.

Assistant to the detective of the RO NKVD
state security sergeant Ogorodnikov

AGREE: Head[al] of the Kuznetsk RO NKVD Zagirov
REFERENCE
1. Attached to the case, as material evidence, is a letter from citizen [citizen] to Moroz of [counter]-r [revolutionary] content.
2. The accused Moroz has been kept in the Kuznetsk prison since April 25, 1938.

Assistant to the detective of the RO NKVD
state security sergeant OGORODNIKOV

*Characteristic on pupil of the Annenkovskiy children's colony
Vladimir Grigoryevich Moroz*

November 6, 1938
Moroz Vladimir Grigoryevich, 17 years old, arrived at the Annenkovskiy children's colony on a special permit from the NKVD of the USSR in October 1937. During his stay in the orphanage, he proved to be isolated from the entire team of pupils. He did not take part in socially useful work; he did not consciously carry out the workload of children's self-government. He did not comply with the internal regulations: he smoked in the bedroom, left the orphanage without permission, did not come to bed on time. He treated the educators and elders with disdain, answered the remarks of the educators with an evil smile and did not follow the orders of the educators. He did not perform labor processes and categorically refused to visit the workshops.
Director of the colony I. Sviridov

Letter from Mother of Vladimir Moroz to L. P. Beria

September 9, 1939
People's Commissar of the NKVD of the USSR Beria Lavrenty Pavlovich
from citizen Kreindel-Moroz Fanny Lvovna,
prisoner in Temlager of the special department of the NKVD
Statement
On September 9, 1937, in Moscow at st. Serafimovicha, 2, apt. 39, entrance number 2 I was arrested by the NKVD. Further, the resolution of the Special Meeting of the NKVD of the USSR was announced to me, that I, as a member of the family of a traitor to the Motherland, was subject to imprisonment in a camp for a period of 8 years.

After my arrest in this apartment, I left children: son Samuil Grigoryevich Moroz, 17 years old; son Vladimir Grigoryevich Moroz, 14 years old; son Alexander Grigoryevich Moroz, 8 years old.

Already in the camp, I asked about the fate of my children, and in March 1938 I was informed that two sons, that is, 15-year-old Vladimir and 9-year-old Alexander, were in an orphanage in Annenkovo, Kuznetsk district, Kuibyshev region. As for the eldest son Samuil, nothing was told to me. I repeatedly applied to the NKVD of Moscow with a request to inform me about my eldest son. And finally, at the end of May 1939, I was informed by the NKVD of Moscow that my sons Samuil and Vladimir had been arrested. When and what followed their arrest, I do not know anything. It is also unknown why the child, who is in the Kuibyshev region in an orphanage, was arrested by the NKVD of Moscow.

The eldest son finished his 10th grade with honors. [...]

The second son Vladimir—a student of the 8th grade, an excellent student, a pioneer, moving from class to class, awarded a certificate of merit, was also of exemplary behavior.

All these data speak for the fact that children could not commit crimes on their own, for which they were arrested by the NKVD. I assume that my children were subjected to repression in the same way as I, that is, as members of the family. But considering the instructions of the party and personally. Comrade Stalin—children are in no way responsible for their father. This instruction of the Leader, uttered repeatedly, gives me the right of a mother to turn to you, Mr. People's Commissar, with a petition—request, in the order of supervision, from the Moscow NKVD a case on charges of my children. Show a sensitive, attentive attitude and release children from custody.

From a very early age I worked honestly, and even in the camp since January 1938 I also work in my specialty—I am a pharmacist. I bravely endure my imprisonment as a member of the family, but that children at such an early age suffer—it takes everything from me, and only the hope of your legitimate intervention and investigation of the children's case gives me the strength to endure this suffering as well.

I beg you, Mr. People's Commissar, do not refuse my request and help the children return to their studies and their former honest life.

Children: Samuil Grigoryevich Moroz, born in 1920; Vladimir Grigoryevich Moroz, born in 1922

I kindly ask you to notify me of your subsequent order at the place of my location.

Kreindel-Moroz

Notes

Introduction

1 GARF, f. 5207, op. 1, d. 1, l. 5.
2 GARF, f. A-406, op. 25, d. 1347, l. 17.
3 Central Archive of the Federal Security Service of Russia (CAFSB), fond 3, op. 4., d. 1949, pp. 478–480.
4 M. N. Gernet, ed et al, *Deti-prestupniki* (Moscow: Znamenskii Publ., 1912), reprint. (Moscow: Kniga po trebovaniiu, 2013), 1.
5 P. I. Ljublinskij, "Okhrana detstva i bor'ba s besprizorn ost'ju za 10 let" in *Pravo i zhizn'*, Vinaver, A. et al, editors (Leningrad: Academiia, 1927), vol. 8, p. 30.
6 I first used this concept of *realpolitik* to explain the Bolshevik population policies, violent food procurement, and later collectivization in Boris B. Gorshkov, *Peasants in Russia from Serfdom to Stalin: Accommodation, Survival, Resistance* (London: Bloomsbury Academic, 2018), see especially chapters 12 and 13.
7 This matter will be explored in more details in the following chapters.
8 There is a misleading assumption that this tradition had already been destroyed earlier by the Provisional Government. See, for example, Potepalov D.V., "Detskaya besprizornost' v pervyye gody Sovetskoy vlasti: istoriograficheskiy ocherk" in *Nauchno-prakticheskiy zhurnal "Gumanizatsiya obrazovaniya"* No. 1 (Moscow, 2012): 23–9, 24. The Provisional Government did not eliminate private, church, and public charity, although it subordinated some of charitable institutions and endowments to the Ministry of Public Education or incorporated them into the Ministry of State Charity in order to coordinate charity nationwide.
9 M. Levitina, *Besprizornye, Sotsiologia. Byt. Praktika raboty* (Moscow: Novaia Moskva, 1925), 66.
10 *Pravda*, February 15, 1924.
11 For example, *Respublika SHKID*, a 1966 film based on the same story (1925) by Grigory Belyh and L. Panteleev and directed by Gennady Poloka talks about lives of pupils (former street children) of a boarding school for difficult children during the revolutionary and Civil War years. An example of street children in arts is "Homeless child Van'ka" (1924), a painting by a social realist artist A. A. Kokel.
12 See, for example, R.M. Bravaya, *Okhrana materinstva i mladenchestva na Zapade i v SSSR*. Moscow, 1929. V. P. Lebedeva, *Nekotoryye itogi*, Moscow, 1928, idem, *Okhrana materinstva i mladenchestva v strane Sovetov*. Moscow-Leningrad, 1934. The authors stress the inadequacy of childcare in western, capitalist, countries, and the advances of the Soviet Union in the matters of motherhood and childcare.
13 A. A. Slavko, "Detskaia Besprizornost' i beznadzornost' v Rossi Kontse 1920-kh—nachala 1950-kh godov: Sotsial'nyi portret, prichiny, formy bor'by." Avtoreferat dissertatsii na soiskaniye uchonoy stepeni doktora istoricheskikh nauk. Samarskii gosudarstvennyi universitet, Samara, 2011.

14 Kuskova Ye. D. "Besprizornaya Rus." Parizh. Sovremennyye zapiski. 1929. Reprint 1990. Cited in D. V. Potepalov, "Detskaya besprizornost' v pervyye gody sovetskoy vlasti: istoriograficheskiy ocherk" in *Gumanizatsiya obrazovaniya*, no. 1, (Moscow, 2012), 23-29:24.
15 A. N. Savel'yev, E. Y. Kostina, "Problema detskoy besprizornosti v SSSR v 20-30 gody," in *Nauchnyye issledovaniya i razrabotki molodykh uchenykh*, no. 5, (Novosibirsk, 2015), 114–16; D. V. Potepalov, S. A. Dneprov, "Blagotvoritel'naya deyatel'nost' v SSSR po Preodoleniyu massovoy detskoy besprizornosti (1917–1935 gg.)," in *Nauka i shkola*, no. 3, (Moscow, 2015), 124–30.
16 Natal'ia Viktorovna Semina, "Bor'ba s detskoy besprizornost'yu v 1920-ye—1940-ye gody v Rossii (na primere Penzenskogo regiona)." Kandidatskaia dissertatsiia, Penzenskiy gosudarstvennyy pedagogicheskiy universitet im. V. G. Belinskogo: Penza, 2007.
17 A. A. Slavko, *Istoria bespizornogo i beznadzornogo detstva Rossii: konets 1920-kh—nachalo 1950-kh godov* (Cheborsary: Perfectum, 2012), 3.
18 P. P. Shcherbinin, *"Pustite detei ko mne ...": "Deti bedy" i popechitel'stvo do i posle 1917 goda* (Tambov: Izdatel'skii dom "Derzhavinskii,") 2018.
19 I noticed at recent Russian and Soviet history conferences that many scholars of late imperial and Soviet Russia stress "neo traditionalism" to evaluate and explain the early Bolshevik and Stalinist government policies, including the food procurement and Stalinist terror, suggesting continuities from the imperial times and underscoring the similarities between late imperial and early Soviet Russia. This approach is misleading.
20 See discussion below in the introduction.
21 Wendy Z. Goldman, *Women, the State and Revolution: Soviet Family Policy and Social Life, 1917–1936* (Cambridge, U.K: Cambridge University Press, 1993), chapter 2.
22 In her review, historian Joan Neuberger rightly noted that Ball's book lacks "the larger cultural and political context that informed social policy and determined its outcome." Neuberger finds problematic the author's hypothesis that "neither the Bolsheviks nor communism should be blamed for widespread besprizornost' but rather pre-existing poverty, the dislocation of war and revolution, and especially the famine of 1920-22." Joan Neuberger, "*Alan Ball, And Now My Soul Is Hardened. Abandoned Children in Soviet Russia* (Berkeley: University of California Press, 1994)" *AHR* April 1995.
23 Alan Ball, *And Now My Soul Is Hardened. Abandoned Children in Soviet Russia* (Berkeley: University of California Press,1994). Among other English-Language studies are "Children of the Revolution: Soviet Russia's Homeless Children (*Besprizorniki*) in the 1920s" by Jennie Stevens in Russian *History* 9, (2–3):242–64; and "Homeless Children in the USSR, 1917–1957" by Margaret K. Stolee in *Soviet Studies* XL (1): 64–83.
24 For more discussion about the Bolshevik food procurement campaign, see Gorshkov, *Peasants in Russia from Serfdom to Stalin: Accommodation, Survival, Resistance*, chapter 12; Michael S. Melancon, "Trial Run for Soviet Food Requisitioning: The Expedition to Orel Province, Fall 1918," *The Russian Review*, 69 (July 2010): 412–37.
25 Semyon Samuilovich Vilensky, Cathy A. Frierson, eds, *Children of the Gulag*. Annals of Communism Series (New Heaven and London: Yale University Press, 2010); Cathy A. Frierson, *Silence Was Salvation: Child Survivors of Stalin's Terror and World War II in the Soviet Union* (New Heaven and London: Yale University Press, 2015).

26 Julie K. deGraffenried, *Sacrificing Childhood: Children and the Soviet State in the Great Patriotic War* (Lawrence, KS: University of Kansas Press, 2014).
27 Catriona Kelly, *Children's World: Growing Up in Russia, 1890–1991* (New Haven: Yale University Press, 2007); Elizabeth White, *A Modern History of Russian Childhood from the Late Imperial Period to the Collapse of the Soviet Union* (New York: Bloomsbury Academic, 2020).
28 GARF, f. 5207, op. 1, d. 1, l. 5.
29 GARF, f. 5207, op. 1, d. 48, l. 7, Kalinina's report.
30 N. Krupskaya, "Bor'ba s detskoi besprizost'iu" *Pravda* (March 7, 1923), no. 51.
31 GARF, f. 5207, op. 1, d. 295, l. 2–9.
32 GARF, f. 5207, op. 3, d. 19, l. 124.

Chapter 1

1 GARF, f. 5207, op. 1, d. 1, p. 5.
2 G. N. Ulyanova, *Philanthropy in the Russian Empire. The 19th and Early 20th Centuries* (Moscow: Nauka, 2005).
3 P. P. Shcherbinin, *"Pustite detei ko mne …": "Deti bedy" i popechitel'stvo do i posle 1917 goda* (Tambov: Izdatel'skii dom "Derzhavinskii," 2018).
4 V. V. Feonychev, "Deyatel'nost' gosudarstvennykh i obshchestvennykh organizatsiy po likvidatsii besprizornosti v Rossii v 1920-ye gody (na primere Penzeskoy, Samarskoy, Simbirskoy guberniy)." Avtoreferat dissertatsii na soiskaniye uchenoy stepeni kandidata istoricheskikh nauk. Kazan', 2017, p. 21.
5 See Adele Lindenmeyr, *Poverty Is Not a Vice: Charity, Society, and the State in Imperial Russia* (Princeton, NJ: Princeton University Press, 1996).
6 M. F. Vladimirskii-Budanov, *Obzor istorii Russkogo prava*, 7th edition (Saint Petersburg, Kiev: Izdatel'stvo knizhnogo magazina N. Ogloblina, 1915), p. 437.
7 Cited in N. L. Rubinshtein, *Sel'skoe khoziaistvo Rossii vo vtoroi polovine XVIII veka* (Moscow: Goslitizdat, 1957), p. 11.
8 Cited in V. P. Mel'nikov, E. M. Kholostova, *Istoriia Sotsial'noi Raboty v Rossi* (Moscow: Marketing, 2002), 187.
9 Boris B. Gorshkov, *Peasants in Russia from Serfdom to Stalin: Accommodation, Survival, Resistance* (London: Bloomsbury Academic, 2018), see the introductory chapter.
10 M. V. Firsov, Istoriia sotsial'noi raboty v Rossi (Moscow: Vlados, 1999), 5.
11 Cited in M. M. Gromyko, *Mir russkoi derevni* (Moscow: Molodaia gvardiia, 1991), 48.
12 Ibid., 43.
13 M. F. Vladimirskii-Budanov, *Obzor istorii Russkogo prava*, 7th edition, (Saint Petersburg, Kiev: Izdatel'stvo knizhnogo magazina N. Ogloblina, 1915), pp. 461–2.
14 V. I. Sergeevich, *Lektsii i issledovaniia po drevnei istorii russkigo prava*, 4th edition (St. Petersburg: Stasiulevich 1910), 506.
15 V. I. Dal', *Tolkovyy s lovar' zhivogo velikorusskogo yazyka* (Moscow: Tsitadel', 1998), 21.
16 Gorshkov, *Russia's Faculty Children*. See especially chapter 1. Also see M. M. Gromyko, *Traditsionnye normy povedeniia i formy obshcheniia russkikh krest'ian XIX veka* (Moscow: Nauka, 1986), 20, 25–6, 31–2.
17 Gorshkov, *Russia's Factory Children*, chapter 1.

18 Engel'gardt, Aleksandr Nikolayevich, *Pis'ma iz derevni* (Moskva: Algoritm, 2010), letter 5; A. N. Engelgardt, *Pis'ma iz derevni* (1872–1877), letter 5, p. 201. Source: http://www.hist.msu.ru/ER/Etext/ENGLGRDT/index.html.
19 This source is in the Electronic Publications of the Institute of Russian Literature (the Pushkin's House) of the Russian Academy of Sciences. http://lib2.pushkinskijdom.ru/tabid-4870.
20 Cited in N. F. Basov, *Istoriia sotsial'noi raboty* (Moscow: Dashkov i K, 2007), 29. See also Blagotvoritel'naia Rossiia. Istoriia gosudarstvennoi, obshchestvennoi i chastnoi blagotvoritel'nosti v Rossii, P. I. Lykoshin, ed., vol. I, part I, (Saint Petersburg: S. Petersburgskaia elektropechatnia, 1901), 58.
21 Makarii (Bulgakov, Mikhail Petrovich). *Istoriia Russkoi tserkvi*, vol. 1, (Saint Petersburg: Tipografiia Imperatorskoi Akademii, 1857), 138; an electric version is available at http://lib2.pushkinskijdom.ru/tabid-4870.
22 B. O. Kliuchevskii, *Istoricheskiie portrety* (Moscow: Pravda, 1990), p. 495; A. S. Gorinskii, "Izmenenie kharaktera deiatel'nosti pedagoga v innovatsionnykh prostessakh obucheniia," in *Innovatsionnye proekty i programmy v obrazovanii*, no 4, (Moscow: Akademiia sotsial'nogo upravleniia, 2012), 24–9; *Blagotvoritel'naia Rossiia*. Vol. 1, 59.
23 A. M. Kapustina "Pravoslavno-khristianskaya traditsiya blagotvoritel'- nosti v Rossii: filosofsko-religiovedcheskiy analiz" Avtoreferat dissertatsii kandidata filosofskikh nauk, (Belgorod: Belgorodskii gosudsrstvennyi universitet, 2007), 15.
24 "Russkaia Pravda. Prostrannaia redaktsiia" in *Русская Правда*. In Y. P. Titov, *Khrestomatiia po istorii gosudarstva i prava v Rossii* (Moscow: Prospekt, 2007), 9–25.
25 Ibid.
26 A. D. Stog, "Ob obshchestvrnnom prizrenii v Rossii," published in St. Petersburg in 1818, reprint in *Antologiia sotsial'noi raboty*, 5 vols, M. V. Firsov, ed. (Moscow: Svarog, 1995), 3:30–1.
27 S. A. Kniazkov, *Golod v drevnei Rossii* (St. Petersburg: K. D. Tikhomirova, 1908), 5–6.
28 Historians of medieval and early modern Russia are increasingly problematizing the idea of "Muscovite autocracy" suggesting reciprocal relations between the ruler and the people. Rulers, including Ivan IV, were expected to seek advice from the wider society, including the peasantry. As historian Nancy Kollmann observed, in Muscovite political culture, "the power of the ruler was *de facto* limited by dense networks of theory, custom, and political pragmatism, 'autocracy' was not absolute, and multiple social forces played a role in keeping the realm legitimate." See Nancy Shields Kollmann, "A Muscovite Republic?," *Slavic Review*, vol. 80, no. 3, (Fall 2021), 492–77: 497.
29 B. V. Agadzhanov, "Sozdateli pervykh uchebnykh knig dlia nachal'nogo obucheniia gramote—buivarei I azbuk XVI—pervoy chetverti XVIII vv" in *Problemy sovremennogo obrazovaniya*, 2010, № 2 (Moskva Moskovskiy pedagogicheskiy gosudarstvennyy universitet, 2010):50–77, 51–2.
30 *Sudebnik tsarya i velikogo knyazya Ivana Vasil'yevicha. Zakony iz Yustianovykh knig. Ukazy dopolnitel'nyye k Sudebniku i Tamozhennyy ustav* (St. Petersburg: Tipografiia Imperatorskoi academii nauk, 1768).
31 "Stoglav" in Khrestomatiya po istorii SSSR XIV—XVII vv., V. A. Aleksandrov, V. I. Koretskii, authors, A. A. Zimin, ed. in chief (Moscow: Sotsekgiz, 1962), 118–20.
32 Ibid.
33 Boris Godunov was the first non-Rurikid ruler of Russia. He came from the oldest Tatar noble family and a descendant of the Tatar prince Chet, who left the Golden Horde for Russia, converted to Christianity, and founded the Ipatiev Monastery

in Kostroma. After Boris Godunov's death, his throne was assumed by his older son Feodor (Feodor II), who ruled for a few months and was assassinated with his mother during an anti-Godunov's plot.
34 A. I. Zagorovsky, *Kurs semeynogo prava* (Odessa: Tip. aktsionernogo Yuzhno-russkogo obshchestva pechatnogo dela, 1909), 103.
35 S. F. Platonov, *Boris Godunov*, reprint (Moscow: Agraf, 1999), 139.
36 Stog, 30–1.
37 I. N. Shamina, "Iz istorii Vologodskikh monastyrey XVI—XVII veka". *Otechestvennaya istoriya*. Vol. 1. (Moscow, 2003), pp. 141–54, 150.
38 Ibid.
39 M. Y. A. Volkov, "Russkaya pravoslavnaya tserkov' v XVIII veke," in *Russkoye pravoslaviye—Vekhi istorii*, ed. Klibanov A. I. (Moscow: Politizdat, 1989), 157.
40 Cited in S. S. Sulakshin, D. V. Bachurina, M. V. Vilisov, G. G. Karimova, I. R. Kish, O. V. Kuropatkina, L. A. Makurina, A. S. Sulakshina, *Blagotvoritel'nost' v Rossii i gosudarstvennaya politika* (Moscow: Nauchnyy ekspert 2013), 19.
41 Ibid.
42 For more discussion about Peter the Great, see Evgenii V. Anisimov, *The Reforms of Peter the Great: Progress through Violence in Russia* (London and New York: Routledge, 2015); Paul Bushkovitch, *Peter the Great* (London and New York: Rowman and Littlefield, 2003); James Cracraft, *The Revolution of Peter the Great* (Harvard: Harvard University Press, 2003); Lindsey Hughes, *Russia in the Age of Peter the Great* (New Heaven and London: Yale University Press, 1998); Basil Dmytryshyn, *Modernization of Russia Under Peter I and Catherine II* (New York and Toronto: Wiley, 1974) among other studies.
43 Sobranie zakonov Rossiiskoi Imperii, vol. 5, 1714, nos. 2844, 2851.
44 P. I. Lytoshkin, *Blagotvoritel'naia Russiia: istoriia gosudarstvennoy, obshchstvennoy i chastnoi blagotvoritel'nosti v Rossii* (Saint Petersburg: Peterburgskaya Elektropechatnya, 1901).
45 M. N. Gernet, *Detoubiystvo. Sotsiologicheskoe i sravnitel'no-yuridicheskoe issledovanie* (Moscow: Izdatel'stvo Moskovskogo universiteta, 1911), pp. 55–6.
46 Sobranie zakonov Rossiiskoi Imperii, vol. 5, 1714, no. 2856.
47 A. V. Bodrin, L. A. Tobol'ko, "Sotsial'naia podderzhka detei v Rossii: Istoticheskii aspekt (X-XIII vek)" in *Molodoi uchenyi* no. 23 (103) (December 2015), 808–11: 809.
48 Sobranie zakonov Rossiiskoi Imperii, 1723, no. 4277.
49 For a discussion about Catherine the Great reign, see John T. Alexander, *Catherine the Great: Life and Legend* (New York: Oxford University Press, 1988).
50 E. E. Vagina A. Yu. Nagornova, "Prizreniye i sotsial'naya zashchita detey-sirot i detey, ostavshikhsya bez popecheniya roditeley, v Rossii s drevneyshikh vremen do vtoroy poloviny XX v," Istoriya i sovremennost', vol. 1, (March 2016), pp. 154–70, 161.
51 Idem.
52 I. A. Stepanova, "Sotsial'no-pravovaya zashchita detstva v rossii v khviii veke," *Pedagogicheskoye obrazovaniye*. 2008. № 3, p. 71.
53 V. V. Beliakov, *Sirotskie detskiie uchrezhdeniia Rossii* (Moscow: Eksmo, 1993).
54 Sotsial'naya podderzhka detey v Rossii: istoricheskiy aspekt (X–XVIII vv.) Bodrin, Aleksey Vladimirovich; Tabol'ko, Lyudmila Anatol'yevna, student, *Molodoy uchonyi*, no. 23 (103), December 2015, p. 809.
55 P. Shcherbako, 31–2; Kuz'michev, Aleksandr Viktorovich, Sozdaniye i deyatel'nost' prikazov obshchestvennogo prizreniya v posledney chetverti XVIII—pervoy polovine XIX veka: na materialakh Verkhnego Povolzh'ya avtoreferat kandidatskoy Orenburgskiy gosud pedagogicheskiy universitet.

56 A. Yu. Nagornova, E. E. Vagina, "Prizreniye i sotsial'naya zashchita detey-sirot i detey, ostavshikhsya bez popecheniya roditeley, v Rossii s drevneyshikh vremen do vtoroy poloviny XX v." in Istoriya i sovremennost'. Vol. 1, (March 2016): 154–70, 161.
57 I. A. Stepanova, "Sotsial'no-pravovaya zashchita detstva v rossii v khviii veke," in Pedagogicheskoye *obrazovaniye*. 2008. № 3, p. 71.
58 Nechaeva, 98.
59 Olonetskie gubernskie vedomisti (April 24, 1865), 255–6; N. A. Korablev, T. A. Moshina, *Pimenovy: dinastiya predprinimateley, blagotvoriteley, obshchestvennykh deyateley* (Petrozavodsk: Periodika, 2016), 107.
60 *Ustavy blagotvoritel'nykh uchrezhdeniy brat'yev P., A. i V. Bakhrushinykh* (Moscow: Gorodskaya tip., 1903), 51.
61 V. A. Bryzgalova "Iz istorii blagotvoritel'nosti," *Innovatsii i investitsii*, no. 12, (2015), pp. 106–9, 108.
62 A. A. Slavko, "Nachalo formirovaniya normativno-pravovoy bazy po bor'be s detskoy besprizornost'yu i beznadzornost'yu v Rossii v pervyye gody sovetskoy vlasti" in *Izvestiya Altayskogo gosudarstvennogo universiteta, Istoriia i arkheologiia*, 2009, p. 129.
63 Boris Gorshkov, Child Factory Labor, see chapter one.
64 *Entsiklopedicheskii Slovar'*, vol. 22 (St. Petersburg: Efron, 1897), 510–11.
65 *Polnoye sobraniye zakonov Rossiyskoy imperii*. Sobraniye 3. 1902. T. XXII. S. 492–5.
66 A. N. Krivonosov, "Istoricheskiy opyt bor'by s besprizornost'yu," *Gosudarstvo i pravo*, vol. 7 (Moscow, 2003), 92–8.
67 Novoye ugolovnoye ulozheniye, utverzhdonnoye 22 marta 1903 goda. Saint-Peterburg: Izdaniye Kamennooyetrovsshcho Yuridncheskago Knizhnogo Magazina V. P. Anisimova, 1903. No. 41, nos. 53–7.
68 *Novoye ugolovnoye ulozheniye, utverzhdonnoye 22 marta 1903 goda.* (Saint Peterburg: Izdaniye Kamennooyetrovsshcho Yuridncheskago Knizhnogo Magazina V. P. Anisimova, 1903); No. 41, nos. 53–7.
69 For example, in the United States, the death penalty has been banned for children who committed crimes only in 1988 and 2005, the death penalty was outlawed for these, who committed murder under the age of 18.
70 For more discussion about child labor laws, see Boris B. Gorshkov, *Russia's Factory Children: State, Society and Law, 1800–1917* (Pittsburgh: University of Pittsburgh Press, 2009).
71 Ibid.
72 Ibid., p. 169.
73 M. A. Galaguzova, Y. N. Galaguzova, *Sotsial'naia pedagogika: Kurs lektsii* (Moscow: Vlados, 2002), 14–15.
74 N. Beliavskii, "Agrarnye lageria dlia sel'skikh sirot" in *Pravitel'stvennyi vestnik*, no. 71 (March 29, 1916).
75 Ibid. "Agrarnye lageria dlia sel'skikh sirot" in *Pravitel'stvennyi vestnik*, no. 71 (March 29, 1916).
76 GARF, f. 5207, op. 1, d. 294, l.1.
77 P. I. Ljublinskii, "Okhrana detstva i bor'ba s besprizorn ost'ju za 10 let," in Pravo i zhizn', Vinaver, A. M. et al, eds (Leningrad: Pravo i zhizn', 1927), vol. 8, p. 28.
78 Beliavskii, "Agrarnye lageria dlia sel'skikh sirot" in *Pravitel'stvennyi vestnik*, no. 71 (March 29, 1916).
79 Krivonosov, 92–8.
80 M. I. Levitiva (Maro), *Besprizornye, sotsiologia. Byt, Practika raboty* (Moscow: Novaia Moskva, 1925), 66.

Chapter 2

1. *Pravda*, February 15, 1924.
2. Nechayeva A. M. *Rossiya i yeye deti: (rebenok, zakon, gosudarstvo)* (Moscow: Graal', 2000), 104.
3. *Bol'shaia Sovetskaia Entsiklopediia*, vol. 5, (Moscow: Entsiklopediia, 1927), 783.
4. *Kommuna*, August 18, 1923.
5. A. V. Obrosov, "Lozhe Sovnarkoma: rasskaz o vremeni, kotoroye nazyvali zolotymi godami nepa." *Rodina*, 1991, no. 9–10, p. 115.
6. I have no direct confirmation of this figure which is taken from Soviet-era historians. See "Sorsial'no-pravovaia ohkrana nesovershennoletnihk" in A. G. Kalashnikov and M. S. Epshtein, eds. *Pedagogicheskaia Entsiklopediia* (Moscow: Rabornik prosveshcheniia, 1930), vol. II, 349–54.
7. In their biography of Felix Dzerzhinsky, the Soviet VCHeKa head, the authors cited the figure of 5 million homeless children in late 1920–early 1921. A. A. Soloviev, S. S. Khromov, and F. E. Dzerzhinsky, *Biographia*. 2nd edition. (Moscow: Politizdat, 1977). Officials from the Commissariat of Enlightenment referred to 7.5 million street children in late 1920. See "O bor'be s detskoi besprizornost'iu. Urverzhdennoe Kollegiei NKP postanovlenie Vserossiiskogo S'ezda ONO," in S. S. Tizianov and M. S. Epshtein, eds., *Gosudarstvo I obshchestvennost' v bor'be s detskoi besprizornost'iu* (Moscow, Leningrad: Narkompros, 1927), 35. English-language studies also suggest similar figures between 5 and 7.5 million. See discussion in Alan Ball, "The Roots of Besprizornost' in Soviet Russia's First Decade" in *Slavic Review*, vol. 51, no. 2 (Summer 1992), 247. Regardless of the exact figure, the proportion of street children to the total children's population of the early Soviet state was astonishingly large.
8. *Izvestia*, February 26, 1928.
9. GARF, f. 5207, op. 1, d. 294, l. 2.
10. *Bol'shaia Sovetskaia Entsiklopediia*, 1st edition, vol. 5, 1926. See "besprizorniki."
11. Poznyshev S. V. *Detskaya besprizornost' i mery bor'by s ney* (Moscow: Novaia Moskva, 1926), 8–9.
12. Rozhkov, A. YU. "Bor'ba s besprizornost'yu v pervoye sovetskoye desyatiletiye." In *Voprosy istorii*. No. 11. 2000.
13. Slavko, *Detskaya besprizornost' v Rossii v pervoye desyatiletiye Sovetskoy vlasti* (Moscow: INION RAN, 2005), 65.
14. T. M. Smirnova, «Detskiye doma i trudkolonii: zhizn' «Gosudarstvennykh detey» v sovetskoy Rossii v 1920–1930-ye gg,» *Vestnik RUDN*, seriya Istoriya Rossii (Moskva, 2012): 16–38, 18.
15. *Pravda*, no. 229 (October 12, 1921).
16. GARF, f. 5207, op. 1, d. 88, l. 38.
17. GARF, f. 5207, op. 1, d. 17, l. 46, 50 and idem, d. 70, l. 31.
18. *Krasnaya Zvezda of the Petrograd* (March 29, 1922).
19. GARF, f. 5207, op. 1, d. 1, l. 5.
20. *Vsesoyuznaya perepis' naseleniya 17 dekabrya 1926 g.: kratkiye svodki*, Tables, Table 1, (Moscow: izd. TSSU Soyuza SSR, 1927), 2–3; *Naseleniye Rossii v XX veke*, 3 volumes. (Moscow: Rospen, 2000),1: 106, 154.
21. In the USSR, the rural population was five times more than the urban population. As of 1923, there were over 133 million inhabitants throughout the Union, of which more than 111 million were in villages and about 22 million in cities. K. Krupskaya,

Pedagogicheskiie sochineniia v desiati nomakh, 10 volumes. (Moscow: Izdatel'stvo Academii pedagogicheskikh nauk, 1959), 6: 26; *Naseleniye Rossii v XX veke*, 1: 60.
22 *Naseleniye Rossii v XX veke*, 1: 99.
23 *Naseleniye Rossii v XX veke*, 1: 44.
24 *Naseleniye Rossii v XX veke*, 3 volumes. (Moskva: Rossiyskaya politicheskaya entsiklopediya (Rospen), 2000), 1: 43.
25 Cited in A. Rozhkov, "Besprizorniki," 8.
26 Alec Nove, *An Economic History of the USSR* (London: Allen Lane/Penguin Press, 1969), 68–74. Cite my article for Orel.
27 GARF, f. 5207, op. 1, d. 88, l. 93.
28 P. I. Ljublinskii, "Okhrana detstva i bor'ba s besprizorn ost'ju za 10 let" in *Pravo i zhizn'*, Vinaver, A. M. et al, eds (Leningrad: Pravo i zhizn', 1927), vol 8, p. 30.
29 *Pravda* (December 17, 1920).
30 GARF, f. 1235, op. 96, d. 36, l. 11.
31 *Pravda* (September 14, 1921).
32 For discussion about collectivization of agriculture in Russia, see Boris B. Gorshkov, Peasants in Russia from Serfdom to Stalin, chapter 13.
33 GARF, f. 5207, op. 3, d. 15, ll. 106–8.
34 *Izvestia VTsIK*, no. 32 (February 4, 1919).
35 See S. S. Tizanov, "Sorsial'no-pravovaia ohkrana nesovershennoletnihk," in A. G.Kalashnikov and M. S.Epshtein, eds. *Pedagogicheskaia Entsiklopediia* (Moscow, 1927–29), vol. II, 349–54.
36 V. I. Lenin, *Unknown documents, 1891–1922* (Moscow: ROSSPEN, 2000), 246.
37 Decrees of the Peoples Commissariat of State Charity of December 12 and 13, 1917. Decree of February 18, 1918. http://www.libussr.ru/doc_ussr/ussr_86.htm.
38 GARF, f. 5207, op. 1, d. 48. l. 26.
39 GARF, f. 130, op. 2, d. 758, l. 623.
40 GARF, f. 5207, op. 1, d. 87, ll 145–6.
41 Gosudarstvennyy obshchestvenno-politicheskiy arkhiv Nizhegorodskoy oblasti (GOPANO), f. 19, op. 1, d. 93, ll. 56–56 ob.
42 GARF, f. 5207, op. 1, d. 87, l. 11.
43 GARF, f. 5207, op 1, d. 48, l. 43 (March 9, 1921).
44 GARF, f. 5207, op. 1, d. 1, l. 41, Ob obespechenii detskikh uchrezhdenii.
45 This discussion is based on my book *Peasants in Russia from Serfdom to Stalin: Accommodation, Survival, Resistance* (London: Bloomsbury Academic Press, 2018), see chapter 12.
46 Discussions can be found in Lars T. Lih, *Bread and Authority in Russia, 1914–1921* (Berkeley: University of California Press, 1990), and Michael Melancon, "Trial Run for Soviet Food Requisitioning: The Expedition to Orel Province, Fall 1918," *The Russian Review*, vol. 69, no. 3 (July 2010), pp. 412–37.
47 A. N. Krivonosov, "Istoricheskiy opyt bor'by s besprizornost'yu," *Gosudarstvo i pravo*, vol. 7 (Moscow, 2003), 92–8.
48 V. I. Lenin, *Polnoe sobranie sochinnii*, 5th edition, vol. 50 (Moscow: Politizdat, 1965), p. 137.
49 GASO, f. R-523, op. 1, d. 8, l. 60.
50 For more discussion about the Tambov province, see Orlando Figes' seminal work *Peasant Rassia, Civil War: Volga Countryside in Revolution, 1917–1921* (Oxford: Clarendon Press, 1989), p. 250.
51 GARF, f. 393, op. 3, d. 44, ll. 172–3; idem, d. 160, ll 91–5; idem, d. 210, l. 50.

52 Ryabinina N. V. Detskaya besprizornost' i prestupnost' v 1920-ye gg. (Po materialam guberniy Verkhnego Povolzh'ya). S. 13.
53 By a decree of the All-Russian Central Executive Committee (VTsIK) and the Council of People's Commissars of October 30, 1918, a one-time emergency ten-billion-dollar revolutionary tax was introduced, which supplemented the system of regular direct taxes. The tax was introduced with the aim of seizing money from parasitic and counter-revolutionary elements and turning them to the urgent needs of revolutionary construction and the defense of the country. This tax was levied according to the layout system; the total amount of the tax was laid out by provinces, cities, counties, and parishes, and then by payers. According to the decree, this layout was to be carried out in such a way that with all its weight the tax would fall on the rich part of the urban population and rich peasants. The urban and rural poor were completely exempted from paying taxes; the middle strata of the population were taxed at low rates. In rural areas, the volost Soviets determined the amount of tax for individual farms in conjunction with the committees of the poor supposedly aimed against the kulaks. Instead, it fell on all but the very poorest peasants (members of the committees of the poor). Rather than the intended 10 billion, the emergency tax yielded only about 1.5 billion rubles.
54 GAPO, f. R-1897, op. 1, d. 80, l. 157. Copy.
55 G. D. Fadeyeva, "Metody bor'by s bezdomnost'yu v Rossii v 1917–1939 gg," in *Molodoy uchenyy*. 2013. no. 12 (59). 767–9.
56 Gosudarstvennyy arkhiv Respubliki Mariy El (GA RME), f. 95 p, op. 1, d. 18, l. 50.
57 GANO, f. p 1, op. 2, d. 31, l. 15. Typewritten copy.
58 GATO, f. R 11, op. 2, d. 183, l. 136. Handwritten original.
59 For more discussion about the procurement campaign, see T. M. Kitanina, *Voina, khleb,i revoliutsiia: Prodovol'stvennyi vopros v Rossii, 1914–oktiabr' 1917 g* (Leningrad: Nauka, 1985); Silvana Malle, *The Economic Organization of War Communism, 1918–1921* (Cambridge, England: Cambridge University Press,, 1985); Orlando Figes, *Peasant Russia, Civil War: The Volga Countryside in Revolution (1917–1921)* (New York: Clarendon Press of Oxford University Press, 1989); Mary McCauley, *Bread and Justice: State and Society in Petrograd 1917–1922* (New York: Clarendon Press of Oxford University Press, 1991); Donald Raleigh, *Experiencing Russia's Civil War: Politics, Society, and Revolutionary Culture in Saratov, 1917–1922* (Princeton: Princeton University Press, 2002); Peter Holquist, *Making War, Forging Revolution: Russia's Continuum of Crisis, 1914–1921* (Cambridge, MA: Harvard University Press, 2002); James Heinzen, *Inventing a Soviet Countryside. State Power and the Transformation of Rural Russia, 1917–1929* (Pittsburgh: Pittsburgh University Press, 2004); Sarah Badcock, *Politics and People in Revolutionary Russia: A Provincial History* (Cambridge, England: Cambridge University Press, 2007); Aaron Retish, *Russia's Peasants in Revolution and Civil War: Citizenship, Identity, and the Creation of the Soviet State, 1914–1922* (Cambridge, England: Cambridge University Press, 2008); Eric Landis, *Bandits and Partisans: The Antonov Movement in the Russian Civil War* (Pittsburgh: Pittsburgh University Press, 2008); Alexander Rabinowitch, *The Bolsheviks in Power: The First Year of Soviet Rule in Petrograd* (Bloomington: Indiana University Press, 2008) and Michael Melancon, "Trial Run for Soviet Food Requisitioning: The Expedition to Orel Province, Fall 1918", *The Russian Review* 69 (July 2010): 412–37.
60 Conversation with M. I. Gorshkova, January 10, 2012.
61 *Krest'ianskaia Revoliutsia v Rossi, 1902–1922: Documenty i materialy*, V. Danilov, T. Shanin, eds, (Moscow: Rosen, 2002), 35.

62 Ibid.
63 GASO, f. R-523, op. 1, d. 8, l. 57, 58.
64 See discussion in chapter 3.
65 RGAE, f. 1943, op. 1, d. 693, ll. 32–3 (about). Script. Manuscript.
66 TOTSDNI, f. 1, op. 1, d. 278, l. 122. Handwritten copy.
67 GANO, f. r 1, op. 2, d. 70, l. 16. Typewritten copy.
68 A. M. Kristkaln, "Golod 1921 g. v Povolzh'ye: opyt sovremennogo izucheniya problemy." Avtoreferat kandidatskoy dissertatsii. Avtoreferat kandidatskoi dissertatsii, Moscow, Moscow State University, 1997.
69 GARF, f. 1064, op. 1, d. 110, l. 13. Certified copy, typescript. Notes: 1. The letter was registered on 12 / IX-1921.
70 *Pravda* (January 27, 1922).
71 *Naseleniye Rossii v XX veke*, 1: 103.
72 *Naseleniye Rossii v XX veke*, 1: 130, 132.
73 *Naseleniye Rossii v XX veke*, 1: 136.
74 The cases of cannibalism were exceptional in response to the famine and hardship. They did not become common place, but they had been documented.
75 Polyakov YU. A. *Perekhod k NEPu i sovetskoye krest'yanstvo* (Moscow: Nauka,1967), 510.
76 AT RT, f. R-4470, op. 1, d. 6, l. 16 rev.
77 Vse—na pomoshch 'Povolzh'yu! Predsamgubkomgoloda. (Samara: Gos.izd-vo, Samar.otd-niye, 1922), 4.
78 NA RT, f. R-4470, op. 1, d. 6, l. 18 ob.
79 GARF, f. 5207, op.1, d. 48, ll. 7–8.
80 Alexander Serafimovich, "Deti", Pravda (Moscow), August 12, 1921.
81 B. Kronin, "Golod i deti" Izvestiia VTsIK (Moscow), March 21, 1922, p. 2.
82 Anatolii Lunacharsky, "Ne zabudem detei" Pravda no. 168 (Moscow), August 2, 1921, p. 1.
83 B. Kronin, "Golod i deti" Izvestiia VTsIK (Moscow), March 21, 1922, p. 2.
84 GARF, f. 5207, op.1, d. 48, ll. 7–8.
85 "Svodka otdela upravleniya Omskogo gubispolkoma sovetov o politicheskom i ekonomicheskom polozhenii gubernii za 1–15 avgusta 1921 goda," GANO, f. r.1, op. 1, op. 661, ll. 178–9. Mashinopisnyy podlinnik.
86 GANO, f. r. 1, op. 1, d. 469, l. 88. Typographic print.
87 GARF, f. 5207, op. 1, d. 48, l. 175.
88 GARF, f. 5207, op. 1, d. 83, l. 56.
89 This discussion is based on my book *Peasants in Russia from Serfdom to Stalin*, chapter 13.
90 *Krest'yanskaia gazetta* (March 26, 1929), TSA FSB, f. 2, op. 7, d. 513, ll. 86–100. Copy.
91 TSA FSB, f. 2, op. 11, d. 42, ll. 151–152. Certified copy no. 278.
92 The scale of hunger is difficult to assess due to the lack of reliable demographic statistics. Recent Russian-language studies based on archival data suggest a range of 3 to 5 million deaths due to starvation and repressions. See V. V. Tsaplin, "Statistika zhertv stalinizma v 30-ye gody." *Voprosy istorii*. Vol. 4. 1989: 177–178. and E. A. Osokina, *Za fasadom "stalinskogo izobiliya": raspredeleniye i rynok v snabzhenii naseleniya v gody industrializatsii, 1927–1941*. Moskva: ROSSPEN, 2008.
93 For more discussion about peasant resistance during collectivization, see Lynne Viola, *Peasant Rebels under Stalin: Collectivization and the Culture of Peasant Resistance* (London and New York: Oxford University Press, 1996) and Sheila Fitzpatrick, *Stalin's Peasants: Resistance and Survival in the Russian Village after Collectivization*, London and New York: Oxford University Press, 1994).

94 *Pravda*, No. 6, March 2, 1930.
95 GARF, f. 5207, op. 3, d.15, ll. 106–8.
96 Amartya Sen, *Poverty and Famines: An Essay on Entitlement and Deprivation* (Oxford, UK: Clarendon Press, 1981). I thank Professor Sheila Fitzpatrick for this citation. See Fitzpatrick, *Stalin's Peasants*, 70.

Chapter 3

1 N. K. Krupskaya, *Izbrannye pedagogicheskiie proizvedeniia*, eds. I. A. Kairov, et al (Moscow: Izdatel'stvoAkademii pedagogicheskikh nauk RSFSR, 1955), 186.
2 N. K. Krupskaya, *Pedagogicheskiie proizvedeniia*, 10 vols., eds. N. K. Goncharov, et al (Moscow: Izdatel'stvo Akademii pedagogicheskikh nauk RSFSR, 1958), 2: 7.
3 "Detskoye dvizheniye i kommunisticheskoye vospitaniye," *Pravda* (2 September 1924).
4 P. I. Lyublinskiy, «Zadachi okhrany detstva» in P. I. Lyublinskiy, S. I. Kapelyanskaya, *Okhrana detstva i bor'ba s besprizornost'yu* (Leningrad: Academia, 1924), 8.
5 A. A. Slavko, "Kontseptsiya bor'by s detskoy besprizornost'yu v otechestvennoy istoriografii 1920-kh gg." *Vestnik IGEU* Vyp. 1 (2010), 2.
6 *Pravda*, no. 2 (January 4, 1921).
7 *Izvestia*, no. 152 of July 20, 1918.
8 V. I. Lenin i A. V. Lunacharskiy. *Perepiska, doklady, dokumenty. Literaturnoye nasledstvo*. Vol. 80. (Moscow: Nauka, 1971), 61, 63.
9 For more discussion about Krupskaya, see Clements, Barbara Evans, *Bolshevik Women* (Cambridge, UK: Cambridge University Press), 1997; Jane McDermid and Anya Hilyar, "In Lenin's Shadow: Nadezhda Krupskaya and the Bolshevik Revolution," in Ian D. Thatcher (ed.), *Reinterpreting Revolutionary Russia* (New York: Palgrave Macmillan, 2006), pp. 148–65 among other studies.
10 Richard Stites, *The Women's Liberation Movement in Russia, Feminism, Nihilism, Bolshevism, 1860–1930* (Princeton: Princeton University Press, 1978), 329.
11 For discussion about some aspects of late imperial schooling, see Boris B. Gorshkov, *Russia's Factory Children*, chapter 4.
12 Julie K. deGraffenried, *Sacrificing Childhood*.
13 Aleksandr Zinovyev, *Homo sovieticus*. (New York: Grove/Atlantic, 1986).
14 I. A. Kairov and N. K. Krupskaya, *Pedagogicheskiie sochinennia v desiati tomakh*, 10 volumes, eds. I. A. Kairov, et al (Moscow: Izdatel'stvo Akademii pedagogicheskikh nauk RSFSR, 1958), 2: 12.
15 Ibid., 6: 29.
16 Tamara Yusufovna Krasovitskaya. "N. K. Krupskaya—ideolog bol'shevistskoy reformy obrazovaniya," in Trudy Instituta rossiyskoy istorii. Vyp. 5 Rossiyskaya akademiya nauk, Institut rossiyskoy istorii; otv. red. A. N. Sakharov. (Moscow: Nauka, 2005), p. 255.
17 Boris B. Gorshkov, *Russia's Factory Children: State, Society, and Law, 1800–1917* (Pittsburgh: University of Pittsburgh Press, 2009).
18 *Pravda*, 34, (April 16, 1917).
19 Krasovitskaya, 247.
20 Krupskaya, *Pedagogicheskiye sochineniya*, vol. 1, p. 278.
21 Krasovitskaya, 247.

22 E. Khazanova, Rost detskoy besprizornosti i organizatsiya bor'by s neyu. Na pomoshch' rebenku. (Petrograd -Moscow, 1923), 47, cited in T. M. Smirnova, 16.
23 E. K. Mineeva, V. A. Morozov, and A. S. Yantseva "Puti preodoleniya detskoi besprizornosti v sovet- skoi Rossii v 1920-1930-e gody," *Vestnik Chuvashskogo gosudarstvennogo pedagogicheskogo universiteta*, no. 2 (2012) (74), 98.
24 A similar observation is made by historian Galina Nikolaevna Ulyanova. Ulyanova suggested that Soviet social support as a whole was not original, but in some ways imitated the later imperial times. G. N. Ulyanova, "Charity, and social security in 1917-1918 in the Politics of the Provisional Government and the Council of People's Commissars," paper delivered at online seminar of the Russian Revolution Research Group of BASEES (British Association for Slavonic and East European Studies), March 23, 2022.
25 Sobranie uzakonenii RSFSR [Collection of laws of the RSFSR], 1917, no. 11, Article 160.
26 Sobranie uzakonenii RSFSR [Collection of laws of the RSFSR], 1917, no. 10, Article 152.
27 *Sobranie uzakonenii RSFSR* [Collection of laws of the RSFSR], 1918, no. 89, Article 906.
28 Decrees of the Peoples Commissariat of State Charity of December 12 and 13, 1917. Decree of February 18, 1918. http://www.libussr.ru/doc_ussr/ussr_86.htm.
29 Ibid.
30 *Pravda*, no. 163 (August 2, 1921).
31 *Izvestia*, May 20, 1919.
32 Ibid; "Pitanie detei," *Izvestia Petrogradskogo Soveta* (Petrograd) June 25, 1919, p. 1, *Bednota* (Moscow) January 14, 1920, 2.
33 *Dekrety Sovetskoy vlasti*, vol. I, 25 oktyabrya 1917 g.—16 marta 1918 g. (Moscow: Gosudarstvennoe izdatel'stvo politicheskoy literatury, 1957).
34 *Detskaya defektivnost', prestupnost' i besprizornost'. Po materialam 1 Vserossiyskogo s"yezda 24/VI—2/VÍI 1920 g.* Redaktsiya Byuro Mediko -Pedagogicheskoy Konsul'tatsii Narkomprosa (Moscow: Gosudarstvennoye izdatel'stvo, 1920), 87.
35 Izvestiia VTsIK, no. 14 (January 22, 1920).
36 Ibid.
37 GARF, f. 5207, op. 1, d. 87, l. 11.
38 The decree on free food, issued in 1919 and signed by Lenin, read: 1) All food items issued by local food agencies to children under the age of 14 inclusive, continue to be issued free of charge at the expense of the state. 2) The effect of this decree shall be extended to the largest factory centers and cities, large towns, etc. (There is a list of 16 provinces). 3) Make all food agencies obligated to sell baby food in the first place. 4) The right to free food is granted to all children of the above age, regardless of the class ration category of their parents. *Pravda*, no. 58 (March 17, 1922).
39 GARF, f. 5207, op. 1, d. 87, l. 11; Izvestiia Petrogradskogo Sovieta, no. 140 (25 June 1919).
40 Among multiple causes of bipolar disorder, there are environmental ones, including child abuse and long-term stress. While one cannot be certain that all members of the Bolshevik government had been abused as children, one can certainly suggest that all of them experienced long-term stress, as revolutionaries. For more information about bipolar disorder, see D. Healy, Mania: A Short History of Bipolar Disorder (Baltimore: Johns Hopkins University Press, 2011).

41 Of note here is that the Stalinist government usually was meeting during night times in the 1930s, when the most outrageous policies and acts were conducted. This may also find its explanation in psychiatry and mental disorders.
42 *Izvestiia*, May 8, 1919.
43 Krivonosov A. N. "Istoricheskiy opyt bor'by s besprizornost'y," *Gosudarstvo i pravo*. No 7. 2003, 93; Rozhkov, 134–5.
44 Rozhkov, 134.
45 Ibid., 135.
46 Burlakova T. T., "Postroyeniye i funktsionirovaniye gumanisticheskoy vospitatel'noy sistemy detskogo doma, osnovannoy na filosofsko-pedagogicheskikh ideyakh L. N. Tolstogo." Dissertatsiya kandidata pedagogicheskikh nauk (Tula, 2001), 34.
47 Rozhkov, 135.
48 TSA FSB, f. 1, op. 6, d. 248, ll. 1–2.
49 TSA FSB, f. 1, op. 6, d. 248, ll. 21–3; Ibid., f. 2, op. 1, d. 180, l. 161.
50 TSA FSB, f. 2, op. 1, d. 180, l. 65.
51 TSA FSB, f. 2, op. 1, d. 180, ll. 167–9.
52 For more discussion about American Relief Administration activities in Russia, see Geller M. YA., Nekrich A.M. *Utopiya u vlasti*. (Moscow: MIK, 2000), 114.
53 *Izvestiia* VTsIK, no. 130 (May 12, 1920).
54 *Pravda*, no. 40 (February 23, 1921).
55 Ibid.
56 GARF, f. 1235, op 96, d. 165, l. 51–2; B. Kronin, "Golod i deti" *Izvestiia*, March 21, 1922, p. 2.
57 *Izvestiia* VTsIK, no. 64 (March 21, 1922).
58 *Pravda*, no. 51 (March 7, 1923).
59 GARF, f. 5207, op. 1, d. 43, l. 7–16.
60 M. Boguslavskiy, "Bor'ba s detskoy besprizornost'yu v RSFSR," 142.
61 GARF, f. 5207, op. 1, d. 48, ll. 1, 123.
62 GARF, f. 5207, op. 1, d. 48, l. 33.
63 B. Kronin, "Golod i deti" *Izvestiia* VTsIK (Moscow), March 21, 1922, p. 2.
64 V. Zenzinov, *Besprizorniki* (Parizh: Sovremennyye Zapiski, 1929), 30–1.
65 Ibid., 33.
66 GARF, f. 5207, op. 1, d. 48, l. 283; d. 4, l. 10.
67 I. Y. Semenova, "Rabota Vserossiiskikh s"ezdov deiatelei po okhrane detstva i yacheek obshchestva 'Drug detei' po ukrepleniiu i okhrane sem'i v molodom sovetskom gosudarstve," *Vestnik Chuvashskogo universiteta*. (2019. No. 4), 193; Mineeva E.K., Morozov V.A., Yantseva A.S. "Puti preodoleniya detskoi besprizornosti v sovetskoi Rossii v 1920–1930-e gody" [Ways to overcome child neglect in Soviet Russia in the 1920s – 1930s]. *Vestnik Chuvashskogo gosudarstvennogo pedagogicheskogo universiteta*, 2012, no. 2(74): 97–101.
68 E. D. Maksimov, *Razvitiye sistemy obshchestvennogo prizreniya detey i podrostkov v Rossii* (Moscow: Akademiya, 2007), 342.
69 *Izvestia* VTsIK (February 24, 1921).
70 Khmel'nitskaya A.P. *Spasennoye detstvo*. M., 1987, 127.
71 M. I. Davydov, "Zabota o detyakh Iz istorii deyatel'nosti Soveta Zashchity detey v 1918–1920 godakh," *Istoriya SSSR*, no. 5 (1979), 163–71.
72 Ibid.
73 Khmel'nitskaya, *Spasennoye detstvo*, (Moscow: Moskovskii pabochii, 1987), 127.

74 A. D. Kalinina, *Desyat' let raboty po bor'be s detskoy besprizornost'yu*. (Moscow, Leningrad, 1928), 38.
75 GARF, f. 5207, op.1, d. 48, l. 7.
76 GARF, f. 5207, op. 1, d. 48, l. 16.
77 Kalinnikova-Magnusson L.V., Magnusson M. "Sotsial'naya politika v otnoshenii detskoy «defektivnosti» v voyenno-revolyutsionnyy period i v pervuyu dekadu sovetskoy vlasti (1914–1927 gg.)," *Vestnik Pomorskogo universiteta*. Seriya: gumanitarnyye i sotsial'nyye nauki, 2015, no. 1, p. 158.
78 T.M. Smirnova, «Detskiye doma i trudkolonii: zhizn' «Gosudarstvennykh detey» v sovetskoy Rossii v 1920–1930-ye gg,» Vestnik RUDN, seriya Istoriya Rossii (Moskva, 1912): 16–38, 20.
79 In his book *Children-Criminals* (1912), M. N. Gernet investigated the ratio of the number of crimes by different age categories (14–17 and 17–21 years old). Based on his findings, he proposed establishing punishment for juvenile offenders for each group separately and to introduce this norm into the Russian criminal law. He drew attention to the constant change in the Soviet legislation of the age for bringing minors to criminal responsibility and argued that these measures had a positive experience of Soviet legislation: the prohibition of the application of capital punishment to minors under the age of 18; mitigation of punishment by half for persons aged 14 to 16 years old, and by one third for persons aged 16 to 18 years old. Garnet also devoted to complex issues of the sanity of juvenile criminals that he considered it appropriate to divide them into two categories. The first is unconditional insanity, when a minor is an irresponsible person and, after committing a crime, cannot be brought to court to determine punishment. The second—sanity is considered only probable, and the question of establishing its presence or absence is brought up for consideration by the court. See *Deti-prestupniki*, M. N. Gernet, Ed at al, (Moscow: Znamenskii Publ., 1912)and M. N. Gernet, *Sotsial'no-pravovaya okhrana detstva za granitsei i v Rossii* (Moscow: Pravo i Zhizn' Publ., 1924).
80 RGASPI, f. 17, op. 2, d. 104; Also see *Izvestia* VTsIK (February 24, 1921); and Zubov N.I., F.E.Dzerzhinsky: Biographia (Moscow: Gospolitizdat, 1963), 257.
81 *Izvestiia*, January 22, 1920; *Izvestiia Petrosoveta*, no. 43 (February 8, 1920); and *Izvestiia*, March 4, 1920.
82 *Izvestiia* VTsIK, no. 14 (January 22, 1920).
83 *Krasnaia Gazeta*, no. 122 (June 6, 1920).
84 GARF, f. 4085, op. 22, d. 22, l. 7.
85 GARF, f. 5207, op. 1, d. 48, l. 317.
86 Dzerzhinskaia, 342; also see Portnov.

Chapter 4

1 F. Dzerzhinsky, Dnevnik zaklyuchennogo. *Pis'ma*, (Moscow: Molodaya gvardiya, 1984), 23.
2 RGASPI, f. 76, op. 3, d. 149, ll. 57–8. Script. Manuscript.
3 GARF, f. 5207, op. 1, d. 2, ll. 462–563.
4 In fact, Felix Dzerzhinsky played a very important role during these years. A Polish revolutionary, Dzerzhinsky from 1917 until his death in 1927 headed the Cheka. Besides the Cheka, he also headed the following key commissariats and

committees: chair of the All-Russian Council of the National Economy (VSNHK) (1921–7), Commissar of the Commissariat of Transportation (1921–7) and chair of the Council of Labor and Defense of USSR. His contemporaries named him "the threatening shield of the revolution" (see A. V. Lunacharsky, "Dzerzhinsky v Narkomprose", in I. E. Polikarpenko, ed., *Rytsar' Revol'utsii. Vospominaniia sovremennikov o F.E Dzerzhinskom* (Moscow: Politizdat, 1967), 277; Stasova E.D., "Vsegda s Massami" in Polikarpenko I. E., 295.

5   S. D. Gladysh, *Deti bol'shoy bedy* (Moscow: Izdatel'skiy dom "Zvonnitsa-MG," 2004), 5–6.
6   GARF, f. 5207, op. 1, d. 43, l. 7–16.
7   N. Ye. Vrangel', *Vospominaniya. Ot krepostnogo prava do bol'shevikov* (Moscow: Novoye literaturnoye obozreniye, 2003). Ebook. https://readli.net/vospominaniya-ot-krepostnogo-prava-do-bolshevikov/?ysclid=l5iny3288m121642066.
8   M. N. Gernet, *Prestupnyy mir Moskvy* (Moscow: Pravo i zhizn', 1926).
9   Gladysh, 7.
10 Ibid., 6.
11 N. V. Riabinina, *Detskaia besprizornost i prestupnost' v 1920-e gody* (Yaroslavl': Yaroslavskii gosudarstvennyi universitet, 1999), 8–9.
12 GASO, f. R. 81, op. 1, d. 331, l. 170.
13 TSGAMO, f. 66, op. 1, d. 483, ll. 195–8 ob. Script. Typescript.
14 SOGASPI, f. 1, op. 1, d. 337, l. 56.
15 Ugolovnoye pravo Rossii. Chast' obshchaya, Ed. in chief Kruglikov L.L. (Moscow: Yurisprudentsiya, 2005), 92.
16 V. Zenzinov, *Besprizornyye* (Parizh: Izdatel'stvo Sovremennyy Zapiski, 1929), 49.
17 Ibid.
18 *Criminal Code of the Russian Soviet Socialist Republic*, 1922 edition.
19 Kruglikov, 92.
20 *Criminal Code of the Russian Soviet Socialist Republic*, 1922 edition, article 56.
21 *Ugolovnyi kodeks Possiiskoi Sovetskoi Federativnoi Sotsialisticheskoi Respubliki*, redaktsiia 1924 goda, (Moscow: Izdaniie voennoi kollegii verkhovnogo tribunala VTsIK, 1925).
22 *Ugolovnyi kodeks Possiiskoi Sovetskoi Federativnoi Sotsialisticheskoi Respubliki*, redaktsiia 1926 goda, (Moscow: Izdaniie voennoi kollegii verkhovnogo tribunala VTsIK, 1927).
23 Nadezhdin, "God v Butyrskoy Tiur'me," in Cheka, Materialy po deiatel'nosti chrezvychaihyhk comissii (Berlin: Orfei, 1922), 149.
24 Ibid.
25 *Kommunicticheskii Trud*, no. 167 (October 10, 1920). Also see MChKa. *Iz Istorii Moskovskoi Chrezvychainoi Kommissii* (Moscow: Moskovsky Rabochii, 1978) 246.
26 GARF. f. 8409, op. 1, d. 67, l. 227. Original. Manuscript.
27 GARF. f. 8409, op. 1, d. 406, l. 104. Original. Typescript.
28 GARF, f. 8419, op. 1, d. 8, l. 54. Typescript.
29 Evgenia Ratner was a Socialist-Revolutionary who advocated the for true soviet power and against the Bolshevik subordination of the Soviets, for which she was persecuted by the Bolshevik authorities. For more discussion, see David Shub, "The Trial of the SRs" *The Russian Review*, vol. 23, no. 4 (October 1964), pp. 362–9.
30 Kalinina, *Desyat' let raboty po bor'be s detskoy besprizornost'yu*, 33.
31 Lunacharsky, "Dzerzhinsky v Narkomprose," 278.
32 GARF, f. 5207, op. 1, d. 1, l. 23.

33 *Izvestiia* (February 12, 1921, February 17, 1921); also see S. S. Dzerzhinskaia, *V Gody Velikikh Boiev* (Moscow: Mysl', 1964), 143–4; and V. P. Portnov, 174.
34 F. E. Dzerzhinsky, *Izbrannyye stat'i i rechi* (Moscow: Politizdat, 1947), 47.
35 TSA FSB, f. 66, op. 1-T, d. 28, ll 96–7. Copy; *Mchka. Iz Istorii Moskovskoy Chrezvychaynoy Kommissii* (Moscow: Moskovskii Rabochii, 1978), 264–6.
36 Polikarpenko, 282.
37 GARF, f. 5207, op. 1, d. 8, l. 20. See also: Ibid., ll. 74, 158; d. 48, ll. 5 ob, 9; d. 82, l. 13; d. 168, l. 126.
38 *Pravda* (February 27, 1921).
39 Dzerzhinsky F. E., *Izbrannyye stat'i i rechi*, M., 1947, 53.
40 Livshits Ye. Sotsial'nyye korni besprizornosti. M., 1925. S. 133.
41 Dzerzhinsky F. E., *Izbrannyye stat'i i rechi*, M., 1947, 53.
42 GARF, f. 5207, op. 1, op. 8, l. 19 ob.
43 Smirnova.
44 GARF, f. 5207, op. 1, d. 48, l. 209.
45 GARF, f. 5207, op. 1, d. 48, l. 200.
46 RGASPI, f. 76, op. 3, d. 204, l. 23. Original. Typescript.
47 *Izvestiia* (February 24, 1921).
48 Dzerzhinskaia, 348.
49 Ibid.
50 *Izvestia*, January 26, 1926, no. 20.
51 "V predchuvstvii pereloma. Poslednie pis'ma i zapiski F. E. Dzherzhinskogo" *Kommunist*, no. 8 (May 1989): 82.
52 GARF, f. 5207, op. 1, d. 88, l. 21.
53 GARF, f. 5207, op. 1, d. 88, l. 21.
54 GARF, f. 5207, op. 1, d. 87, l. 36.
55 GARF, f. 5207, op. 1, d. 94, l. 87.
56 GARF, f. 5207, op. 1, d. 293, ll. 27, 28.
57 A. V. Puzykin, "Razvitie gazetnoi periodicheskoi pechati na territorii sovremennoi Kemerovskoi oblasti v 20-e gg. XX v." *Izvestiia Altaisogo gosudarstvennogo universiteta* no 4-4 (Barnaul, 2008), p. 164.
58 *Izvestia*, December 18, 1923.
59 GARF, f. 5207, op. 1, d. 85, l. 9.
60 Ibid.
61 Ibid.
62 GARF, f. 5207, op. 1, d. 303, l. 33.
63 Ibid.
64 Ibid.
65 TSDNIKK, f. 1. Kubano-Chernomorskiy obkom RKP(b), op. 1, op. 173. Materialy oblastnoy komissii po uluchsheniyu byta detey, ll. 1–1 ob.
66 GAVO, f. 37, op. 1, d. 117, ll. 202.
67 Blonsky, "Nedeli pomoshchi detyam kak effektivnaya forma bor'by s besprizornost'yu v sovetskoy Rossii nachala 1920-kh gg."
68 V. Nevzorov, «Deti posle voyny i goloda v Krymu,» *Krasnaya nov'*, 1923, no. 5, p. 207.
69 *Pravda*, no. 64 (March 23, 1923).
70 *Krasnaia Nov'. Litaraturno-khudozhestvennyi i nauchno-publitsesricheskii zhurnal* (Moscow-Leningrad: Gosudarstvennoe izdatel'stvo, August 1927), 146.
71 Krivonosov A. N. Istoricheskiy opyt bor'by s besprizornost'yu, *Gosudarstvo i pravo*. No. 7, 2003, 92–8.

72   GARF, f. 5207, op. 1, d. 85, l. 2.
73   *Besprizornye v trudovykh kommunakh: Praktika raboty s trudnymi det'mi*, V. L. Shveitser, S. M. Shabalova, eds, (Moscow: Glavsotsvos NKP, 1926), 6.
74   GARF, f. 5207, op. 1, d. 306, ll. 5–6.
75   GARF, f. 5207, op. 1, d. 301, l. 3.
76   RGASPI, f. 76, op. 3, d. 149, ll. 57–8.
77   Krivonosov, 97.
78   Matvey Samoylovich Pogrebinsky (1895, Belilovka, Russian Empire—April 4, 1937, Gorky, USSR)—employee of the Cheka-OGPU-NKVD of the USSR, founder, and head of the Bolshevskaya Labor Commune (1926–8), Commissar of State Security 3rd rank (1935). Plenipotentiary Representative of the OGPU under the Council of People's Commissars of the USSR for the Gorky Territory, Head of the NKVD Directorate for the Gorky Territory. Under the threat of imminent arrest, he committed suicide.
79   Pogrebinskiy, M.S. Trudovaya kommuna OGPU. M.: Gosizdat, 1928. 26–42.
80   Pogrebinskiy, M.S. Trudovaya kommuna OGPU. M.: Gosizdat, 1928. 15.
81   T. A. Antonova, «Sotsial'no-pedagogicheskaya rabota s besprizornymi det'mi i nesovershennoletnimi pravonarushitelyami v Bolshevskoy trudovoy kommune» Vestnik Novgorodskogo gosudarstvennogo universiteta, 64, 2011 (Novgorod, 2011), 12–13.
82   Ibid., 14.
83   Ibid.
84   A. S. Makarenko. Shkola zhizni, truda, vospitaniya. Uchebnaya kniga po istorii, teoriii praktike vospitaniya. Chast' 9. Frolov, A. A., ed. in chief. (Nizhniy Novgorod: Minskiy universitet, 2017), 74, 78.
85   Boris Paramonov, *MZh: Muzhchina i zhenshchina* (Mocosw: Act, 2010), 92.
86   Idem.
87   Gotts Khillig, *V poiskakh istinnogo Makarenko. Russkoyazychnyye publikatsii, 1976–2014* (Poltava: PNGU im. V.G. Korolenko, 2014), 195.
88   *Izvestia*, July 17, 1928.
89   GARF, f. 5207, op. 2, d. 1, l. 56; also see K. S. Tsvigun, ed., F. E. Dzerzhinsky. *Biographia* (Moscow: Politicheskaia literatura, 1977), 286.n.
90   *Pravda*, no. 51 (March 7, 1923). Nadezhda K. Krupskaya was the wife of Vladimir I. Ulyanov (Lenin); during these years she chaired the editorial staff of a journal *Narodnoe Obrazovanie* (People's Education), an official organ of the Commissariat of Education.
91   O mestnykh fondakh imeni V. I. Lenina dlya organizatsii pomoshchi besprizornym detyam (Post. VTsIK i SNK RSFSR ot 26 yanvarya 1925 g.) *Sobranie uzakonenii*, 1925 g., No. 8, s. 52.
92   Ibid. (February 13, 1924).
93   Ibid., no. 40 (February 19, 1924).
94   Ibid. (February 22, 1924).
95   GARF, f. 5207, op. 1, d. 1, l. 5.
96   M. Boguslavskiy, "Bor'ba s detskoy besprizornost'yu v RSFSR," 143.
97   Koroleva V.M. Sotsial'no-pravovaya okhrana nesovershennoletnikh (20–30-ye gg.). S. 12.
98   Pravda (February 27, 1924).
99   Pravda (February 29, 1924).
100 Ibid., no. 59 (March 3, 1925).

101 GARF, f. 5707, op. 1, d. 306, l. 19.
102 GARF, f. 5707, op. 1, d. 306, l. 4.
103 GARF, f. 5207, op. 1, d. 292, l. 39.
104 Yekaterina Alekseyevna Bender, Bor'ba s besprizornost'yu i beznadzornost'yu nesovershennoletnikh v RSFSR v 1920–30-ye gg (na materialakh Leningrada i Leningradskoy oblasti) Dissertatsiya kandidata istoricheskikh nauk (Sankt-Peterburg: Sankt-Peterburgskiy Gosudarstvennyy universitet, 2015), 77.
105 GARF, op. 1, d. 293, l. 17.
106 A. N. Krivonosov and A. Rozhkov, "Besprozorniki" in *Kommuna v Nikolo–Ugreshe. g. Dzerzhinsky Moskovskoy oblasti. Dokumenty, stat'i, ocherki, vospominaniya* (Dzerzhinsky Moskovskoy oblasti: DMUP «Informatsionnyy tsentr»; MAUK «Kul'turno-esteticheskiy tsentr», 2012), 16.
107 Ibid.
108 Rozhkov, "Bor'ba s besprizornost'yu v pervoye sovetskoye desyatiletiye," *Voprosy istorii*, vol. 3 (Moscow, 2000), 138.
109 Ibid., 137.
110 RGANI, f. 6, op. 13, d. 71, ll. 135–39. Script.

Chapter 5

1   I. V. Stalin. *Sochineniia*, 18 vols., vol. 13, 1930–1934 (Moscow: Pilitizdat, 1951), 270.
2   GARF, f. 5207, op. 1, l. 125.
3   *Komsomol'skaia pravda* (January 29, 2015).
4   *Deti GULAGa: 1918–1956*, S.S. Vilenskiy, A.I. Kokurin, G.V. Atmashkina, I.YU. Novichenko.
5   Sheila Fitzpatrick, *Stalin's Peasants: Resistance and Survival in the Russian Village after Collectivization* (London: Oxford University Press, 1996), 219.
6   GARF, f. 5207, op. 3, d. 15, ll. 106–8.
7   Pis'mo zaveduyushchego detskoy trudovoy koloniyey Fokinskogo rayona Zhikina v redaktsiyu rayonnoy gazety «Kolkhoznik-l'novod». November 15, 1930. GASO, f. r-233, op. 1, d. 1377, ll. 125–29ob.
8   Semyon Samuilovich Vilensky, Cathy A. Frierson, eds, *Children of the Gulag. Annals of Communism Series* (New Heaven and London: Yale University Press, 2010); Cathy A. Frierson, *Silence Was Salvation: Child Survivors of Stalin's Terror and World War II in the Soviet Union* (New Heaven and London: Yale University Press, 2015).
9   For informative discussions of this topic, see Robert Conquest, *The Harvest of Sorrow: Soviet Collectivization and the Terror-Famine* (New York: Oxford University Press, 1986); Lynne Viola, *Peasant Rebels under Stalin: Collectivization and the Culture of Peasant Resistance* (New York: Oxford University Press, 1996); Lynne Viola, *The Unknown Gulag. The Lost World of Stalin's Special Settlements* (New York: Oxford University Press 2007); Sheila Fitzpatrick, *Stalin's Peasants: Resistance and Survival in the Russian Village after Collectivization* (New York: Oxford University Press, 1994).
10 T. A. Solov'yeva, «Povsednevnaya zhizn' sovetskogo provintsial'nogo goroda v 1920–1930-ye gg.: na materialakh g. Saratova," avtoreferat kandidatskoy dissertatsii. Saratovskiy gosudarstvennyy universitet imeni N. G. Chernyshevskogo. Saratov, 2014.

11 Samara Regional GASPI, f. 1141, op. 14, d. 7, ll. 136–136ob.
12 Ibid.
13 "Spetsial'naya dokladnaya zapiska GPU" (Special memorandum of the GPU). January 28, 1932.Top secret. GANISO, f. 1, op. 1, d. 2086, ll. 16–18. Script.
14 "Spetsial'naya dokladnaya zapiska GPU" (Special memorandum of the GPU). January 28, 1932.Top secret. GANISO, f. 1, op. 1, d. 2086, ll. 16–18. Script.
15 Ibid.
16 TSA FSB, f. 2, op. 10, d. 513, l. 258.
17 TSA FSB, f. 2, op. 10, d. 508, ll. 41–3.
18 TSA FSB, f. 2, op. 10, d. 508, ll. 105–107.
19 GA Rostov region, f. R-1485, op. 8, d. 272, l. 201.
20 GAOPI Voronezh region, f. 2, op. 1, d. 2459, l. 15. Original.
21 TSA FSB, f. 3, op. 1, d. 35, l.140.
22 Ibid.
23 TSA FSB, f. 3, op. 4, d. 1949, ll. 478–80. Copy.
24 TSA FSB. f. 3, op. 1, d. 35, l. 141.
25 GANO. f. P-47, op. 5, d. 200, ll. 86–7 rev. Copy.
26 Samara Regional GASPI. f. 1141, op. 14, d. 7, l. 136–36ob.
27 *Pionerskaya Pravda*, 1930, no. 87.
28 Tragediya sovetskoy derevni. Kollektivizatsiya i raskulachivaniye. Dokumenty i materialy Tom 5. 1937–1939. Kniga 2. 1938–1939. Moskva ROSSPEN 2006. Str. 383–4 Arkhiv: GARF. f. 8131, op. 37, D. 141. L. 56–7.
29 Ibid.
30 Tragediya sovetskoy derevni. Kollektivizatsiya i raskulachivaniye. Dokumenty i materialy Tom 5. 1937–1939. Kniga 2. 1938–1939. Moskva ROSSPEN 2006. Str. 383–4 Arkhiv: GARF. f. 8131, op. 37, d. 141, l. 56–7. Kopiya.
31 *Krest'izanskaia pravda*, February 27, 1929.
32 TSA FSB. f. 2, op. 9, d. 695. ll. 142–59.
33 Ibid.
34 *Tragediia Sovetskoi derevni*, vol. 2, p. 376.
35 Cited in Irina Valentinovna Goncharova, "Krest'yanstvo Tsentral'no-Chernozemnoy oblasti v usloviyakh podgotovki i provedeniya kollektivizatsii v 1928–1932 gg." Doctoral dissertation. Rossiyskaya akademiya narodnogo khozyaystva i gosudarstvennoy sluzhby pri Prezidente Rossiyskoy Federatsii (Moscow 2015), 292.
36 GAOO. f. P-48, op. 1, d. 431, l. 109; Goncharova, 292.
37 Yuri Druzhnikov, Informer 001: The Myth of Pavlik Morozov Rutledge.
38 For an informative discussion ofMorozov's story see Catriona Kelly, *Comrade Pavlik: The Rise and Fall of a Soviet Boy Hero* (London: Granta Books, 2005).
39 Goncharova, 292.
40 Cited in V. A. Ippolitov, "Raskulachivaniye v Tsentral'nom Chernozem'ye na rubezhe 1920-kh – 1930-kh godov: rol' komsomola" in Genesis: istoricheskiye issledovaniya. – 2016. – No 3. – S. 42.
41 GARF, f. 3316, op. 1, d. 448, ll. 66–8.
42 GARF, f. 3316, op. 1, d. 448, l. 45.
43 GANO. f. 1353, op. 3, dll. 67. l. 11.
44 GANO. f. 1353, op. 3, d. 70. ll. 157, 158.
45 A special settlement for dispossessed peasants in the Kulai tract in the northeast of the modern Omsk region existed from 1930 to 1947. The Kulay commandant's office included twenty-two settlements. In the 1930s, there was a high mortality rate of

special settlers due to hunger, difficult living conditions and lack of medical care. The exact death toll is unknown. Apparently there was no common cemetery on Kulai; the dead were buried in the forest near the settlement in which they lived.

46   TSA FSB, f. 2, op. 10, d. 379a, ll. 96–7.
47   TSA FSB. f. 2, op. 10, d. 513, ll. 93–103.
48   GANO. f. 47, op. 5, d. 177, ll. 2–5, 7, 8.
49   GANO. f. 288, op. 5, d. 11, ll. 127–128ob. 1933.08.02.
50   GANO. f. 1353, op. 1, d. 97, l. 33. Original.
51   GARF. f. P-2306, o. 69, d. 242, l. 85. Typescript. Script.
52   RGANI. f. 6, o. 13, d. 71, ll. 135–9. Script.
53   RGANI. f. 6, o. 13, d. 21, ll. 154–6. Certified copy.
54   Georgy Ivanovich Blagonravov was the Deputy People's Commissar of Railways. On May 25, 1937, he was arrested, sentenced to death in a "special order" on December 2, 1937, on charges of "participation in an anti-Soviet counter-revolutionary organization in the NKVD," and shot on June 16, 1938.
55   RGASPI f. 81, o. 3, d. 99, ll. 121–3. Autograph.
56   GDA SBU, f. 16, on. 1, ref. 340, arch. 11–42. Original. Typescript.
57   TSA FSB, f. 3, o. 2, d. 799, ll. 1–11.
58   TSA FSB. f. 3, o. 1, d. 317, ll. 36–44. Certified copy.
59   TSA FSB. f. 3, o. 1, d. 317, ll. 41–21.
60   Istoriya stalinskogo Gulaga. Konets 1920-kh—pervaya polovina 1950-kh godov. Sobraniye dokumentov v 7 tomakh. T. 1. Massovyye repressii v SSSR / Otv. red. N. Vert, S. V. Mironenko; otv. sostavitel' I. A. Zyuzina.—M.: Rossiyskaya politicheskaya entsiklopediya (ROSSPEN), 2004.—S. 258.
61   Aleksandr Orlov, *Taynaya istoriya stalinskikh prestupleniy* (Moskva: Izdatel'stvo Vsemirnoye Slovo, 1991), 51.
62   Alexander Orlov (Leib Lazarevich Feldbin), the author of the memoirs, was respected and normally trustworthy. Leib was born on August 21, 1895, in a Jewish family living in the city of Bobruisk, Minsk province. In 1916 he was drafted into the ranks of the tsarist army but did not get to the front. In February 1917, he joined the Mezhraionka Social Democrats, a group of SDs who wished to unite the Bolshevik and Menshevik parties, and during the Civil War became a member of the Bolshevik Party. In 1920, he became an employee of the Special Department of the 12th Army and took part in the disclosure and liquidation of counter-revolutionary organizations in Ukraine. In 1921, the party sent Lev Lazarevich to Arkhangelsk to lead the secret operational unit there. After a short time, he was appointed head of the intelligence and investigation department and authorized to release White Guard officers who were given the opportunity to leave Russia. In the same year, Nikolsky, as a promising worker and member of the RCP(b), received a referral to study in Moscow, where he spent the next four years as a student at the School of Law, created on the basis of Moscow University. All this time, he combined study in classrooms with practical work in law enforcement agencies, and upon completing his studies, he enlisted as an employee of the economic department of the GPU, headed by his cousin Zinovy Katsnelson. The career of intelligence officer Lev Lazarevich began in 1926, with enrollment in the staff of the foreign department of the OGPU. The specifics of his future work forced him to continue his life under an assumed name. From then on, his documents named him as: Orlov Alexander Mikhailovich. The former name and surname remained only in the secret folders of the personnel department. Having passed the appropriate training and being

fluent in several foreign languages, he performed various tasks in many countries of Europe and America. In particular, it was Orlov who worked directly with Kim Philby, a high-ranking British intelligence officer recruited by the Soviet special services. Thanks to Orlov, a whole network of agents working for the Soviet Union was created around him. This was the famous "Cambridge Group," which entered the world history of intelligence services. In 1936, after Civil War broke out in Spain, Orlov Alexander Mikhailovich was sent there to help the republican government as a specialist in internal security and counterintelligence. Here, with his participation, an operation was prepared and brilliantly carried out to transfer a significant part of the gold reserves of Spain to the Soviet Union, as a result of which 510 tons of precious metal turned up in Moscow safes, which accounted for almost 73 percent of everything that the Spanish State Bank had. He also performed many other tasks given to him by the People's Commissariat of Internal Affairs of the USSR. In 1936, Stalin set in motion the process that led to one of the darkest periods in Soviet history, known as the Great Terror. In those years, the country was swept by a wave of mass repressions, the victims of which were overwhelmingly innocent people. They also touched the political and military leadership. Many founders and veterans of the Cheka were removed from their posts, and later arrested and shot on clearly trumped-up charges. Among them were many with whom Orlov began his service. Alexander Mikhailovich was well aware that sooner or later the same fate awaited him. Confidence in this was reinforced by the numerous responses to Moscow from diplomats who worked abroad. They received an order to arrive on official business and were arrested along with family members right at the gangway. In February 1938, Orlov finally made up his mind to break with the state, whose regime he considered criminal and posed a mortal danger to him and his family. At this time, under very mysterious circumstances, Orlov's immediate superior, the head of the foreign department of the NKVD, Abram Slutsky, died unexpectedly, and S. M. Shpigelglas was appointed in his place. On February 17, Alexander Mikhailovich received an order to meet him on board the Soviet ship Svir, which arrived in Antwerp. However, he had every reason to believe that having climbed the ladder to the ship, he would be trapped. He never showed up to meet his new boss. Instead, taking his wife and daughter, along with sixty thousand dollars from the service fund, Orlov Alexander Mikhailovich secretly left for France and, traveling through Canada, he arrived in the United States.

63 AP RF. f. 3, op. 57, d. 42, ll. 15–42. Script. Typescript.
64 Samarskiy oblastnoy GASPI. f. 1141, op. 14, d. 7, ll. 136–136ob. Podlinnik.
65 GANISO, f. p-5, op. 2, d. 1583, ll. 159–62.
66 TSA FSB, f. 3, op. 1, d. 317, ll. 14–21.
67 Ibid.
68 Ibid.
69 Ibid.
70 GARF. f .9474, op. 16, d. 137, l. 72.
71 GARF. f. 9401, on. 1a, d. 65, ll. 172–3. Certified copy. Typescript.
72 *GULAG (Glavnoye upravleniye lagerey). 1917–1960* (Moskva: MFD, 2000), 106–10.
73 Tomsk Memorial Museum, https://nkvd.tomsk.ru/media_news/criminal_kids/?yscli d=l7ykwvw3rs847841111.
74 Komsomol'skaia pravda (January 29, 2015).
75 Arkhiv UFSB po g. Moskve i Moskovskoy obl. Sledstvennoye delo Moroza Vladimira Grigor'yevicha. ll. 1–2, 6–10, 19–20, 23–24, 32–34, 45, 47–8.

76 The criminal law specifies that the Article 58-10, Propaganda or agitation containing a call to overthrow, undermine or weaken Soviet power or to commit individual counter-revolutionary crimes (also Articles 58-2–58-9), as well as the distribution or production or storage of literature of the same content, entail – imprisonment for a period not less than six months.
77 For a discussion about this soviet government house, see Yuri Slezkine, *The House of Government: A Saga of the Russian Revolution* (Princeton: Princeton University Press, 2017).
78 For reference notes, see Appendix 2.
79 GARF. F. 5207., op. 1, d. 1618, l. 5.
80 TsDOOSO. F. 4. On. 15. D. 54. L. 22v., 23.
81 Deti GULAGa. 1918-1956/Sost. S.S. Vilenskiy, A.I. Kokurin, G.V. Atmashkina, I.YU. Novichenko. — M., 2002. S. 316–17.
82 Ekho bol'shogo terrora T.3, M. 2018, 500.
83 TsDOOSO. f. 4, on. 31, d. 41, ll. 34–7. Typescript. Script.
84 GASO. f. p-321. on. 1, d. 73, ll. 51, 52.
85 Krivonosov, 98.
86 For more discussion about children's homelessness during World War Two, see S. M. Yemelin, "Bor'ba s detskoy besprizornost'yu i beznadzornost'yu v gody Velikoy Otechestvennoy voyny (1941–1945 gg.)" http://juvenjust.org/index.php?showtopic=1443.

Epilogue

1 Melancon.

Appendix

1 Source: FSB Archive for Moscow and the Moscow Region. Investigation case of Moroz Vladimir Grigoryevich. L. 1–2, 6–10, 19–20, 23–4, 32–4, 45, 47–8.

Cited Materials

Archives:

Documentation Center for the Contemporary History of the Krasnodar Territory (TSDNIKK)
Gosudarstvennyy obshchestvenno-politicheskiy arkhiv Nizhegorodskoy oblasti [State Archival Service of the Nizhny Novgorod Region] (GOPANO)
Rossiyskiy gosudarstvennyy arkhiv ekonomiki [Russian State Archive of Economics] (RGAE)
Rossiyskiy gosudarstvennyy arkhiv sotsial'no-politicheskoy istorii [Russian Government Archive for Socio-Political History] (RGASPI)
Samarskiy oblastnoy gosudarstvennyy arkhiv sotsial'no-politicheskoy istorii [Samara Regional Government Archive for Socio-Political History] (SOGASPI)
State Archive of Novgorod Province (GANO)
State Archive of the Russian Federation (GARF)
State Archive of Sverdlovsk Province (GASO)
State Archive of the Tatar Republic (GART)
Tsentral'nyi arkhiv federal'noi sluzhby bezopasnosti [Central Archive of the Federal Security Service of Russia] (TSA FSB)Gosudarstvennyi arkhiv Respubliki Mariy El [State Archive of Mariy El Republic] (GA RME)
Tsentral'nyi gosudarstvennyi arkhiv Moskovskoi oblasti [Central State Archive of Moscow Province] (TSGAMO)
Tsentr dokumentatsii obshchestvennykh organizatsii Sverdlovskoi oblasti [Center for Documentation of Public Organizations of the Sverdlovsk Region] (TSDOOSO)
Tyumen Regional Center for Documentation of Contemporary History (TOTSDNI)

Newspapers and Periodicals

Bednota
Izvestia
Izvestiia Petrogradskogo Sovieta
Kommuna
Kommunist
Kommunicticheskii Trud
Krasnaia Gazeta
Krasnaya nov'
Krest'izanskaia pravda
Olonetskie gubernskie vedomisti
Pionerskaya pravda
Pravda
Pravitel'stvennyi vestnik
Rossiyskaya Gazeta

Published Primary Sources (Legislative Documents, Statistics, Letters and Memoirs):

Bol'shaia Sovetskaia Entsiklopediia. Moscow: Entsiklopediia, 1927.
Children of the Gulag. Annals of Communism Series. Semyon Samuilovich Vilensky, Cathy A. Frierson. Eds. New Heaven and London: Yale University Press, 2010.
Dekrety Sovetskoy vlasti. Moscow: Gosudarstvennoe izdatel'stvo politicheskoy literatury, 1957.
Deti GULAGa: 1918–1956. S. S. Vilenskiy, A. I. Kokurin, G. V. Atmashkina, I.YU. Novichenko. Eds. Moscow: MFD, 2002.
Detskaya defektivnost', prestupnost' i besprizornost'. Po materialam 1 Vserossiyskogo s"yezda 24/VI —2/VII 1920 g. Redaktsiya Byuro Mediko -Pedagogicheskoy Konsul'tatsii Narkomprosa. Moskva: Gosudarstvennoe izdatel'stvo, 1920.
Dzerzhinskaia Sof'ia Sigizmundovna. *V Gody Velikikh Boiev*. Moscow: Mysl', 1964.
Dzerzhinsky, Felix Edmundovich. *Izbrannyye stat'i i rechi*. Moscow, 1947.
Dzerzhinsky, Felix Edmundovich. *Dnevnik zaklyuchennogo. Pis'ma*. Moscow: Molodaya gvardiya, 1984.
Ekho bol'shogo terrora T.3, M. 2018.
Entsiklopedicheskii Slovar'. Vol. 22. St. Petersburg: Efron, 1897.
Istoriya stalinskogo Gulaga. Konets 1920-kh — pervaya polovina 1950-kh godov. Sobraniye dokumentov v 7 tomakh. T. 1. Massovyye repressii v SSSR. Otv. red. N. Vert, S. V. Mironenko; otv. sostavitel' I. A. Zyuzina. Moscow: Rossiyskaya politicheskaya entsiklopediya (ROSSPEN), 2004.
Kalinina, Asya Davydovna. *Desyat' let raboty po bor'be s detskoy besprizornost'yu*. Moscow Leningrad: Moskovskii rabochii, 1928.
Krest'ianskaia Revoliutsia v Rossi, 1902–1922: Documenty i materialy. V. Danilov, T. Shanin, eds. Moscow: Rosen, 2002.
Krupskaya, Nadezhda Konstantinovna, *Izbrannye pedagogicheskiie proizvedeniia*, eds. I. A. Kairov, et al. Moscow: Izdatel'stvo Akademii pedagogicheskikh nauk RSFSR, 1955.
Krupskaya, Nadezhda Konstantinovna, *Pedagogicheskiie proizvedeniia*, 10 vols. eds. N. K. Goncharov, et al. Moscow: Izdatel'stvo Akademii pedagogicheskikh nauk RSFSR, 1958.
Lenin (Ulyanov), Vladimir Il'ich. *Polnoe sobranie sochinnii*. 5th edition. Moscow: Politizdat, 1965.
Lenin (Ulyanov), Vladimir Il'ich. *Unknown documents, 1891–1922*. Moscow: ROSSPEN, 2000.
Lunacharcky, Anatolii Vasil'evich, "Dzerzhinsky v Narkomprose". I. E. Polikarpenko, ed. *Rytsar' Revol'utsii. Vospominaniia sovremennikov o F.E Dzerzhinskom*. Moscow, 1967.
Naseleniye Rossii v XX veke. 3 volumes. Moscow: Rospen, 2000.
Novoye ugolovnoye ulozheniye, utverzhdonnoye 22 marta 1903 goda. Saint Peterburg: Izdaniye Kamennooyetrovsshcho Yuridncheskago Knizhnogo Magazina V. P. Anisimova, 1903.
Polnoye sobraniye zakonov Rossiyskoy imperii. Sobraniye 3. Saint Petersburg: Gosudarstvennaia Tipografiia, 1885–1916.
Pravda Russkaya. Akad. nauk SSSR, In-t istorii; pod obshch. red. B. D. Grekova. - Moskva- Leningrad: Izd-vo Akad. nauk SSSR, 1940–1963.
"Russkaia Pravda. Prostrannaia redaktsiia" in Русская Правда. In Y. P. Titov, *Khrestomatiia po istorii gosudarstva i prava v Rossii*. Moscow: Prospekt, 2007, 9–25.
Sobraniye kodeksov R.S.F.S.R. Prodolzheniye II k sobraniyu kodeksov RSFSR izdaniya 1927 goda po zakonodatel'stvu, opublikovannomu na 1 marta 1928 g. v Sobranii uzakoneniy

RSFSR. Izdaniye ofitsial'noye. Rossiyskaya Sotsialisticheskaya Federativnaya Sovetskaya Respublika. Moskva: Yuridicheskoye izd-vo N.K.YU. R.S.F.S.R., 1928.
Stasova, Elena Dmitrievna. "Vsegda s Massami" in I. E. Polikarpenko, ed., *Rytsar' Revol'utsii. Vospominaniia sovremennikov o F.E Dzerzhinskom*. Moscow: 1967.
Stoglav. Kazan': Tip. gubernskogo pravleniya, 1862.
Sudebnik tsarya i velikogo knyazya Ivana Vasil'yevicha. Zakony iz Yustianovykh knig. Ukazy dopolnitel'nyye k Sudebniku i Tamozhennyy ustav. St. Petersburg: Tipografiia Imperatorskoi academii nauk, 1768.
Tragediya sovetskoy derevni. Kollektivizatsiya i raskulachivaniye. Dokumenty i materialy. Tom 5. 1937–1939. Kniga 2. 1938 – 1939. Moskva: ROSSPEN 2006.
Ugolovnoye pravo Rossii. Chast' obshchaya, Ed. in chief Kruglikov L.L. Moscow: Yurisprudentsiya, 2005.
Ugolovnyi kodeks Possiiskoi Sovetskoi Federativnoi Sotsialisticheskoi Respubliki, redaktsiia 1924 goda. Moscow: Izdaniie voennoi kollegii verkhovnogo tribunala VTsIK, 1925.
Ugolovnyi kodeks Possiiskoi Sovetskoi Federativnoi Sotsialisticheskoi Respubliki, redaktsiia 1926 goda. Moscow: Izdaniie voennoi kollegii verkhovnogo tribunala VTsIK, 1927.
Ustavy blagotvoritel'nykh uchrezhdeniy brat'yev P., A. i V. Bakhrushinykh, Moscow: Gorodskaya tip., 1903.
V. I. Lenin i A. V. Lunacharskiy. Perepiska, doklady, dokumenty. Literaturnoye nasledstvo. Vol. 80. Moscow: Nauka, 1971.
Vse na pomoshch 'Povolzh'yu! Predsamgubkomgoloda. Samara: Gos.izd-vo, Samar.otd-niye, 1922.
Vsesoyuznaya perepis' naseleniya 17 dekabrya 1926 g.: kratkiye svodki, Moscow: izd. TSSU Soyuza SSR, 1927, 2–3.

Secondary Literature

Agadzhanov, Borislav Vladimirovich. "Sozdateli pervykh uchebnykh knig dlia nachal'nogo obucheniia gramote bukvarei i azbuk XVI—pervoy chetverti XVIII vv" in *Problemy sovremennogo obrazovaniya*, 2010. No. 2. Moskva: Moskovskiy pedagogicheskiy gosudarstvennyy universitet, 2010, 50–77.
Alexander, John T. *Catherine the Great: Life and Legend*. New York: Oxford University Press, 1988.
Anderson, B. A., and Silver, B. D. "Demographic Analysis and Population Catastrophes in the USSR." *Slavic Review*. Vol. 44, no. 3. (1985): 517–36.
Anisimov, Evgenii V. *The Reforms of Peter the Great: Progress through Violence in Russia*. Routledge, 2015.
Badcock, Sarah. *Politics and People in Revolutionary Russia: A Provincial History*. Cambridge, England: Cambridge University Press, 2007.
Ball, Alan "The Roots of Besprizornost' in Soviet Russia's First Decade." *Slavic Review*. Vol 51. no. 2. (Summer 1992).
Ball, Alan. *And Now My Soul Is Hardened. Abandoned Children in Soviet Russia*. Berkeley: University of California Press,1994.
Basov, Nikolai Feodorovich. *Istoriia sotsial'noi raboty*. Moscow: Dashkov i Ko., 2007.
Beliakov, Viacheslav Viktorovich. *Sirotskie detskiie uchrezhdeniia Rossii*. Moscow: Eksmo, 1993.

"Blagotvoritel'naya deyatel'nost' v SSSR po preodoleniyu massovoy detskoy besprizornosti (1917–1935 gg.)" Potepalov, D. V., S. A. Dneprov. Eds. Nauka i Shkola, no. 3, Moscow, 2015.

Blagotvoritel'naia Rossiia. *Istoriia gosudarstvennoi, obshchestvennoi chastnoiblagotvoritel'nosti v Rossii.* P. I. Lykoshin, ed. Vol. I, part I. Saint Petersburg: S. Petersburgskaia elektropechatnia, 1901.

Blagotvoritel'nost' v Rossii i gosudarstvennaya politika. S. S. Sulakshin, D. V. Bachurina, M. V. Vilisov, G. G. Karimova, I. R. Kish, O. V. Kuropatkina, L. A. Makurina, A. S. Sulakshina. Eds. Moscow: Nauchnyy ekspert, 2013.

Bodrin, Aleksey Vladimirovich, Liudmila Anatol'evna Tobol'ko, "Sotsial'naia podderzhka detei v Rossii: Istoticheskii aspekt (X-XIII vek)." *Molodoi uchenyi* No. 23 (103) (December 2015): 808–11.

Bravaya, R. M. *Okhrana materinstva i mladenchestva na Zapade i v SSSR.* Moscow, 1929.

Bryzgalova, Victoria Andreevna. "Iz istorii blagotvoritel'nosti" in *Innovatsii i investitsii*, No 12, (2015): 106–9.

Burlakova, Tamara Tikhonovna. "Postroyeniye i funktsionirovaniye gumanisticheskoy vospitatel'noy sistemy detskogo doma, osnovannoy na filosofsko-pedagogicheskikh ideyakh L. N. Tolstogo." Dissertatsiya kandidata pedagogicheskikh nauk. Tula, 2001.

Bushkovitch, Paul. *Peter the Great.* London and New York: Rowman and Littlefield, 2003.

Clements, Barbara Evans. *Bolshevik Women.* New York: Cambridge University Press, 1997.

Conquest, Robert. *The Harvest of Sorrow: Soviet Collectivization and the Terror-Famine.* London and New York: Oxford University Press, 1986.

Cracraft, James. *The Revolution of Peter the Great.* Harvard: Harvard University Press, 2003.

Dal', Vladimir Ivanovich. *Tolkovyy slovar' zhivogo velikorusskogo yazyka.* Moscow: Tsitadel', 1998.

Davydov, M. I. "Zabota o detyakh. Iz istorii deyatel'nosti Soveta Zashchity detey v 1918–1920 godakh." Istoriya SSSR. 1979. № 5. S. 163-71. deGraffenried, Julie K. *Sacrificing Childhood: Children and the Soviet State in the Great Patriotic War.* Lawrence KS: University of Kansas Press, 2014.

Dmytryshyn, Basil. *Modernization of Russia under Peter I and Catherine II.* Wiley, 1974.

Dzerzhinsky. Biographia. Doroshenko, Ilya Akimovich. Ed et al. 2nd edition. Moscow: Politizdat, 1983.

Engel'gardt, Aleksandr Nikolayevich. *Pis'ma iz derevni.* Moskva: Algoritm, 2010.

Fadeyeva, Galina Dmitrievna. "Metody bor'by s bezdomnost'yu v Rossii v 191–1939 gg." *Molodoy uchenyy.* No. 12 (59). (December 2013): 767–9.

Feonychev, V. V. "Deyatel'nost' gosudarstvennykh i obshchestvennykh organizatsiy po likvidatsii besprizornosti v Rossii v 1920-ye gody (na primere Penzeskoy, Samarskoy, Simbirskoy guberniy)." Avtoreferat dissertatsii na soiskaniye uchenoy stepeni kandidata istoricheskikh nauk. Kazan', 2017.

Firsov, M. V. *Istoriia sotsial'noi raboty v Rossi.* Moscow: Vlados, 1999.

Figes, Orlando. *Peasant Russia, Civil War: Volga Countryside in Revolution,1917–1921.* Oxford: Clarendon Press, 1989.

Fitzpatrick, Sheila. *Stalin's Peasants: Resistance and Survival in the Russian Village after Collectivization.* London: Oxford University Press, 1996.

Frierson, Cathy A. *Silence Was Salvation: Child Survivors of Stalin's Terror and World War II in the Soviet Union.* New Heaven and London: Yale University Press, 2015.

Galaguzova, Minnennur Akhmetkhanovna. Galaguzova, Yuliia Nikolaevna. *Sotsial'naia pedgogika: Kurs lektsii.* Moscow: Vlados, 2002.

Geller Mikhail, Yakovlevich, A. M. Nekrich. *Utopiya u vlasti*. Moscow: MIK, 2000.
Gernet, Mikhail Nikholaevich. *Sotsial'no-pravovaya okhrana detstva za granitsei i v Rossii*. Moscow: Pravo i Zhizn' Publ., 1924.
Gernet, Mikhail Nikholaevich. *Prestupnyyi mir Moskvy*. Moscow: Provo i zhizn', 1926.
Gernet, Mikhail Nikholaevich. Ed et al, *Deti-prestupniki*. Moscow: Znamenskii Publ., 1912. Reprint. Moscow: Kniga po trebovaniiu, 2013.
Gladysh, Svetlana D. *Deti bol'shoy bedy*. Moscow: Izdatel'skiy dom "Zvonnitsa-MG," 2004.
Goldman, Wendy Z. *Women, the State and Revolution. Soviet Family Policy and Social Life, 1917–1936*. Cambridge, UK: Cambridge University Press, 1993.
Goncharova, Irina Valentinovna, "Krest'yanstvo Tsentral'no-Chernozemnoy oblasti v usloviyakh podgotovki i provedeniya kollektivizatsii v 1928–1932 gg." Doctoral dissertation. Rossiyskaya akademiya narodnogo khozyaystva i gosudarstvennoy sluzhby pri Prezidente Rossiyskoy Federatsii. Moscow 2015.
Gorinskii, A. S. "Izmenenie kharaktera deiatel'nosti pedagoga v innovatsionnykh prostessakh obucheniia." Innovatsionnye proekty i programmy v obrazovanii. No. 4. Moscow, 2012.
Gorshkov, Boris B. *Peasants in Russia from Serfdom to Stalin: Accommodation, Survival, Resistance*. London: Bloomsbury Academic, 2018.
Gorshkov, Boris B. *Russia's Factory Children: State, Society and Law, 1800–1917*. Pittsburgh: University of Pittsburgh Press, 2009.
Gromyko, Marina Mikhailovna. *Traditsionnye normy povedeniia i formy obshcheniia russkikh krest'ian XIXveka*. Moscow: Nauka, 1986.
Gromyko, Marina Mikhailovna. *Mir russkoi derevni*. Moscow: Molodaia gvardiia, 1991.
Heinzen, James. *Inventing a Soviet Countryside. State Power and the Transformation of Rural Russia, 1917–1929*. Pittsburgh: Pittsburgh University Press, 2004.
Holquist, Peter. *Making War, Forging Revolution: Russia's Continuum of Crisis, 1914–1921*. Cambridge, MA: Harvard University Press, 2002.
Hughes, Lindsey. *Russia in the Age of Peter the Great*. New Heaven and London: Yale University Press, 1998.
Ippolitov, V. A. "Raskulachivaniye v Tsentral'nom Chernozem'ye na rubezhe 1920-kh – 1930 kh godov: rol' komsomola." Genesis: istoricheskiye issledovaniya. Vol. 3. 2016.
Istoriia Sotsial'noi Raboty v Rossi V. P. Mel'nikov, E. M. Kholostova, Moscow: Marketing, 2002.
Kalinnikova-Magnusson Liia Vladimirovna, M. Magnusson. "Sotsial'naya politika v otnoshenii detskoy «defektivnosti» v voyenno-revolyutsionnyy period i v pervuyu dekadu sovetskoy vlasti (1914–1927 gg.)," *Vestnik Pomorskogo universiteta. Seriya: gumanitarnyye i sotsial'nye nauki*, no 1. (2015): 157–66.
Kapustina, A. M. "Pravoslavno-khristianskaya traditsiya blagotvoritel'- nosti v Rossii: filosofsko-religiovedcheskiy analiz." Avtoreferat disertatsii kandidata filosofskikh nauk. Belgorod, 2007.
Kelly, Catriona. *Comrade Pavlik: The Rise and Fall of a Soviet Boy Hero*. London: Granta Books, 2005.
Khmel'nitskaya, Anna Pavlovna. *Spasennoye detstvo*. Moscow: Moskovskii pabochii, 1987.
Kitanina, Taisiia Mikhailovna. *Voina, khleb,i revoliutsiia: Prodovol'stvennyi vopros v Rossii, 1914–oktiabr' 1917 g.* Leningrad: Nauka, 1985.
Kliuchevskii, B. O. *Istoricheskiie portrety*. Moscow: Pravda, 1990.
Kniazkov, Sergey Alessandrovich. *Golod v drevnei Rossii*. Saint Petersburg: K. D. Tikhomirova, 1908.
Korablev, Nikolai Aleksandrovich, Tatiana Aleksandrovna Moshina, *Pimenovy: dinastiya predprinimateley, blagotvoriteley, obshchestvennykh deyateley*. Petrozavodsk: Periodika, 2016.

Krasovitskaya, Tamara Yusufovna. "N.K. Krupskaya – ideolog bol'shevistskoy reformyreform obrazovaniya." *Trudy Instituta rossiyskoy istorii*. Vyp. 5. Rossiyskaya akademiya nauk, Institut rossiyskoy istorii; otv. red. A. N.Sakharov. Moscow: Nauka, 2005.

Kristkaln, A. M. "Golod 1921 g. v Povolzh'ye: opyt sovremennogo izucheniya problemy." Avtoreferat kandidatskoy dissertatsii. Avtoreferat kandidatskoi dissertatsii. Moscow: Moscow State University, 1997.

Krivonosov, A. N. "Istoricheskiy opyt bor'by s besprizornost'yu," *Gosudarstvo i pravo*. Vol. 7 Moscow, 2003: 92—98.

Kuskova, Ye.D. *Besprizornaya Rus'*. Paris: Sovremennyye zapiski. 1929.

Landis, Eric. *Bandits and Partisans: The Antonov Movement in the Russian Civil War*. Pittsburgh: University of Pittsburgh Press, 2008.

Lebedeva, Vera Pavlovna. *Nekotoryye itogi*. Moscow: Okhrana materinstva i mladenchestva NKZ, 1928.

Lebedeva, Vera Pavlovna. *Okhrana materinstva i mladenchestva v strane Sovetov*. Moscow: tipo-lit. im. Vorovskogo, 1934.

Levitina, Mariia Iisakovna (Maro). *Besprizornye: Sotsiologia. Byt. Praktika raboty*. Moscow: Novaia Moskva, 1925.

Lih, Lars T. *Bread and Authority in Russia, 1914–1921*. Berkeley: University of California Press, 1990.

Lindenmeyr, Adele. *Poverty Is Not a Vice: Charity, Society, and the State in Imperial Russia*. Princeton, NJ: Princeton University Press, 1996.

Lyublinskiy, P. I. «Zadachi okhrany detstva» in P. I. Lyublinskiy, S. I. Kapelyanskaya, *Okhrana detstva i bor'ba s besprizornost'yu*. Leningrad: Academia, 1924.

Ljublinskij, P. I. "Okhrana detstva i bor'ba s besprizorn ost'ju za 10 let." *Pravo i zhizn'*, Vinaver, A. M. et al, ed. Leningrad: Academiia, 1927.

Makarii (Bulgakov, Mikhail Petrovich) *Istoriia Russkoi tserkvi*, vol 1. Saint Petersburg: Tipografiia Imperatorskoi Akademii, 1857.

Maksimov, Evgenii Dmitrievich. *Razvitiye sistemy obshchestvennogo prizreniya detey I podrostkov v Rossii*. Moscow: Akademiya, 2007.

Malle, Silvana. *The Economic Organization of War Communism, 1918–1921*. Cambridge, England: Cambridge University Press, 1985.

Mania, D. Healy. *A Short History of Bipolar Disorder*. Baltimore: Johns Hopkins University Press, 2011.

McCauley, Mary. *Bread and Justice: State and Society in Petrograd 1917–1922*. Oxford, 1991.

McDermid, Jane, Anya Hilyar. "In Lenin's Shadow: Nadezhda Krupskaya and the Bolshevik Revolution," in Ian D. Thatcher (ed.). *Reinterpreting Revolutionary Russia*. New York: Palgrave Macmillan, 2006.

MChKa. *Iz Istorii Moskovskoi Chrezvychainoi Kommissii*. Moscow: Moskovsky Rabochii, 1978.

Melancon, Michael. "Trial Run for Soviet Food Requisitioning: The Expedition to Orel Province, Fall 1918," *Russian Review* 69 (July 2010): 412–37.

Mineeva Elena, Konstantinovna, Morozov, V. A., Yantseva, A. S. "Puti preodoleniya detskoi besprizornosti v sovetskoi Rossii v 1920–1930-e gody," *Vestnik Chuvashskogo gosudarstvennogo pedagogicheskogo universiteta*. No. 2(74). (2012).

Nadezhdin, "God v Butyrskoy Tiur'me." *Che-Ka, Materialy po deiatel'nosti chrezvychaihyhk comissii*. Berlin: Orfei, 1922.

Nagornova, Anna Yur'evna, Elena Evgen'evna Vagina. "Prizreniye i sotsial'naya zashchita detey-sirot i detey, ostavshikhsya bez popecheniya roditeley, v Rossii s drevneyshikh

vremen do vtoroy poloviny XX v." *Istoriya i sovremennost'*. Vol 1 (March 2016): 154–70.
Nechayeva, Aleksandra Matveevna. *Rossiya i yeye deti (rebenok, zakon, gosudarstvo)*. Moscow: Graal', 2000.
Neuberger, Joan. "Alan Ball, and Now My Soul Is Hardened. Abandoned Children in Soviet Russia. Berkeley: University of California Press,1994." *American Historical Review*. April 1995.
Nove, Alec. *An Economic History of the USSR*. London: Allen Lane/Penguin Press, 1969.
Osokina, Elena Aleksandrovna. *Za fasadom "stalinskogo izobiliya": raspredeleniye i rynok v snabzhenii naseleniya v gody industrializatsii, 1927–1941*. Moskva: ROSSPEN, 2008.
Platonov, Sergey Feodorovich. *Boris Godunov*. Reprint. Moscow: Agraf, 1999.
Polyakov, Yurii Alessandrovich. *Perekhod k NEPu i sovetskoye krest'yanstvo*. Moscow: Nauka, 1967.
Polikarpenko, I. E. Ed. *Rytsar' Revol'utsii. Vospominaniia sovremennikov o F.E Dzerzhinskom*. Moscow: Politizdat, 1967.
Potepalov, D. V. "Detskaya besprizornost' v pervyye gody Sovetskoy vlasti: istoriograficheskiy ocherk." Nauchno-prakticheskiy zhurnal "Gumanizatsiya obrazovaniya". No. 1 Moscow, 2012: 23–9.
Poznyshev Sergei, Viktorovich. *Detskaya besprizornost' i mery bor'by s ney*. Moscow: Novaia Moskva, 1926.
Puzykin, A. V. "Razvitie gazetnoi periodicheskoi pechati na territorii sovremennoi Kemerovskoi oblasti v 20-e gg. XX v." *Izvestiia Altaisogo gosudarstvennogo universiteta* no 4-4. Barnaul, 2008.
Rabinowitch, Alexander. *The Bolsheviks in Power: The First Year of Soviet Rule in Petrograd*. Bloomington: Indiana University Press, 2008.
Raleigh, Donald. *Experiencing Russia's Civil War: Politics, Society, and Revolutionary Culture in Saratov, 1917–1922*. Princeton: Princeton University Press, 2002.
Retish, Aaron. *Russia's Peasants in Revolution and Civil War: Citizenship, Identity, and the Creation of the Soviet State, 1914–1922*. England: Cambridge, 2008.
Riabinina, Natal'ia Valer'ianovna. *Detskaia besprizornost i prestupnost' v 1920-e gody*. Yaroslavl': Yaroslavskii gosudarstvennyi universitet, 1999.
Rozhkov, Aleksandr Yur'evich. "Bor'ba s besprizornost'yu v pervoye sovetskoye desyatiletiye." In Voprosy istorii. No. 11. 2000: 134–9.
Rubinshteyn, N. L. *Sel'skoe khoziaistvo Rossii vo vtoroi polovine XVIII veka*. Moscow: Goslitizdat, 1957.
Ruzhnikov, Yuri. *Informer 001: The Myth of Pavlik Morozov* Rutledge.
Ryabinina, Natal'ia Valer'ianovna. "Detskaya besprizornost' i prestupnost' v 1920-ye gg. (po materialam guberniy Verkhnego Povolzh'ya)." Avtoreferat kandidatskoy dissertatsii. Penza, 2007.
Savel'yev, E. A. N., Y. Kostina, "Problema detskoy besprizornosti v SSSR v 20-30 gody." *Nauchnyye issledovaniya i razrabotki molodykh uchenykh*, No. 5. Novosibirsk, 2015: 114–16.
Semenova, Inna Yur'evna "Rabota Vserossiiskikh s"ezdov deiatelei po okhrane detstva I yacheek obshchestva "Drug detei" po ukrepleniiu i okhrane sem'i v molodom sovetskom gosudarstve." *Vestnik Chuvashskogo universiteta*. Vol. 4. (2019): 192–200.
Semina, Natal'ia Viktorovna "Bor'ba s detskoy besprizornost'yu v 1920-ye – 1940-ye gody v Rossii (na primere Penzenskogo regiona)." *Kandidatskaia dissertatsiia, Penzenskiy gosudarstvennyy pedagogicheskiy universitet im. V. G. Belinskogo*. Penza, 2007.

Sen, Amartya. *Poverty and Famines: An Essay on Entitlement and Deprivation* (Oxford, UK: Clarendon Press, 1981
Sergeevich, V. I. *Lektsii i issledovaniia po drevnei istorii russkigo prava*, 4th edition. Saint Petersburg: Stasiulevich, 1910.
Shamina, I. N. "Iz istorii Vologodskikh monastyrey XVI–XVII veka (sostav nasel'nikov). *Otechestvennaya istoriya*. Vol. 1. Moscow, 2003: 141–54.
Shcherbinin, Pavel P. *"Pustite detei ko mne ...": "Deti bedy" i popechitel'stvo do i posle 1917 goda* Tambov: Izdatel'skii dom "Derzhavinskii," 2018.
Shub, David. "The Trial of the SRs" *The Russian Review*. Vol. 23, No. 4. (1964): 362–9. ***
Slavko, Andrei Aleksandrovich. *Detskaya besprizornost' v Rossii v pervoye desyatiletiye Sovetskoy vlasti*. Moscow: INION RAN, 2005.
Slavko, Andrei Aleksandrovich. "Kontseptsiya bor'by s detskoy besprizornost'yu v otechestvennoy istoriografii 1920-kh gg." *Vestnik IGEU Vyp*. Vol. 1 (2010): 1–5.
Slavko, Andrei Aleksandrovich. "Detskaia Besprizornost' i beznadzornost' v Rossi Konstantinos 1920-kh—nachala 1950-kh godov: Sotsial'nyi portret, prichiny, formy bor'by." *Avtoreferat dissertatsii na soiskanie uchonoy stepeni doktora istoricheskikh nauk*. Samara: Samarskii gosudarstvennyi universitet, 2011.
Slavko, Andrei Aleksandrovich. *Istoria bespizornogo i beznadzornogo detstva Rossii: konets 1920-kh—nachalo 1950-kh godov*. Cheborsary: Perfectum, 2012.
Smirnova, Tat'iana Mikhailovna. «Detskiye doma i trudkolonii: zhizn' «Gosudarstvennykh detey» v sovetskoy Rossii v 1920–1930-ye gg,.» *Vestnik RUDN. Seriya Istoriya Rossii*. Moskva, 2012: 16–38.
Solov'yeva, T. A., "Povsednevnaya zhizn' sovetskogo provintsial'nogo goroda v 1920–1930-ye gg.: na materialakh g. Saratova." *Avtoreferat kandidatskoy dissertatsii*. Saratovskiy gosudarstvennyy universitet imeni N. G. Chernyshevskogo. Saratov, 2014.
Stepanova, Irina Al'fredovna. "Sotsial'no-pravovaya zashchita detstva v rossii v khviii veke." *Pedagogicheskoye obrazovaniye*. No 3. 2008.
Stevens, Jennie "Children of the Revolution: Soviet Russia's Homeless Children (Besprizorniki) in the 1920s" *Russian History*, Vol. 9, No. (2–3): 242–64.
Stites, Richard. *The Women's Liberation Movement in Russia, Feminism, Nihilism, Bolshevism, 1860—1930*. Princeton: Princeton University Press, 1978.
Stog, A. D. "Ob obshchestvrnnom prizrenii v Rossii." Published in St. Petersburg in 1818, reprint. Antologiia sotsial'noi raboty. 5 vols. M. V. Firsov, ed. Moscow: Svarog, 1995, 3: 30–1.
Stolee, Margaret K. "Homeless Children in the USSR, 1917–1957." *Soviet Studies* XL, No. 1 (January 1988): 64–83.
Tizanov, Semeon Sergeevich. "Sorsial'no-pravovaia ohkrana nesovershennoletnihk." *Pedagogicheskaia Entsiklopediia*. A. G. Kalashnikov and M. S.Epshtein. Eds. Vol 2. Moscow: Rabotnik Prosveshcheniia, 1930, 349–54.
Tizanov, Semeon Sergeevich, M. S. Epshtein, eds. *Gosudarstvo i obshchestvennost' v bor'be s detskoi besprizornost'iu*. Moscow-Leningrad: Gosizdat, 1927.
Tsaplin, Vsevolod Vasil'evich. "Statistika zhertv stalinizma v 30-ye gody." *Voprosy istorii*. Vol. 4. (1989): 177–8.
Ulyanova, Galina Nikolaevna. *Philanthropy in the Russian Empire. The 19th and early 20th Centuries*. Moscow: Nauka, 2005.
Viola, Lynne. *Peasant Rebels under Stalin: Collectivization and the Culture of Peasant Resistance*. Oxford University Press, 1996.
Viola, Lynne. *The Unknown Gulag. The Lost World of Stalin's Special Settlements*. Oxford University Press, 2007.

Vladimirskii-Budanov, M. F. *Obzor istorii Russkogo prava*. 7th edition. Saint Petersburg, Kiev: Izdatel'stvo knizhnogo magazina N. Ogloblina, 1915.

Volkov, M. YA. "Russkaya pravoslavnaya tserkov' v XVIII veke." *Russkoye pravoslaviye Vekhi istorii*. Ed. Klibanov A. I. Moscow: Politizdat, 1989.

White, Elizabeth A. *Modern History of Russian Childhood from the Late Imperial Period to the Collapse of the Soviet Union*. London: Bloomsbury Academic, 2020.

Zagorovsky, A. I. *Kurs semeynogo prava*. Odessa: Tipografiia aktsionernogo Yuzhno-russkogo obshchestva pechatnogo dela, 1909.

Zinovyev, Aleksandr. *Homo sovieticus*. Grove/Atlantic, 1986.

Zubov, Nikolai Ivanovich. *F. E.Dzerzhinsky: Biographia*. Moscow: Gospolitizdat, 1963.

Index

A
adoption(s) 21, 33, 36, 81–83, 85, 129, 167, 177
age
  at labor obligations 22, 38, 90, 141
  at transition to adulthood 22, 31, 32, 33, 35
  of criminal liability 6, 38, 98, 104, 105, 106, 108, 122, 133, 152, 159, 160, 191n69, 199n79
  of majority 1, 45
agitprop 75
agriculture 66–67
  collectivization of, *see* collectivization (of agriculture)
  subsistence 68
American Red Cross 86–87
American Relief Administration, the 86–87, 115, 198n52

B
Benevolence 22–23, 26–29, 34–35, 169
besprizorniki, see homeless children
besprizornost, see homeless children
Bipolar disorder 84, 109, 166–167, 197n40, 213
Bolshevik perceptions of homeless children as defective 5, 46, 84, 95–96, 105, 122, 126–127, 168
Bolshevik *realpolitik, see* Realpolitik of Bolsheviks

C
Catherine II 18, 30, 199n42, 211
Caucasus region (North and South) 51–52, 67–68, 93, 95, 120
Censorship, *see* Stalinism
Cheka viii, 2, 12, 15, 54, 59, 61, 65, 86, 87, 89, 93, 95, 101–104, 107–117, 119–122, 126, 134, 175, 165, 167, 171–173, 192n7, 199n4, 202n78, 206n62; also *see* NKVD

Childcare 4, 8–9, 13–14, 17–18, 25, 29, 32–33, 36, 38–40, 42, 44–45, 48, 50–51, 53–55, 73–74, 76, 78, 80–82, 84–85, 89, 91, 94, 103, 113, 125, 128, 133, 153, 167, 186n12
Childhood
  All-Russian Congress for the Protection of, the 88
  early Soviet 43, 54, 56, 60, 71, 74–76, 78, 85, 163
  historiography of 6–7, 9–12, 54, 80
  ideals of 9, 73, 75–76, 80, 84, 133, 158
  in Imperial Russia 25, 36, 38, 41
  official Soviet image of 7, 15–16
  under Stalin 133–135, 145, 156, 158, 160, 162
Children
  "defective", *see* Bolshevik perceptions of homeless children as
  definition of 1, 5, 43–45, 50, 164, 170
  evacuation(s) of 15, 88–90, 95, 101, 121, 127, 166
  homeless, *see* homeless children
  institutions for, *see* children's homes
  life expectancy of 6, 49
  mortality among viii, 2–4, 6, 10–11, 14–15, 25, 32–33, 44, 48–49, 56, 58, 62, 64, 89, 91, 135, 145–146, 149, 161, 163, 165, 176
  rural 22, 31, 39–41, 43, 49–51, 53–54, 56–58, 60–62, 64, 69, 141–142, 144, 169
  starvation among viii, 3–5, 8–9, 12–15, 17, 20, 22, 28, 42, 46, 48–52, 54, 56–58, 62, 65–66, 71, 73–74, 85–86, 89–90, 92–93, 96, 101, 103, 115, 125, 130, 133–134, 136–141, 144, 147, 160–161, 163–165, 167, 195n92

Children's
  Commission (*Detkomissia*) 12, 80, 103, 109–119, 121, 125, 128, 152, 165, 167, 174, 176–178
  homes
    Bolshevik's 91–92, 103, 113, 115
    Cheka's 115, 119–121, 125, 128, 130
    Imperial 30, 33, 39–40, 47, 53, 55, 80–82, 86, 88–89, 91; *see also* labor campsfor children
    Stalinist 140, 151, 153, 155, 176; *see also* labor camps for children
  Week, campaign, the 74, 94–95
Collectivization (of agriculture) 4, 5, 11, 15, 49, 52, 65, 135
Commissariat
  for Enlightenment, the 13, 17, 46–47, 55, 59, 64, 74–75, 81, 85, 88–89, 92, 94–95, 103, 107, 113–114, 120, 122, 192n7
  for Food Supplies, the 58, 86
  for railroads 110
  for State Charity, the 81, 92
Communist Youth Union (Komsomol) 66, 93, 121, 128–129, 134, 144, 160, 177
Crimea 48, 51, 68, 73

D
dekulakization 5, 52, 69, 134, 135, 167
Detkomissia, *see* Children's Commission (*Detkomissia*)
disease 12, 46, 49, 56, 62–63, 88, 95, 136–129, 147, 153
domestic policy, *see* population policies
Dzerzhinsky, Felix Edmundovich 8, 12, 84, 86, 93, 95, 101–103, 108–116, 121–122, 125–126, 173–174, 192n7, 199n4
Dzugashvilli, Iosif (Joseph) Vissarionovich (Stalin) vi, vii–ix, 5–6, 8, 15, 45, 47–48, 66–68

G
Godunov, Boris Feodorovich 27, 189n33
Gorbachev's perestroika 7–8, 49, 169
Gorky, Maxim, (Gorky, Aleksei Maksimovich) 86
  labor commune 122, 125

Gorky region 159, 175, 202n78
Great Soviet Encyclopedia, the 1, 5, 6, 43, 44, 45, 47

H
Homeless children
  crime among 96, 103
  defective, *see* Bolshevik perceptions of homeless children as
  definition of 4–6, 44–45, 50
  demography of 46–50, 53, 168
  during the early Bolshevik government viii, ix, 2–6, 8, 13, 15, 23, 41, 43–54, 57, 64–65, 73–74, 83, 85, 88, 90, 92, 95–96, 98–99, 102, 109–110, 112, 114–117, 123, 126–131, 172, 186n8, 187n22
  during the Industrial Revolution 4
  during the Stalinist years viii, ix, 2, 14–15, 52, 65, 71, 134, 136, 150–155, 158, 160, 164, 166–168, 175, 177–178
  Historiography about 8–12
  in ancient Greece 4
  in Ancient Rome 4
  in the post-Stalinist period 168–169
  in tsarist Russia 4, 28, 33, 39
  in Ukraine 2
  life expectancy of 6
  Russian-language scholarship about 8
  Statistics on 46–47, 51, 53–54, 57, 169–170, 192n7

I
Ivan IV 25–27, 31, 189n28
Ivan Fedorov 25

K
Kazan 49, 58, 87
Kelly, Catriona Helen Moncrieff 11, 143, 204n38
Komsomol, *see* Communist Youth Union
Kornev, Vasilii Stepanovich 12, 111, 116
Krupskaya, *see* Ulyanova, Nadezhda Konstantinovna
Kulak(s) 11, 52, 54, 61, 66–67, 69–70, 134–135, 140, 142–151, 194n53; *see also* deculakization
  children of 142–146, 160
Kuskova, E. D. 8, 86, 187n14

L

Labor camps for children 15, 70, 103, 119, 140, 143, 153–155, 157–159
Larek 15, 103, 116–118, 121, 167
League for the Rescue of Children 86
Lenin, *see* Ulyanov, Vladimir Ilyich
Leningrad, *see* St. Petersburg
Lunacharsky, Anatolii Vasil'evich 47, 55, 64, 73, 75, 84–85, 92–93, 110, 114

M

Makarenko, Anton Semenovich 123–125
Marxist (Marxist-Leninist) 3–4, 9, 165–166
Messing, Stavislav 107
monastery 28, 189n33
Moroz, Vladimir 133, 156–158, 162, 179–185
Morozov, Pavel (Pavlik) 143–144, 156, 204n38
Mortality, *see also* Children, mortality among 49, 56, 62, 66, 204n45
Moscow
    Agency for rural manufacturing (Mossel'prom) 116
    Butyrka prison, of 109
    Cheka Department of 107
    city 1, 14, 17, 25, 27–28, 31–32, 35–37, 48–51, 55, 60, 68, 73–75, 82, 85, 88–89, 91–97, 107–109, 112, 122
    City Soviet 82
    concentration camps 65
    Criminal Investigation Department 105
    customs 87
    Department of People's Education 86
    depopulation of 53
    Orphanage 32, 56, 57figure6
    police 117
    share partnership of Larek 118
    Sukharevka, district of 107

N

Nabokov 163, 170
Narkompros, *see* the Commissariat for Enlightenment
NKVD viii, 2, 12, 14–15, 49, 60, 103, 107, 110–111, 115, 122, 124, 134, 136, 139–140, 142, 146, 149–150, 152–161, 179–185, 202n78, 206n62; *see also* Cheka
North Caucasus, *see* Caucasus

P

Pavlik Morozov, *see* Morozov, Pavel
People's Commissariat for Education, *see* Commissariat for Enlightenment
Peter I 18, 29–30, 190n42, 211
Petrograd, *see* St. Petersburg
Population
    decline of 29, 49
    policies, Soviet 9, 65, 71, 186n6
    rural 4, 49, 58, 192n21
    urban 192n21, 194n53
Pskov, region, the 27, 32, 82, 88, 142

R

Realpolitik 3, 4, 134
    definition of 3–4
    of Bolsheviks 3, 4, 5, 6, 10–12, 16, 44, 48, 53–54, 81, 84, 95, 102, 107, 109–111, 115, 126, 128, 130
    Stalin's 65–71, 135, 144
Russian backwardness 9, 11, 17
Russian society 5, 9, 18–23, 41, 86
Russian Truth 24

S

Samara, city 49, 93, 111, 154, 176–178
Samara province 51, 58, 61–64, 87, 93, 105
Siberia 3, 9, 11, 14, 52, 59, 61
Soviet statistics, *see* Statistics
St. Petersburg 31–32, 34, 36, 39–40, 48–51, 67–68, 73–75, 82, 85, 87–88, 93–94, 104, 109, 131, 142, 150, 155–156, 168
Stalin, *see* Dzugashvilli, Iosif (Joseph) Vissarionovich (Stalin)
Stalin's censorship, *see* Stalinist government
Stalin's collectivization, *see* collectivization
Stalin's realpolitik, *see* realpolitik
Stalinism vii, 2, 4, 6, 8, 11, 15, 106, 134–136, 144–146, 149–151, 153, 156–157, 168, 170, 180, 197n19, n41
Stalinist era, *see* Stalinism
Stalinist children's homes, *see* children's homes
Stalinist government, *see* Stalinism
Stalinist period, *see* Stalinism
Stalinist regime, *see* Stalinism
Stalinist state, *see* Stalinism

Statistics 12, 29, 46, 47, 48, 49, 55, 57, 68, 71, 120, 128, 136, 145, 152, 161, 169, 195n92, 209
Statistics Records Committee, the 136
street children, *see* homeless children

T
Tambov region, the 9, 17, 49, 51, 58, 65, 114, 193n50
Tula, region, the 32, 88, 95
Tver region, the 32, 82

U
Ukraine 2, 50, 52, 65, 67–68, 73, 120, 136, 154, 178, 205n62
Ulyanov, Vladimir Ilyich (Lenin) 8, 54–57, 61–62, 70, 75, 83, 85–86, 92–94, 108, 110–111, 126, 143, 157, 165, 179, 193n36, n48, 196n8, n9, 197n38, 202n90, n91, 209–210, 213
Ulyanova, Galina Nikolaevna 17, 188n2, 196n24, 215
Ulyanova, Nadezhda Konstantinovna (Krupskaya) 13, 43–44, 47, 51, 73, 75–79, 85, 93, 103, 121, 123, 125–127, 140–141, 149, 166, 188n30, 192n21, 196n1, n2, n9, n14, n16, n20, 202n90, 209, 213

V
Vladimir
Monomakh (Vladimir II) 25
Prince 22–24
region, the 32, 82, 95

Volga region, the (Lower and Middle) 14, 48–52, 60–65, 67–68, 73–74, 88, 95, 136–138, 151, 154, 176–178
Vologda 28, 82, 145
Voronezh 1, 34, 49, 51, 88, 141

W
War
Civil, the 8–10, 13–14, 17, 48, 58, 62, 84, 111, 124, 151, 163–164, 167, 186n11, 205n62
Communism (1918–21) 5, 11, 13, 53, 83, 84, 95, 164
First World, the 8–9, 13, 17, 39–42, 48–49, 71, 78, 95, 126, 128, 151, 164, 174
Great Patriotic, the, *see* the Second World War
Imperialist, *see* the First World War
Revolutionary, the, *see* War communism (1918–21)
Second World, the viii, 3, 6, 11–12, 76, 134–135, 160, 163–164, 168
War(s) 19, 25, 27, 29, 112
in a figurative sense 135, 152
Napoleonic, the 33
Women's Department (*Zhenotdel*) 75, 77, 94, 121, 134, 171

Z
Zemsky Sobor 26
Zhenotdel, *see* Women's Department

www.ingramcontent.com/pod-product-compliance
Lightning Source LLC
Chambersburg PA
CBHW052107300426
44116CB00010B/1570